CW00704903

Conter

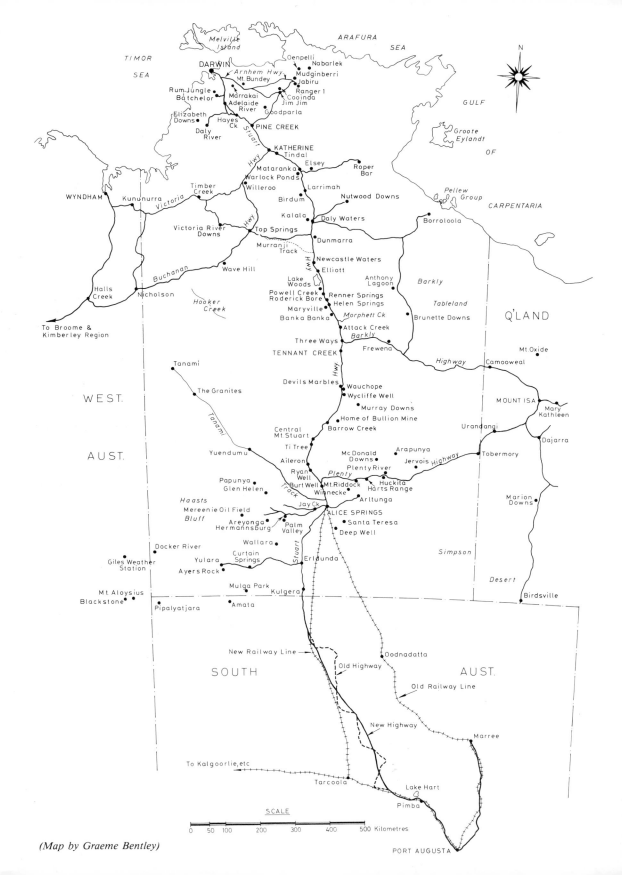

(Map by Graeme Bentley)

A HISTORY OF ROAD TRAINS
IN THE NORTHERN TERRITORY 1934-88

A History of
ROAD TRAINS
in the
NORTHERN TERRITORY

John Maddock

Kangaroo Press

ACKNOWLEDGMENTS

I gratefully acknowledge the valued assistance given to me in many and various ways by organisations and individual people, including:

C. H. Currey Memorial Fellowship;
Northern Territory Road Transport Association;
Northern Territory Government;
Australian National Railways (Mr Lou Marks, Dr Fred Affleck);
Department of Works & Transport, Northern Territory (Mr John Svenson, Mr Larry Bannister);
Main Roads Department, Western Australia (Mr A. J. O'Neill);
Highways Department, South Australia (Mr R. B. Ide);
Main Roads Board, Queensland;
Australia Post (Mrs R. M. Bradshaw, Adelaide);
Department of Primary Production, Northern Territory (Mr John Tobin);

Centralian Advocate, Alice Springs;
State Reference Library of the Northern Territory;
Northern Territory Archives Service;
Mr and Mrs Win and George Maff, Darwin;
Mr Laurie Pearson, Northern Territory owner–driver;
Mrs Pearl Tuit, Buderim, Queensland;
Ansett Trailways (Mr John Sinclair);
Truck & Bus Transportation (Mr Colin Horne, Mr Steve Brooks);
Mr Ted Joyce, Winnipeg, Canada;
Mr Ian Hammond, Banksia Park, South Australia; Mrs Geraldine Hogben, Shell Co., Melbourne; Mr Paul Michael, Shell Co., Darwin.

My sincere thanks also are extended to all the people mentioned in the book, whether by way of interview or loan of photographs.

JOHN MADDOCK

A Note on Metrication

Between the introduction of decimal currency in 1966, and 1974 Australia introduced metric to replace imperial measures. This continues to pose problems for many people, including those recording history. In a book such as this one, the issue is complicated by truck and engine specifications using both systems, as well as the fact that metrication is still often honoured more in the breach than in the observance. It is not unusual to be told of a 12-metre double-decker with 5 foot 6 inch internal height!

Accordingly I have used each measure where appropriate, retained imperial measures in the recorded recollections of road train operators and other historical material, and included conversions in parentheses so those readers not equally familiar with each system can assess distance, dimensions and specifications with relative ease.

Cover/jacket design by Darian Causby showing one of Tanami Transport's 460 horsepower Mack Superliners pulling three Haulmark double-deck cattle trailers west of Alice Springs.

Reprinted 1992
First published in 1988 by Kangaroo Press Pty Ltd
3 Whitehall Road (P.O. Box 75) Kenthurst 2156
Typeset by G.T. Setters Pty Limited
Printed in Singapore by Kyodo Printing Co (S'pore) Pte Ltd

ISBN 0 86417 187 0 (paperback)

PART ONE

The Old and the Bold

Big Country, Big Vehicles

Road trains and the Australian outback are synonymous. There's a correlation of bigness and vastness, of imposingly large vehicles serving a region where neighbouring homesteads can be hundreds of kilometres apart. Admired and at times detested by other road users, road trains have played a similar role in opening up the nation's more remote regions to that which the iron railroad did elsewhere in Australia and in other countries.

It was the reluctance of successive Australian governments to extend rail routes beyond termini established in the early part of the twentieth century that led to the development of the trackless multi-unit vehicle which has become a unique part of Australia's history and is regarded almost with awe and a touch of envy in other countries of the world, especially in the older and more closely settled parts of the Northern Hemisphere.

The birthplace of modern Australian road train operation was Alice Springs, and its genesis was an unfulfilled agreement and a successful experiment with an unusual vehicle in the 1930s.

The agreement was that the Federal government of the day, upon taking over the area at the time known as North Australia from the South Australian government, would complete the rail line which had been planned for many years between Adelaide and Darwin. But that never came about. The experiment was conceived in Britain by the Oversea Mechanical Transport Directing Committee to meet the problems of transport in undeveloped regions of the British Empire. It involved a multi-wheeled road vehicle designed and built to run on rough bush roads, pulling a set of trailers.

In 1934 the Australian government imported one such vehicle and put it into service in the Northern Territory, operating out of Alice Springs and at times moving north to Katherine to serve the Victoria River region. It alternated between these towns according to the seasons.

And so the camel trains which had served the Territory since the days when the Afghans and other teamsters had supplied the needs of the construction gangs on the Overland Telegraph Line in the 1870s, faded into the background of transport.

The 'government road train', as it became known, was a big advance in motor vehicle technology since trucks of the early '30s were of elementary design and questionable reliability. Yet they and their owners battled on and coped with an unforgiving environment to carry supplies and mails to settlements along the OTL. The road train did not compete with these pioneers; its task was to extend the supply routes beyond those served by the likes of Dave Baldock, Len Tuit, the Kittle brothers Len and Geoff, father Gerhardt and son Kurt Johannsen, Stan Cawood and others.

A Changing Land

The Northern Territory is a land of contrasts. In the 1,745 road kilometres from Kulgera to Darwin the climate, soil and vegetation vary widely.

Occasional sandhills and claypans between the border and Alice Springs are reminders of the presence of the Simpson Desert occupying the south-eastern corner and spilling over into South Australia and Queensland. Saltbush, spinifex and low scrub have led to the 'dead heart' label for this region, but it's anything but dead; it's cattle country, where man and beast not merely survive but thrive. There are no major rivers in the 'Red Centre', as it is described in tourist literature. The streams which appear on maps are usually the flood plains of rivers and creeks that only flow after rains, which are not very frequent. In fact rainfall for The Centre averages round 16 cm a year. The Finke River, which is joined by numerous creeks and by rivers such as the Palmer and the Hugh before it disappears hundreds of kilometres away in the Simpson Desert, can cause havoc to land transport in times of flood but eventually becomes a string of waterholes which dry up completely during a drought.

In the north the picture is entirely different. There are numerous big rivers which, encouraged by an average annual rainfall of 120 cm, flow constantly and in large volume. There's the Roper—the Territory's largest river—which flows into the Gulf of Carpentaria, and others such as the Victoria and the Daly flowing westwards, as well as the Adelaide, Mary, South Alligator and North Alligator flowing to the north, and the McArthur and Cox running into the Gulf of Carpentaria.

Near Alice Springs there are the MacDonnell Ranges whose spectacular colours and features have been made familiar to the outside world by Aboriginal artists. Geologically these mountains are in complete contrast with the regions to the north and south; numerous gorges and canyons, some with lush vegetation and rock pools, emphasise the distinctiveness and the differences of the Territory.

Strange as it may seem even to those who have visited it, Alice Springs is approximately 600 metres above sea level, but for the most part the Territory is below the 450 metre level, forming part of the continent's central lowlands.

There is a notional dry belt across the Territory between Barrow and Tennant Creeks which, in theory at least, separates the Centre from the Top End. A series of bores tapped into underground sources ensures the availability of water up along the central route roughly along the original line of the overland telegraph. From about Renner Springs the rainfall increases and the vegetation changes progressively and becomes taller and more lush as the sub-tropic zone unfolds. Pandanus and coconut palms as well as eucalypts, paperbarks and cypress pine appear in increasing numbers.

To the east of Newcastle Waters, approximately half-way between Alice Springs and Darwin, there's the Barkly Tableland with its vast tracts of grass plains extending through to the Queensland border, and to the west there's the Victoria River district which also provides pasture for beef cattle production.

By Darwin the 'feel' is distinctly tropical. Billabongs, palms, flocks of wheeling kite hawks and a warm, humid atmosphere complete the picture of differentiation from the arid southern sector of the Territory.

Settlement in the Northern Territory was slower than in other parts of Australia. It did not have the impetus of a convict population thrust on it as did the eastern side of the continent, nor were there the immigrant settler programs which gave the south and the west their beginnings.

Had the Dutch followed up their contact with the Northern Territory coast in the *Arnhem* in 1623, it goes without saying that the Territory's—and Australia's—history might have been entirely different. It was 200 years after this brief visit by Jan Carstens that the British hoisted their flag at Port Essington and established Fort Dundas on Melville Island, declaring the area to be part of New South Wales. Elsewhere in the young colony there was only desultory interest in the Territory's vast lands. Explorer Ludwig Leichhardt crossed part of the top section in his 1845 expedition from Moreton Bay to the Gulf of Carpentaria and across to Port Essington, and A. C. Gregory in 1856 traversed much the same area in his expedition from the Victoria River to Port Curtis (near Gladstone) in Queensland.

But the Centre remained silent and unexplored until 1862 when John McDouall Stuart established a route from the settled regions of the south by leading an expedition from Adelaide to Chambers Bay on the Arafura Sea. Following Stuart's success the South Australian government moved to extend its northern boundary and in 1863 it took over from New South Wales the whole of the area now known as the Northern Territory. This deflected a proposal by A. C. Gregory, whose explorations had disclosed valuable tracts of land in northern Australia, that Queensland should annex a large area south of the Gulf of Carpentaria and that the rest of northern Australia as far west as the De Grey River in Western Australia should be formed into a new (possibly penal) settlement to be named Albert.

Next the South Australians contracted with the British Australian Telegraph Company to construct the Overland Telegraph Line from Port Augusta to Palmerston (now Darwin) for £120,000. This was completed in 1872 and resulted in Australia being connected by submarine cable which, as is noted on a commemorative tablet in Darwin, 'provided the first means of telegraph communication between Australia and other countries. . . It was taken out of service in 1938 and finally abandoned in 1950.'

The 3,200 km single-wire telegraph line strung over 36,000 poles across the continent provided the key to opening up the Territory. Eleven repeater stations were spaced out along the line—at Beltana, Strangway Springs, The Peake, Charlotte Waters (all in South Australia), Alice Springs, Barrow Creek, Tennant Creek, Powell Creek, Daly Waters, Katherine and Yam Creek (Northern Territory). These stations, and the men who spent long, lonely shifts receiving and passing on Morse code messages, gave life to what in essence was a lifeline through the Territory and put Australia into what Charles Todd, the progenitor of the line, picturesquely described as 'the giant electric chain which unites all nations of the earth'.

Except for these fortified repeater stations there was virtually no settlement through the centre. But slowly prospectors moved in seeking what mineral wealth there might be in the region. Gold was discovered at Pine Creek in 1872 and copper at Daly River in 1882. Grazing leases in the Alice Springs district were acquired, the first big grazing properties on the Barkly Tableland being established by 1880 and opening the way for the arrival of the 'cattle kings'.

In spite of the efforts and enthusiasm of the South Australian government to promote and develop the Territory, at the turn of the century it remained sparsely inhabited. Pastoral leases and permits of various kinds had been granted over 104 million acres (40 million hectares), leaving 231 million acres unoccupied. The 1911 census showed a population of 3,310 whites and an estimated 13,600 Aborigines.

After protracted negotiations which began at the time of Federation, the Northern Territory was transferred to the Commonwealth in 1911. Fifteen years later the Territory was subdivided into Central Australia and Northern Australia but this state of affairs only lasted four years and in 1930 it became a single entity.

With the spread of settlement, slow as it was, came the need for transport to carry the stores, materials, mails, etc., that are basic to people's existence. In the loneliness of the outback the mail is an all-important contact with civilisation and the men who carried the mails and station supplies were, like the early settlers, in a pioneer class.

The packhorse was widely used but it had its limitations in dry country with vast stretches of sand. However, it was preferred by the early mailmen, among whom was 'The Fizzer' immortalised in Mrs Aeneas Gunn's *We of the Never Never*. Henry Peckham was his name; in the early 1900s he had the mail run from Katherine to Anthony Lagoon via Powell Creek, roughly 800 km each way, which took 16 days out and 16 back.

'The Fizzer' was one of hundreds who, before the advent of the motor vehicle and later the light plane, contracted with the Postmaster-General to carry mails by packhorse to the remotest stations.

The camel was a major means of freight transport in outback Australia for over 60 years. Teams in strings of up to 40 beasts, carrying supplies or pulling big flat-top wagons, dominated the carrying scene, particularly in the arid, sandy regions. They were usually owned by Afghans who set up big depots at Cloncurry, Bourke,

Marree, Oodnadatta, Marble Bar, Broken Hill and other places from which major routes radiated—such as along the OTL. Subsidiary 'lines' were developed to remote stations.

Mr Ted Hayes, of Undoolya Station, 20 kilometres east of Alice Springs, whose forbears settled in the Territory in the 1880s, told of the early days of transport in an address to the National Trust of Australia (Northern Territory) in 1983. Delivering the Doreen Braitling Memorial Lecture he said:

The twice-a-year arrival of station supplies was always a welcome sight, as much for the material to build furniture from as the goods they contained. All groceries, plus flour, sugar, salt etc., were ordered by the ton, as supplies had to last for the next six months.

Station supplies were mostly carried by camel strings from Oodnadatta... The stores here in Alice—Wallis and Company and Fogarty's—ran their own teams and hired men to run them until the motor trucks eventually took over in the late 1920s. Camels were still on the road in a limited way up until the completion of the railway in 1929.

Today I often hear the Afghans were the people that opened this country up, and if people would only stop and think, they would realise the Afghans were only carrying the supplies to the people who were opening up the country as pastoralists or mining this area.

The early trucks carrying from Oodnadatta to Alice, were by today's standard almost like toys, but they did a marvellous job... The drivers of these vehicles were great workers, as it was not unusual for them to unload part of their load and carry it across some of the very sandy river crossings, after getting their trucks across.

THE OLD AND THE BOLD

Early Road Train Ventures

Road trains as a means of developing and supplying the Australian outback have exercised the minds of people since the 1860s.

In 1863 the Yudnamutana Mining Company, which extracted copper ore at the northern end of South Australia's Flinders Ranges, decided to import three steam traction engines, each to haul six waggons, to cart stores from Port Augusta to the mines and back-load with ore. Each was designed to haul 50 tonnes over the 195 km route in two days. Although they ran for a year or so these road 'trains' were costly to operate and unable to cope with the primitive road conditions of the time. As one writer put it: 'The chief feature of their progress to the mine was the speed at which they stripped the country along which they passed of wood and water'. They were eventually sold as scrap iron in Port Augusta.

A more successful venture was that of John Napier whose general store was an important feature of the business life of Farina, a once-thriving town 180 miles on the rail line to Marree and Oodnadatta. In 1912 Napier imported from England a Daimler-Renard road train—complete with driver! He used it to cart stores to the copper mines at Yudnamutana and returned with copper ore.

A unique feature of the Napier road train, as it came to be known, was that each trailer had drive wheels: the central of each trailer's three axles was driven by a prop shaft; a power take-off from the prime mover drove a shaft which was connected by universal joints, etc., to the first trailer's drive axle; and in turn the power was carried to the other trailers' axles by shafts connected to the unit ahead of it.

The name Daimler-Renard stemmed from a move by Daimler to acquire sole British rights for the manufacture of what Daimler described as 'an unusual machine'—a road train invented by Frenchman, M. Renard. The 'mechanised monster' had its first public showing in 1903 and Daimler apparently thought it had sufficient buyer appeal to obtain manufacturing rights four years later, their road trains being supplied to India, Canada, Australia, U.S.A., South America and several European countries. Then came the final seal of approval: Lord Kitchener ordered one for military use in Egypt.

Presumably the Daimler-Renard road train concept, with its 8 mph (11 km/h) top speed, proved too ponderous and it was shouldered off the road by vehicles of improved technology stimulated by the onset of World War I.

Writing in the British publication, *The Autocar*, in August 1910, S. C. H. Davis commented on demonstrations of Daimler-Renard road trains built for Australia and Canada:

Perhaps the most astonishing feature of all, when watching these huge motor trains moving on smooth road or rough field, is the wonderful silence of the whole mechanism. This is, of course, due primarily to the Knight engine, and secondly to the efficient transmission system which has been adopted.

The engine, Daimler Knight type, has six cylinders cast in pairs and listed as 80 hp. A very large radiator is provided in front, and above, running the whole length of the bonnet, is a large water tank which would obviously appear to be a necessity, especially in hot climates. From the engine, power is taken through a very large diameter cone clutch and flexible shaft to a gearbox containing four speeds forward and reverse.

The Knight engine, incidentally, was fitted in later years to the Willys Knight motor car; the sleeve-valve principle was also used in World War II in the engines fitted to the Bristol Beaufighter aircraft dubbed 'whispering death'.

In the days leading up to World War I a German, Major W. A. Muller, invented a system of powering a string of trailers by electric motors which received their current through cables running from a power car or prime mover. The train, designed and built by Muller, consisted of the engine car and ten waggons, powered by two Austro-Daimler 6-cylinder petrol engines of 125 hp each. The engines were sited at each end of the power car and drove a large centrally located dynamo which provided current for 22 12 hp electric motors driving the wheels on each axle by means of a differential, jackshaft and chains.

The power car did not pull the waggons, each of which was independently powered by its own pair of electric motors. Thus each trailer could be disconnected from the train and manoeuvred about as long as it remained connected to the electric cable. The tare weight of each trailer was 3.5 tonnes and the power car weighed 8.5 tonnes. The wheels were 4 feet (1.2 m) diameter and the iron tyres were 10 inches (25 cm) wide. Carrying capacity of each trailer was 6 tonnes.

A prominent Australian pastoralist from western New South Wales heard of the Muller road train and decided to order one at a price of £12,500 on condition that it would meet certain criteria of load and speed on outback tracks. On arrival the road train was put through a series of tests in Albert Park, Melbourne, with its ten trailers loaded to a gross train weight of 100 tonnes, of which 43.5 tonnes were tare weight. It soon became evident that the unit was underpowered and the purchaser stipulated that larger engines be fitted.

The Western Australian government also became interested and indicated that if trials were successful an order for six road trains would be placed. The test assignment was to haul a load of 60 tonnes of stores from Melbourne via Albury to Wagga Wagga over the then very poor roads. It was mid-summer at the time and it soon became obvious that instead of fitting larger engines the manufacturer had simply speeded-up the existing ones from their normal operating speed of 900 rpm to 1500 rpm which led to various troubles, including overheating.

The test journey was completed but World War I was looming and Muller and his men decided to quit Australia. Muller got away but his two assistants were not so fortunate and were interned.

Some time later the purchaser made one more attempt to put the road train into operation. It was loaded with sheep fodder and driven to a property 150 miles north of Hay, N.S.W. For the return journey it was loaded with wool. Heavy rains turned the plains into mud and although the outfit coped with these extremely difficult conditions the engine only lasted as far as Hay and eventually the whole outfit was shipped back to Melbourne where it was stored for the duration of the war and later destroyed by fire. Both Muller's firm and the grazier ended up losing heavily on the experiment which just might have revolutionised transport in distant regions.

Another early entrant in the road train field was the Caldwell-Vale. Between 1910 and 1914 approximately 40 of these prime movers were built by the Caldwell-Vale Motor and Tractor Construction Company of Auburn, N.S.W., to a design by two brothers, Felix and Norman Caldwell, who were financed by a well known Sydney engineering firm, Henry Vale & Co., builders of locomotives and rolling stock for the New South Wales Railways. Several Caldwell-Vales were used in the early development of Canberra; the Australian Pastoral Company purchased some for hauling wool by road in the Longreach (Qld) area; and a number of mining and construction companies worked them in various parts of Australia.

They had wide-tread spoked iron wheels approximately 5 feet (1.5 m) in diameter and were powered by a 4-cylinder 14-litre petrol engine with a bore and stroke of 6½ inches (165 mm). Power output was 80 hp (59 kW) and the engine consumed fuel at the rate of one mile per gallon (2.82 litres per km). The axle shaft was 4½ inches (114 mm) thick; there was no differential but there was said to be sufficient pinion lash to allow moderate turns! Steering was power-assisted, and a

3-speed gearbox allowed it to travel at a maximum of 6 mph. It could haul a load of 40 tonnes—16 tonnes on each of the two trailers and 8 tonnes on its tray.

The Holt Manufacturing Co., of Stockton, California, forerunner of the Caterpillar Tractor Co., whose engines nowadays power many heavy transport vehicles throughout the world—including those of Co-Ord Transport, the big Territory road train operator—produced the Holt 75 in the early 1900s for the task of hauling heavy loads in a road train configuration.

One of these was imported by station owners C. & S. Officer Pty Ltd, of Bourke, in the north-west of New South Wales.

An obviously impressed reporter from the *Western Herald* (Bourke) wrote on 11 November 1914: 'The strength of the tractor can be imagined when we state its own weight is over 10 tons and the two lorries [trailers] which it pulls weigh over 4 tons each. The width of the tyres on each vehicle is 16 inches.' On each of three trial runs from Bourke to Kallara station, 113 miles (181 km), it covered the distance in five days, averaging 22 miles per day hauling 18 tonnes. The report continued:

As the road was in the very worst possible state owing to the severe drought, the vehicle has done remarkable work and, moreover, has not given any trouble or caused delay. Anyone acquainted with this road, in its present condition, can estimate the immense hauling power of this tractor, in so successfully carrying out the trials, and it certainly appears that there are enormous possibilities before it in solving the vexed and harassing problem of road carriage in the back country of Australia. Sand, the bugbear of all other forms of tractors, traction engines and motor lorries, is no obstacle to it. It carries enough water to last 200 miles, enough fuel for 150 miles, and fuel used is a mixture of naphthilate and kerosene.

The Holt 75 was first produced in 1913 and thousands of them were built before production was discontinued in 1924. It was equipped with tracked wheels at the rear and a single wheel at the front for steering. Its 4-cylinder overhead-valve gasoline engine had a bore and stroke of 7½ and 8 inches (190.5 and 203.2 mm) respectively, and it produced 75 bhp (55 kW). Its usual engine speed was a leisurely 550 rpm.

In 1925 when the Holt company became the Caterpillar Tractor Co., experiments with diesel engines commenced, resulting in the production of the first Caterpillar diesels in 1931.

The difficulties experienced in handling quagmire and sandy conditions undoubtedly led to Mr Frank Botterill's 'Dreadnought' invention which consisted of a series of flat bearers for attachment to wheels. As the wheels turned the bearers revolved with them and each one in turn became a flat 'bed' on the surface of the road or paddock, which prevented the wheel from sinking while at the same time enabling the engine to apply full tractive effort.

The success of the 'pedrails', as they were known, encouraged Botterill in 1914 to design a large prime mover or tractor to haul trailers carrying wool and wheat in country areas. The machine, dubbed 'Big Lizzie', had a 60 hp (44 kW) Blackstone crude oil engine with a 7-foot (2.1 m) flywheel weighing three tonnes. It had four forward and two reverse gears which provided speeds ranging from 0.5 to 2 mph (0.8 to 3.2 km/h) and the main (drive) wheels were 4 feet 6 inches (1.3 m) high.

The vehicle was 34 feet (10.3 m) long, 11 feet wide and 18 feet high. It weighed 45 tonnes and could carry 10 tonnes; it could also haul two 32-foot (9.7 m) trailers which each carried 35 tonnes, making an 80-tonne load capacity and an overall length of over 100 feet.

'Big Lizzie' carried 9,000 litres of fuel and 1,300 litres of water in tanks on both the prime mover and the trailers.

Between 1917 and 1929 it worked in north-western Victoria hauling wheat, railway sleepers, timber posts, etc., and on land-clearing projects for soldier settlement schemes—on which operation a 30-metre steel cable was attached and 'Big Lizzie' pulled trees, stumps, etc., and cleared thousands of hectares of agricultural land.

The remains of 'Big Lizzzie' are on permanent display at Red Cliffs, near Mildura, Victoria.

In the immediate post-World War II years a British company, Heavy Tractor and Carrier Co. Ltd, of Hounslow, announced that it was designing a cross-country vehicle named the Translandic Train, comprising a series of trailers of a capacity of 40 to 50 tonnes each mounted on wide pneumatic tyres similar to those developed for wartime aircraft. It was to be basically an off-road vehicle operating on routes with 'the fewest natural obstacles'. All-up weight of the Translandic Train was planned for 275 tonnes, which included 30 to 35 tonnes for the tractor itself, plus four trailers weighing 10 tonnes each carrying payloads of 50 tonnes each.

The design envisaged an engine of approximately 700 bhp (524 kW) with tracked driving wheels, hauling the train at 5 mph. No specific type of transmission was mentioned although diesel-electric operation was put forward as an available option.

Advance publicity for the Translandic Train stated that

Holt 75 tractor pulling two trailers with wide iron wheels operated in the Bourke (N.S.W.) area in 1914. Its average speed was around 22 miles per day and the engine fuel was a mixture of naphthilate and kerosene. *(W. G. Cameron, Bourke Historical Society)*

EARLY ROAD TRAIN VENTURES

careful attention is being paid to the protection of all moving parts from dust; war-time desert and other experience has taught us much in this sphere. The engine selected will be of the diesel type but the precise make will only be fully decided on after selective tests in the light of the proposed route. Cooling will be adequate for the worst tropical conditions, with easy adjustment for cold climates. Air cleaning is of the utmost importance and, as stated above, advantage is being taken of experience gained during the War in regard to air cleaning for the engines of tanks in North Africa, where dust conditions were far more severe than would normally be experienced. The air intake has been raised as far above ground level as is practicable so as to escape dust raised by the train when working over dry earth surfaces.

The design for the trailers was to incorporate self-tracking steering and power-assisted over-run braking.

Estimated first cost of a Translandic Train and accessories was approximately £52,000 plus another £5,000 to cover transport to destination and delivery in working order.

It is not known if any of these trains were ever built but certainly none came to Australia, although the promoters mentioned its possibilities 'in countries such as China, South Australia, North-West Canada, in African and other Colonies'.

In the August 1956 issue of *Truck & Bus Transportation* the Le Tourneau organisation of the U.S.A. provided details of its off-road trains for which propulsion was by means of 'electric wheels' for which this company became famous. A diesel generator running at a constant speed of 1800 rpm generated current to drive electric motors in the wheels of each unit of the train. As the pulling load came on a controller was opened to provide more electric power but the engine of the power unit remained at a constant speed of 1800 rpm. Thus there was no need for any type of gearbox or axle differentials, nor was there any requirement to fit brakes because the wheel motors were reversible. However, each wheel contained a magnetically controlled spring-loaded multiple disc brake for emergency stops and parking. Oscillating axles provided an element of 'walking' over obstacles and all wheels of the power unit were steerable by means of controlled current. Speed control was effected by a small rheostat-type handle and all other requirements such as steering and braking were controlled by the manipulation of small switches on a panel in front of the driver.

The Le Tourneau Freighters, as they were named, provided payload capacities ranging from 35 to 185

Translandic Train was a post-World War II proposal by a British company for use in undeveloped regions. A 200-ton payload carried on four trailers pulled by a tractor fitted with a 700 bhp engine were features of the design.

THE OLD AND THE BOLD

tonnes. The 185-tonne model was purchased in some numbers by the U.S. Army, but perhaps the best-known of these trains was that produced for Alaska Freight Lines to carry heavy consignments from the road head at Fairbanks, Alaska, to an air warning radar station being built on the north-west coast of Canada. It consisted of a power car and five trailers, all shod with tyres 3 metres in diameter and 1.5 metres wide. Two 600 bhp (447 kW) Cummins diesel engines provided the power for the electric generators, and the overall length of the train was 295 feet (90 m).

Although the Le Tourneau organisation had an Australian branch at Rydalmere, N.S.W., to assemble and service its earthmoving equipment, the company's road train did not find any takers in Australia.

Even some suburbs saw 'road trains' in the early 1900s. A 120-bale load being hauled along Parramatta Road, Annandale, by a steam tractor. The cyclist at right would have had little difficulty overtaking.

Manufactured in Auburn (N.S.W.), Caldwell-Vale prime movers were used in various parts of Australia to haul multiple trailers. The unit shown here, in tip-truck configuration, was owned by the South Australian Roads and Bridges Department. (Ian Hammond)

EARLY ROAD TRAIN VENTURES

Government Road Train

The convulsive progress of the proposed transcontinental rail line from south to north spanned a period of nearly 50 years.

Initial planning envisaged simultaneous commencement of construction from Palmerston (now Darwin) in the north and from Port Augusta in the south. Port Augusta was seen by visionaries of the 1870s such as Sir William Jervois who was then governor of South Australia, as

the harbour to which all the pastoral, agricultural and mineral resources of the country to the North, North-East and North-West will converge. It will, ere long, be the port of the produce of a large portion of the Western part of New South Wales and the South-Western portion of Queensland. It will be the southern terminus of a Transcontinental Railway, about 1,800 miles in length, which will ultimately be carried through the Province of South Australia to Port Darwin.

In 1878 work commenced on the construction of the southern section of the line but it was another eight years before a start was made from the Darwin end.

From Port Augusta the narrow-gauge (3 ft 6in, or 106 cm) line reached Marree in 1884 and Oodnadatta in 1891. There the project stalled, 477 miles from Port Augusta and 688 miles from Adelaide. For the next 38 years the planned link between the northern and southern shores of the continent stopped at Oodnadatta. Camel trains, owned mostly by Afghans, were used to ferry passengers and freight to The Alice and beyond and when the railway line eventually reached Alice Springs in 1929 the fortnightly passenger train acquired the title of the Ghan.

In the meantime the top section of the line reached Pine Creek from Palmerston in 1889 (145 miles/232 km) but the next section of 55 miles to Katherine was not completed until 1917. This extension was carried out as part of an agreement with Vestey Bros, who had built an abattoir there and a freezing works in Darwin. The line eventually and finally reached Birdum in the same year that the Oodnadatta–Alice Springs length was completed.

When the Territory was transferred to the Commonwealth of Australia in 1911, responsibility for loans spent on the Territory was assumed by the Commonwealth government which also agreed to complete the missing link between Oodnadatta and Pine Creek. Although the Central Australia Railway was extended to Alice Springs and the North Australia Railway to Birdum, the 1,000-kilometre gap between these two termini was never bridged; in fact it was

increased to 1,470 kilometres in 1976 when the Darwin–Birdum line was closed.

The isolation of the Territory and the problems of providing it with an effective form of transport exercised the minds of the British and Australian governments in the 1930s and the Oversea Mechanical Transport Directing Committee, which had been formed in Britain to study such difficulties in undeveloped regions of the British Empire, saw the answer in an ingenious concept of trackless train which had a four-axle all-wheel-drive prime mover and two eight-wheel self-tracking trailers. It was a type of go-anywhere vehicle.

The combination which the Australian government imported from England in 1934 was one of two constructed to the committee's specification. The first was a petrol-powered version which went to the Gold Coast (now Ghana); Australia's road train was fitted with a diesel engine. The prime mover was built by the Associated Equipment Company Ltd (AEC), of Southall, and the trailers were constructed by R. A. Dyson & Co Ltd, of Liverpool.

Overall length of the complete train was 71 feet 8 inches (just under 22 m) and the carrying capacity was 15 tonnes—three on the prime mover and six tonnes on each trailer. Maximum design speed was 28 mph (45 km/h). Specifications of the prime mover were:

Overall width	7 ft 6 in	(2.5 m)
Wheelbase (1st to 4th axles)	14 ft	(4.2 m)
Bogie spacings	5 ft	(1.5 m)
Track (1st to 4th axles)	6 ft 4½ in	(1.9 m)
Track (2nd & 3rd axles)	6 ft 1 in	(1.8 m)
Body length	11 ft 2½ in	(3.4 m)
Ground clearance (min.)	11 in	(279 mm)
Platform height	4 ft 6 in	(1.3 m)
Turning circle	58 ft	(17.6 m)
Chassis weight (inc. 227 litres of fuel)	7 tons 19 cwt	(8067 kg)

The AEC diesel engine was similar to the standard production unit then fitted to London buses. It was an 8.8 litre unit of 115 mm bore and 142 mm stroke, producing 130 bhp (97 kW). The clutch, main gearbox, axles and the 20-inch (500 mm) wheels were, with slight modifications, standard AEC products.

However, the method of transferring the power to the wheels was unusual and ingenious. A 4-speed main gearbox was mounted in conventional fashion behind the engine, and further back was a 3-speed auxiliary box from which the prop shaft ran to a point almost above the last axle where, by means of gearing in a type of transfer case, the power was delivered to a series of four shafts running through each axle from the rear to the front. Each axle had a differential but each diff was independent of the other. Thus, should wheelspin occur in one axle it would not have any effect on the other three.

The 4-speed main box and 3-speed auxiliary did not provide 12 gear ratios because the boxes were interlocked so that auxiliary low was only available when main-box low was selected, and auxiliary top could only be engaged when the main-box gears were in top. The ratios available and corresponding road speeds at 2000 rpm are shown in this table.

Gear	Main Box	Auxiliary Box	Overall Ratio	Speed m.p.h.
Top	Top	Top	8.25	28.4
Fourth	Top	Second	13.1	17.8
Third	Third	Second	20.6	11.3
Second	Second	Second	35.4	6.6
First	First	Second	57.5	4.0
Emergency	First	First	91.5	2.56
Reverse	Reverse	Second	67.5	3.48

The front and rear axles were equipped with steering mechanism but did not have any brakes. The two central axles were fitted with brakes, which were Westinghouse air, operating at between 70 and 80 psi (482 and 551 kPa). The air tanks were mounted at the rear of the cab and a hose was provided for tyre inflation. Prime mover and trailer brakes were operated by the foot pedal, with air going to the trailers first. A mechanical handbrake was also fitted.

Each pair of axles on the tractor shared a set of semi-elliptic springs. The springs were inverted, with the ends attached to the axles and the centre bolted to the chassis frame. A special swivel joint mounting at the axle ends of the springs allowed for articulation as the vehicle travelled over rough ground, and this movement was enhanced by another swivel joint where the spring was mounted to the chassis, so that on rough terrain the wheels of each pair shared the load equally.

Tyre equipment was 24 10.50 × 20 low-pressure wide-section tyres running at 38 psi (262 kPa); two spare wheels were carried at the front but they were later removed from this position due to mounting-bracket breakages and were carried on the tray.

Although an electric starter was fitted, provision was also made for hand-starting by two men, each using a crank handle to turn pulleys which were connected by belts to the engine mainshaft.

The radiator was mounted high up at the rear of the cab to reduce as far as possible the intake of grass seeds, insects and general bush debris. In front of it was a large slow-speed fan driven by belt from an auxiliary shaft on the engine which also drove the air compressors for the brake system. An article in the British publication, *The Engineer*, 21 July 1933, noted: 'This fan forces a copious flow of air through the radiator and as it draws from the front of the vehicle it creates a cooling draught in the cab. Thus [it] is conducive to the comfort of the driver and his assistant.'

Drivers, however, saw it differently.

The cooling water was circulated around the engine by conventional water pump. A smaller fan mounted on the engine drew air through a duct opening in the front of the cab to cool the area under the bonnet.

The two Dyson self-tracking trailers were eight-wheelers arranged in bogie-bogie style. Each bogie was fitted with a turntable and each turntable was connected to the other by a spring-loaded link.

The braking arrangement on the trailers was such that only two wheels on each bogie were fitted with brake drums. The thinking behind this was the prevention of wheel skid under heavy brake applications. Even if the brakes were locked 'hard on' four wheels would be left revolving. No brake reaction was felt by the springs; the force was taken by the radius rods. A

The AEC Government Road Train is shown here being checked on a rough track at the British Army proving grounds before being shipped to Australia in 1934. It was loaded with heavy steel plates for the trial. *(The Engineer)*

handbrake was provided for use when the trailer was detached from the prime mover. The brakes on each bogie were operated from an air cylinder connected with the main brake controls and supply bottles on the tractor by a flexible pipe with quick-connection devices similar to those used by the railways at the time.

In a letter to the author, Mr R. A. (Bob) Fryars, a retired AEC executive engineer, provided some interesting additional information.

The road train, he said, was designed by Hardy Motors of Slough, England, which was a subsidiary of AEC. Supplementing the technical data recorded elsewhere in this chapter, he said that the clutch was a 16-inch (406 mm) dry plate and the gearbox was a single countershaft 4-speed type in the D124 series with sliding gears.

The suspension was fully articulated and was a classic design, with leaf springs on central pivots pinned into swivelling fork jaws mounted on the axles. This provided very high levels of articulation and obstacle clearance ability required by Army specifications. This design was carried on AEC prewar Army 6 × 4 vehicles and in strengthened form on World War II models, including an armoured command type of vehicle which was used in the Western Desert. One of these was captured by the German forces and Rommel used it throughout his desert campaign, speaking very highly of his 'Mammoth' which was the AEC name for their six-wheelers at the time.

The road train was accompanied on its voyage to Australia by British Army Captain E. C. Roscoe, RASC, and two army sergeant drivers. In Australia this team was joined by Captain E. M. Dollery who at that time was in charge of development of motor transport in the Australian Army. It was to Dollery that the Australian government turned when this revolutionary new vehicle arrived, and when the acceptance tests under his instruction had been completed the unit was handed over to the Department of Works. During World War II Brigadier Dollery was commander of the Northern Territory Line of Communications Area.

Reporting the arrival of the road train on the *Largs Bay* on 3 April 1934, the *Adelaide Advertiser* said that a test run from Adelaide to Bordertown was to be made with 15 tons of superphosphate and returning with a similar weight of wheat. The news item also gave an indication of the condition of this section of the interstate highway system in those days:

This will be over sandy, unmade road for the greater part of the way along the main line through the desert, and will correspond as near as possible to some of the tracks outback. The distance is about 180 miles and the trip will probably take place next Monday.

The test run had its moments. An *Advertiser* reporter accompanying the official test party phoned this story from Kumorna Siding on 12 April:

The unloading of four and one half tons of superphosphate and the advent of rain to bind the sand tracks enabled the

Prime mover of the Government Road Train undergoing an articulation and traction test to check the efficiency of the suspension of the four driven axles under extreme operating conditions. *(The Engineer)*

THE OLD AND THE BOLD

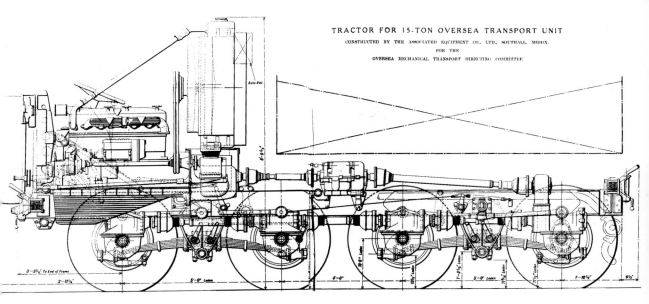

Profile drawing of the AEC prime mover showing details of the suspension and the drive train system. Fan and radiator were behind the driver, with long pipe (top, left) carrying cooling water to the engine. *(The Engineer)*

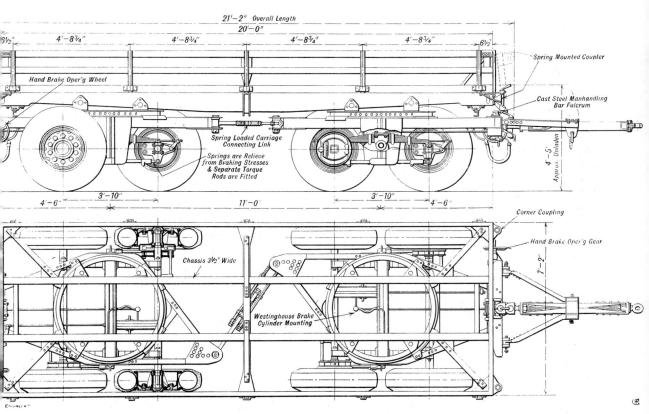

Views of the trailer suspension (top) and the inter-connected turntables which provided the self-tracking feature which the British designers deemed necessary for operations on twisting bush tracks and in confined areas. *(The Engineer)*

GOVERNMENT ROAD TRAIN

motor transport unit to reach Kumorna Siding from Tintinara in the 90-Mile Desert with ease today. It left Tintinara at 2.30 p.m. and reached Kumorna at 5.30. The eleven miles was made in three hours in spite of the unit covering three miles of the journey twice for experimental reasons, and several voluntary stops. The tractor is now carrying three and a half tons of fertiliser and equipment after the removal of half a ton of super at Tintinara, and each trailer is now carrying four tons of useful load. Captain E. C. Roscoe who is in charge of the unit said it was definitely not designed as a cross-country carrier but to run on cheap developmental roads.

Commenting on the test, Mr G. A. Helling, owner of Tintinara home station and a pioneer of motor transport in the upper South-East, said he was profoundly impressed with the work of the unit. He had seen many forms of non-rail transport in the 90-Mile Desert, and the outfit appeared to him to be superior to any other.

At one stage today the tractor went on with one trailer and after uncoupling it returned for the other in fast time, as it was able to follow its own tracks.

Complete success crowned the attack on a stretch of sandhill named by the party the 'Witch's Cauldron', the deep sand of which had been expected to bog the unit. In drenching rain, part of the track had to be cleared with axe and tomahawk.

After consultation, Captain Roscoe decided this morning to ease the load by taking off 54 bags of super, which have been consigned on the railway to Bordertown.

Where there was a fair holding surface, the road train showed itself an ideal means of transport for heavy loads over broken country.

Next came the delivery run to Alice Springs. This took three weeks, so bad were the road conditions, particularly north of Oodnadatta. The *Advertiser* of 20 May 1934 carried this report datelined Alice Springs and bylined 'From Our Travelling Staff Representative':

Arriving at Alice Springs on Friday night, the 15-ton transport unit brought the 1,100 mile journey to a successful conclusion.

Early next week the unit will be loaded with building material for the new Tennant's Creek Hotel and will return over the 350 miles stretch from there with a load of ore, which has been packed in 1 cwt bags. Thereafter, further loadings have been arranged for Tennant's Creek and Newcastle Waters, whence several journeys will be made between Muckadee, 100 miles south of Newcastle Waters. The unit will then return to Alice Springs for future operations.

The journey from Oodnadatta to Alice Springs was of a varied nature. Progress was necessarily slow because of the number of creek bed crossings which had to be carefully reconnoitred before crossing, and along narrow winding tracks through the mulga—boughs had to be cut and stumps removed.

The Alberga, the Palmer, the Finke and the Kurullula River beds presented difficulties, but in no case were they serious obstacles. Captain E. C. Roscoe, Captain E. M. Dollery and the driver have learned by experience how to cross sand, and former difficulties have been overcome by the proper use of matting.

The last stage of the journey on Friday proved to be the most arduous. The track follows the course of the Hugh River, and through the mountains the river bed had to be crossed 11 times in 22 miles. Each crossing involved a separate method of treatment.

The successful accomplishment of the long journey to Alice Springs over tracks far more difficult than it will operate over with its pay loads in the Northern Territory is a vindication of the careful attention to design displayed by the Oversea Mechanical Transport Committee and the confidence in such a means of transport for the outback shown by the Commonwealth Department of the Interior in arranging the experiment. Graziers expressed the opinion that such a method of transport would be of the utmost benefit to them in assisting with the quick carriage of their produce to the railway and that the possibility of the shifting of stud stock might be exploited in the future by this means.

A picturesque touch was afforded this morning when practically everyone in Alice Springs turned out to inspect the unit. The old means of transport, the camels and the donkey teams, are rapidly passing, and the Afghans and Aborigines, although interested in the big unit, viewed it with mixed feelings. One old Afghan said, 'My people pioneered the transport in the outback, but the train and the motor car have come, and now they can run a train without building a line.'

A week later the *Advertiser* ran this item:

The 15-ton transport unit arrived at Newcastle Waters on Sunday, completing another successful test from Alice Springs. A full load was carried on the journey, consisting of material for Tennant's Creek and Muckadee Dip, and stores for Newcastle Waters, besides 1,000 gallons of fuel for the unit's use while in the district. Notwithstanding the rather severe nature of the track for 15 miles on both sides of Powell Creek and the deep gutters which had to be negotiated, fair time was made and the vehicle came through without trouble.

Fifteen tons of timber rails will now be carried to Muckadee Dip on Tuesday, and then the unit will make four journeys from Birdum to stations with stores and bore equipment. The return to Alice Springs will be made early in July.

The standard charge for carrying in Central Australia is 1/- a ton a mile and at that price few carriers have been able to carry on successfully. The accountancy cost on the transport unit allowing for generous depreciation, garaging and upkeep, is 4¼d a ton-mile. The load from Alice Springs to Tennant's Creek was carried at 6¼d a ton-mile, and, although much time was lost in clearing the track, this load was carried at a profit.

The inaugural trip from Alice Springs to Tennant Creek took 23½ hours. The load comprised building materials for an hotel being erected at the Tennant for Mr J. Kilgariff.

It was the legendary D. D. Smith, Resident Engineer in Central Australia for the Commonwealth government, who inaugurated the Territory's government road services. Speaking to the author in 1979, Mr Smith said:

After Captain Roscoe left I made a special trip to Melbourne and Canberra to discuss the setting-up of a road and mail service with the Minister of the Interior who by that time was Sir John McEwan; he had taken over from Tom Patterson. Then I had a long session with George Gahan who was Commissioner for Commonwealth Railways. That was about 1935. Eventually the service became a reality.

All supplies for Northern Territory stations came in to Alice Springs, Darwin and Mt Isa. When I came here in 1926 the stations got their supplies by camel teams; everything came into this region by camel from Oodnadatta, and Sam Irvine the mailman brought some small items up on his truck but he couldn't carry much as he only had a small vehicle.

The cartage rates for the road train were set at 3½d per ton mile for station equipment such as boring plant, fencing, windmills and general items; for household supplies such as tea, flour, sugar, etc., the charge was 6d a ton-mile.

The operation started off in Alice Springs and we carted as far north as Newcastle Waters. It built up until we had the AEC road train and six 10-ton AEC trucks. We had our own workshops in Alice Springs to handle all our equipment.

To collect the freight charges we instituted a system whereby all stations that wished to be served by the road and rail service agreed to lodge with their bank a guaranteed sum to cover these charges. So, when the freight arrived, we would pay the Commonwealth Railways their charges, add our own on, and charge it against the bank guarantee which was subsequently replenished by the station client.

When our service finally folded we were handling over 2,000 tons of freight per year to outback stations. Had it not been operating during World War II a lot of station people would have had to walk off their properties or make some other arrangements to get their food supplies. There was no other way.

During the time the road and rail service was in operation we carted from Alice Springs to Halls Creek via the Granites and Tanami and from Alice Springs to Wave Hill via Hooker Creek. We also operated to places like Anthony Lagoon and Borroloola and Brunette Downs. It worked in such a way that when we carted stuff from Alice Springs to, say, Brunette Downs we would send the vehicle over to Mt Isa to pick up a load there and come back into the Territory. We also operated from Katherine. It was completely coordinated. For that reason we were able to keep our rates down and still make a break-even profit.

We didn't do any carting in the north during the Wet. We'd go up to Katherine at the end of March or April and cart all the stations' supplies to the north-western area. They'd come down from Darwin by rail; we didn't cart out of Darwin. We'd stay in that region until a month or so before the wet season was due to start and we'd cart all their wet-season supplies out to them before we left. Then we'd come down south to Alice Springs to help move the stuff that had built up there.

The Payne Report on land use and development in the Northern Territory in 1937 had this comment on the road train:

A development of outstanding importance in inland transport was the introduction three years ago, of a trial 15-ton motor transport unit. This is, in effect, a small road train. After operating less than three years it has succeeded in redeeming its cost paying all working expenses and making a small profit. It is estimated that it could be operated at a cost of about three and one half pence per ton mile without loss if there were both forward and back loading.

The only disadvantage attaching to the transport unit now in use, is its wide gauge, 5 ft 9 in. In consequence of this wide gauge, its wheels do not conform to the track made by the ordinary motor vehicles. It is thus only able to use one of the motor wheel tracks, the other set of wheels having to cut a new track outside the existing one. Apart from the damage to the road, this has the effect of reducing the speed at which the unit can travel. The consequent roughness in running is detrimental to the vehicle and in some instances, may entail risk of damage to the freight being conveyed. Any further units introduced would be designed to the standard 4 ft 8 in. gauge.

While this, and any new transport units, are utilized for miscellaneous loading, it is fitting that the service be controlled by the Works Section of the Department of the Interior, but if the service were developed and regular timetables run between specified places such as Alice Springs and Tennant Creek, then we think that the road transport service should be controlled by the Commonwealth Railways Commissioner, when it would become a valuable adjunct to the railways.

Ewan Clough was the first regular driver of the road train. He drove it from October 1934 until November 1936, having taken it over from Bentley Greenwood who drove it after the Army drivers had left the Territory in the previous June. Other drivers who 'piloted' the road train during its 12 years of operation included Bill Goodsell, Ted Carlton, George Nicholls and Jack King. All trucks operated by the department, as well as the road train, had two-man crews, and off-siders included Roy Parker, Frank Morton, 'Shorty' Fulton, 'Pudden' Peterson and Charlie Wright.

Ewan Clough told the author that as a driver he would be away from Alice Springs for months at a time, working mainly in the Top End:

The first trip from Katherine to Wave Hill, 287 miles, took three weeks. We had to make new tracks in most places because they had disappeared in some places during the Wet and river banks were cut away where old crossings had been. My offsider and I had to walk up and down creek beds to find suitable crossings and then sometimes we'd have to dig away part of the bank so that we would get the prime mover across and then haul the trailers over with a long cable.

In boggy or sandy country we would disconnect the trailers, get some planks or tree trunks to put under the wheels of the prime mover and drive it out. Then we'd either find or make a new track with the prime mover by running backwards and forwards for some distance to consolidate the surface, and then we'd go back for the trailers and haul them through.

GOVERNMENT ROAD TRAIN

The late Ewan Clough, first regular driver of the Government Road Train. His wage was £15 a week, which was 'good money' in the mid-1930s. The road train's principal task was to carry supplies and materials to remote stations.

That AEC prime mover would go anywhere and could haul anything—it was like a tractor. In fact it would still be useful on the roads in the Territory today. It was more maneouvrable than any existing road train.

Fencing wire and pickets, fuel, food and general station supplies were our usual loadings. We were supposed to carry only 15 or 16 tons but as often as not the loading would be heavier. I remember one load of 24 tons, and on another occasion we must have exceeded even that when we took a water boring plant from Alice Springs up to Murranji, which is about 550 miles north of The Alice.

I thought it was a great vehicle, although some drivers after me didn't have much luck with it.

There was quite a bit of trouble with the aluminium heads at times, and I remember when it first went on the road the diffs used to get so hot that they used to glow a dull red! But some modifications to the bearings overcame that trouble.

I think the worst feature was that thundering great fan behind the engine. It used to suck air through the cab—which, incidentally, had no windscreen—at such a rate that I had to wear a heavy coat in winter to keep myself from freezing.

You had to be very careful that you didn't let the engine over-rev when going down a hill or into a creek bed. The sheer weight of the prime mover and its trailers tended to push it rapidly downhill if you weren't ready to check it with the brakes. I think that's what happened to it finally; the engine over-revved on a down-grade and a con-rod went through the side of the crankcase.

In winter it was often cantankerous and difficult to start. Its electrical system was 24 volts from four 6-volt batteries, with 22 volts required by the starter motor, 6 volts for the lights, and 2 volts for the engine heaters which had been fitted to assist starting. However, the latter weren't always effective, and Ewan Clough had his own method of providing some warmth for the engine to assist starting in winter when working out of Alice Springs. When he stopped for the night he would make camp, drain the water out of the radiator, and after cooking his meal he would shovel

The Government Road Train in action in the Northern Territory, with a third trailer hooked on at the rear. At difficult creek crossings all trailers had to be disconnected and hauled over one at a time, sometimes by winch cable.

THE OLD AND THE BOLD

The Government Road Train in 'winter rig' (no hood) with Ewan Clough at the wheel. Note the twin belts below the engine fan. To start the engine, two men using crank handles wound these belts to turn the main pulley on the end of the engine crankshaft.

the coals under the engine. In the morning his camp fire would cook his meal, heat the radiator water, and warm the sump when the embers were spread under the engine. Wherever possible he took the precaution of stopping for his camp on a rise so that if battery power was doubtful he could clutch-start on the downgrade.

In those days Ewan Clough's wage was £15 a week and the offsider's was £13. When the AEC first went into service the so-called road north of Alice Springs was a snake-like track which wound in and out of the Overland Telegraph Line poles. An early problem that he encountered was caused by the width of its track, which was 18 inches wider than that of most other vehicles of the day. Hundreds of conical-shaped anthills, some of them nearly two metres high, had to be cut down; those of only minor height required the speed to be reduced but still caused damage to loads.

The biggest load ever carried by the famous road train was two railway carriages weighing 45 tons each—a triple overload!—from Alice Springs to Larrimah for use by the Red Cross following the bombing of Darwin by the Japanese.

One of its last big jobs was moving 126 bales of wool from McDonald Downs station, 260 kilometres from Alice Springs, into the railhead at Alice.

After his two-year stint driving the largest vehicle in Australia, Ewan Clough went down the power scale and bought himself a Bedford five-ton truck with a 4-cylinder Perkins Leopard diesel engine, and began carting to stations along the Tanami Track and to mining companies spread in a wide radius around the Alice Springs region. 'It was only a table-top truck,' he said, 'but I made good money with it.'

According to his long-time friend Jim Morgan of Katherine, Ewie Clough's business prospered and he moved up to a Leyland and then an International semi-trailer outfit. However, in the 1950s he decided to quit road transport and he established a small farm on the Katherine River about 12 kilometres east of Katherine where he grew peanuts and some vegetables. But the rainfall was inconsistent so he abandoned that project and worked as a mechanic with the Department of Interior for some years.

When the author met him in Katherine in 1976 he was semi-retired and driving a small tanker on street watering for the local council. He died in 1978.

When Jim McConville was superintendent of the Department of Works workshop at Alice Springs in the late 1930s the department's fleet consisted of a Maple Leaf Chev truck, a Dodge tipper, three Leyland

Cubs used on local road works, two Buick utilities for the resident engineer and the deputy administrator, a number of Chev utilities, plus the AEC road train, an AEC Mammoth Major bogie-drive and three AEC Matadors. All the AECs were used on road-rail transport, principally from Katherine to Wave Hill, Victoria River Downs and other stations in that region.

The AECs had diesel engines. The single-axle Matadors were powered by a 125-horsepower unit and the Mammoth Major's engine which produced 130 hp was identical to that in the road train. The Matadors and Mammoth Major operated as rigid trucks; occasionally they pulled a small three-tonne dog trailer, depending on the amount of loading that had to be moved. Later on the department acquired Ford semi-trailer seven-tonners with Hercules 4-cylinder DOOC engines.

McConville described the all-wheel-drive AEC road train as the most technically up-to-date vehicle of its time. The front and rear axles steered, which was rather early for that principle; the vehicle could turn in almost any street in Alice Springs. He said that whereas in World War II vehicles a big ball-and-trunnion universal joint was developed for steerable drive wheels, the road train had a big Spicer-type joint; two large yokes came down and the Spicer joint was in between the drive axle and the stub axle on the steerable wheel. He said it was like two Spicers bolted together to form a sort of double universal. The wartime types had two big yokes with big balls and trunnions and were fully articulated. The springs were inverted semi-elliptics and gave very little trouble. Those on the trailers did not have spring eyes; they rode in a slipper-type arrangement with torque rods to locate the axles. The turntables on the trailers were well designed but gave trouble until they were reinforced and rebuilt.

The clutch and gearbox stood up to the work quite well but the engine wasn't always reliable. Due to the loads and the high revs that had to be used to keep the vehicle moving there was considerable bearing trouble. This engine had a centrifugal filter in the crankshaft; the crank pins were hollow and there was a one and a half inch (38 mm) hollow through the shaft which picked up sludge and caused blockages. There was also the usual oil filter.

The road train was based in Katherine from about April to December each year and was then moved down to Alice Springs in the wet season. From Alice Springs it operated to Hermannsburg, Aileron, Henbury and numerous other places.

Lionel Whittaker, BEM, was a mechanic with the Caterpillar organisation and shortly before World War II he went to Alice Springs and joined the department's staff when the workshop was in Parsons Street, on the

'The office' of the AEC prime mover. The handbrake and two gear levers can be seen, as well as the long water pipe connection from the rear-mounted radiator to the engine. Note the large fan alongside the driver's seat.

site of the present government offices opposite the police station.

He recounted that for a time the road train's diffs gave trouble, much of which was attributed to tyres of different circumference but ostensibly the same size being fitted to the same axles. With one tyre bigger than the other, it created pressure on the crown wheel and pinion and caused overheating. Careful attention to tyre matching, plus the use of a special diff oil, alleviated much of this trouble.

Whittaker said that with all the jerking and jolting caused by rough roads the batteries used to get the life shaken out of them. When they were low on 'juice' the driver and his offsider would have to start the engine with two crankhandles, inserting them into the sprockets, pushing in two spring-loaded 'dogs' to engage the sprockets, and then winding like hell! There was no valve lifter or any other device to reduce the compression, as there was on some other engines of those days; it was simply a matter of strength and stamina to get it started.

He added that the turntables on the trailers were said to be the same as those on gun carriages: big and much more stable than the relatively narrow ones on modern semi-trailers. If they'd been like the semi-trailer type and the load moved or was over to one side the trailers probably would have capsized, or the turntable would have buckled. It was like a big swivelling ring, and it took the load right out to the wheels, making the whole set-up very stable.

Although the men who handled the AEC road train might have been regarded by some as the 'gun' drivers, others in the department's employ were no less skilful and carried out equally important tasks with the relatively smaller AECs which over the years included

The AEC prime mover has been restored by the Northern Territory Museum Authority after lying derelict for many years in a wrecker's yard. This photograph was taken when it was on display at The Residency, Alice Springs.

A rear-end view of the prime mover, showing the worm drive and the steering knuckles on the rear axle. The front and rear axles steered and the middle two were fixed. Note the pintle-type towing connection mounted on a leaf spring to absorb shock.

One of the AEC Monarchs which the Department of Works operated in prewar days. It is shown here with a dog trailer behind, emerging from a sandy creek crossing. Among its drivers were Spurge Nichols and Frank Fidler.

Spurge Nichols.

Monarchs, Matadors and Mammoth Majors. These vehicles were much larger than the Fords and Internationals and other similar marques that private enterprise hauliers were using.

One of the 'other drivers' was Thomas Spurgeon ('Spurge') Nichols who drove for the Department of Works in the immediate postwar years.

I never got to drive the 'old girl', *said Spurge*. Jack King and George Nicholls were its drivers at the time and anybody else had a hard time getting a 'go' at it. One of the things I vividly remember about it was that big fan right behind the driver; it was a helluva size and I often heard drivers complaining about pains in their back. Perhaps it was a good thing I didn't get chosen!

I mainly drove AEC Monarchs on the road and rail service. They were good vehicles but they didn't like the sandy country; the back axle would 'chatter' and would quickly bog down. We used to like having a Matador somewhere around, preferably travelling with us, because it could give us a pull; it crawled over the sand without trouble.

We would be away from our base at Alice Springs for up to two weeks at a time. Then we'd go up to Katherine for a while and cart from the railway up there out to various stations.

While we were away we carried tinned food and a water bag; the station people were good to us in those days—we could always get a meal or some fresh (or cooked) meat—and if we met up with a drover who'd just killed a beast we'd finish up with a good feed of rib bones which we'd cook on a shovel. At night we'd roll out the swag and sleep under the stars; there were no sleeper cabs in those days.

I wouldn't know how many times I've dug out bogged vehicles. On one trip through Finke (dry river), the truck went down so far that I just walked off the truck tray on to the ground! It wasn't so bad if the load was, say, tins or drums of petrol; you could simply roll them off and then heave them back on again when the vehicle was up out of the bog.

We used to carry those big wallaby jacks, to raise the vehicle and then we'd corduroy under the wheels with saplings or scrub or whatever was available. Sometimes if we were pulling a trailer and it went down too we'd have to unload both the truck and the trailer—eight tons and four tons—and load them up again after we'd got out of the soft stuff.

At times we ran into trouble with tyres, particularly in the summer. Big stones and gidgee were the main culprits; they'd damage a tyre and then in the heat it would blow at the weakened spot.

The high summer temperatures in the Centre together with engine heat in the cab made driving unpleasant at times but with the 'air conditioning' switched on—that is, with the windows down and the windscreen open—plus an occasional slosh of water over the head and chest from the water bag, we'd manage okay. We'd pull up at a bore and put a siphon hose in the tank and give ourselves a cool shower and then get on our way once more.

Most tyre trouble was experienced on the bitumen, it was much hotter than the dirt roads. We always carried two spare tyres mounted on wheels. We often used both of them and came home on singles on the rear. Fortunately there wasn't much back-loading, only empty drums, so we usually had no weight to carry and could get home without further worry.

We didn't have much mechanical trouble; the AECs were very reliable. On one occasion I was stranded for three days when a con rod snapped; I had about a ten-mile walk to Nicholson Station to get a radio message out and a new con rod was flown out by plane. I removed the broken one, fitted the new one, and we were soon mobile again.

The road and rail service finally ceased about 1950 when private carriers began to serve places off the highway. The Martin Brothers were among the early ones to cart to outlying stations. Then some of the big station companies got their own cattle transports and they began to cart their own supplies.

Frank Fidler was one of a number of Department of Works drivers who later became road transport operators in their own right. Frank went to Alice Springs from Clare (S.A.) in 1947. He got a job with the government road and rail service and stayed with

Frank Fidler.

the organisation until it got out of day-to-day transport operations in 1950.

Frank related his career with the Department and subsequently in this interview:

The government road and rail service used to carry to all the stations inland from the highway. We didn't see much of The Bitumen; we'd go up as far as Newcastle Waters and then take the Murranji Track to Victoria River Downs, Wave Hill and other stations.

My 'mount' was a 6-cylinder AEC Monarch. Sometimes we'd pull an 18-foot trailer, but it never really had enough power for the loads it hauled. For instance, the banks of the Wickham River were pretty steep and we'd give the motor all the revs we could get. Gradually it would die right down till it was just ticking over; we'd apply the brakes, check the trailer, unhook, drive the truck up to level ground, get the steel cable out and hook on to the trailer and pull it up!

We carted the first buildings out to the Aboriginal settlements at Hooker Creek and Yuendumu. We used to put eight tons on the Monarch's tray and about four on the trailer.

Gilbert Creek, between Hermannsburg and Areyonga, was a trouble spot for us. We've been there for up to seven hours at a time, getting out of sand. On one trip we had a young woman with us; she boiled the billy for us, and when we eventually got out you could see a string of small ash heaps where she'd kept making new fires as we progressed! The only way to get out was to corduroy with gum saplings; we couldn't let down the tyres because there was no way to pump them up again, as the Monarchs didn't have any means of supplying air for tyres.

If we got bogged in sand in the heat of summer we simply had to get the vehicle out; we didn't wait till night time. We

got used to that sort of thing. We always had plenty of water with us, usually in a 44-gallon drum slung under the truck.

We didn't have any radio communication, so that if we broke down we could easily be out there for up to three weeks. You see, some of the trips would be away from base for three weeks, which meant that nobody would know anything was amiss until we didn't turn up! There was no one on those back roads in those days; we had them to ourselves.

We used to take plenty of tucker with us just to make sure we survived if we met with serious trouble. First day out was always the best, with plenty of fresh food. Then we'd be into the tinned stuff. Sometimes the labels would come off the tins and we wouldn't know what was in them; there was often an element of surprise.

When I operated my own trucks I always carried strips of Marsden matting if I knew I was going into sandy country. They were almost as good as driving on bitumen; you simply re-laid the strips in front of the wheels and drove over them.

Commenting on the fade-out of the government road freight operation, D. D. Smith said:

The service folded when the Allied Works Council came into this area during the latter part of the war. They took over the whole thing. They put all our vehicles into a pool. The AEC road train ceased operating just after the war and the Allied Works Council then began disposing of a lot of equipment which they had declared surplus after the cessation of hostilities and the AEC was among them.

At this time pressure was building up both outside and inside government for private enterprise to take over this sort of work and eventually the government of the day decided that its official road and rail service would cease. That was about 1946 or 1947. The vehicles were sold off and that was that. Private enterprise took over and in the 1950s the private operators and the Commonwealth Railways got together in the Co-Ord operation, and so another phase of transport in the Territory began.

Mr Smith said that in its 12-year life in government service the road train covered approximately 850,000 ton-miles and earned £21,909 for an expenditure of £19,102. Its original cost was £2,500.

In 1946 the AEC prime mover and its trailers were sold at a disposal of surplus government equipment at Darwin and were acquired by Territory Timber who used it for some time in the Pine Creek area. A conrod through the side of the crankcase wrote 'finis' to its career as a haulage vehicle. It was removed to a scrap yard at Berrimah, near Darwin, where it lay derelict for many years. In 1980 it was acquired by the Northern Territory Museums Board and restored; it was placed on exhibition at The Residency Museum, Alice Springs.

Along the Telegraph Line

The Overland Telegraph Line was an important part of the Territory's history. It connected Australia with the rest of the world, led to the movement of pastoralists and other settlers into the region, and, equally importantly, formed the original south-north track. On each side of the Line a strip 20 metres wide was kept clear by regular patrols of linesmen who also kept the Line itself operational. Vehicles followed this cleared space weaving between the poles where necessary—there were approximately 20 poles to the mile—and thus the first vehicular route to the north was formed.

It was along this so-called road that men such as Dave Baldock, Len and Geoff Kittle, Len Tuit, Stan Cawood, Kurt Johannsen and others pioneered road freight services as well as mail and passenger operations. From the railway termination point at Alice Springs the government road train and ancillary vehicles moved supplies, materials, etc., to remote stations off the Track and a handful of individual carriers handled general freight and perishables consignments for settlements along the Track while the mail contractor looked after the Postmaster-General's requirements and transported the occasional passenger.

It was the likes of these men, in particular Baldock and Johannsen, who saw the potential for multi-unit operation in the early postwar years. Their ingenuity and inventiveness adapted wartime equipment to create the concept of the modern road train and it was the isolation of the Territory and the absence of regulations governing size and weight which gave these enterprising transport operators their once-in-a-lifetime opportunity to design and implement a transport format which was indigenous to the Territory and unique in the world. They showed the way; others followed and honed the system to make it one of the most efficient operations in the Australian transport industry.

During the Depression Dave Baldock began his Alice Springs-Tennant Creek carrying service which later became D. R. Baldock & Co., operators of a fleet of Foden and Leyland road trains hauling general freight north and ore south from the mines at Tennant Creek.

Dave was 21 when he went to the Northern Territory in 1934. At Quorn (S.A.) he'd met Bob Rumball, the Shell representative for northern South Australia and the Northern Territory, who was on his way back from Tennant Creek and said that that was the place to go for work. So he travelled by road to Alice Springs and then on to Tennant Creek where things did not turn out as well as he expected:

I had a lean time there for a while. I was told there was miles of gold and miles of work there but there was nothing doing, really. There were a lot of small mining shows working but they weren't employing anybody. I just sat around for six weeks. Things were pretty bad in '34.

In those days there were about 600 people in Tennant Creek and about the same number in Alice Springs. Everything was very dear, except beef which was sixpence a pound all round and bread was a shilling a loaf. I eventually got a temporary job in the mines; in those days the unemployed got nothing—no money, no rations. It was tough! Later I got a job with Harold Williams; I helped in his store and drove his truck to Alice Springs for his supplies. There was only one train a fortnight in those days; later it was weekly.

Dave Baldock.

Dave Baldock's first truck—a forward-control Ford V8—with which he started running between Alice Springs and Tennant Creek in 1937 carrying general freight and later perishables.

THE OLD AND THE BOLD

Then in mid-1936 I moved down to Alice Springs and did a bit of driving for Eric Miller on his mail run. I also drove on the Huckita mail run east of Alice and out around the stations for some months and then I drove a couple of trips a week from Alice Springs to Tennant Creek for other carriers.

By Easter 1937 Dave Baldock decided he'd get into the carrying business himself. He acquired a forward-control Ford V8 three-tonner and began to run to Tennant Creek from Alice Springs with general freight. A few months later he decided to carry perishables as well:

The perishables came to Alice Springs in a railway 'cool cars' with ice packed in each end. We would unload them into an ordinary truck, put a tarpaulin over them and head out for Tennant Creek. We'd go as quick as we could; if the train was somewhere near on-time we'd get away between 8 p.m. and 10 p.m. and drive all night. We'd arrive next day. The journey used to be about 320 miles but when the new road was put through during the war it was shortened a bit. In the early days of the perishables side of the business we used to do the trip in about 18 hours, but once the road was improved we could get the time down to about 15 hours.

In 1937 trucks were relatively small but more often than not they carried loads twice as heavy as their rated capacity. Thus it was not unusual for Dave to be seen carrying six tons over the bush track that wound in and out of the OTL, over stony and sandy creek crossings, through the hills and across the antbed flats to Tennant Creek. His truck had single tyres on the rear because it was not possible to run with duals as the wheel tracks were so deep they were only suitable for single-tyred vehicles. In fact, the truck would follow them without being steered:

I could set the hand throttle and the vehicle would plug along steadily while I had a nap! You'd seldom meet anyone, of course.

I used to travel at about 20 to 30 miles an hour, mainly at night to avoid the heat. In those days we had plenty of tyre troubles; there was a lot of stone damage, mainly in creek crossings and watercourses after rains which washed away the

sand and soil and left the stones sticking up. It would be months before any repairs would be carried out to these scoured-out crossings. Up near the Devil's Marbles there was a very bad section for about 14 miles; we had to follow the creek for most of that distance. We'd probably bruise or damage a tyre there, and it would go okay for a week but it would be fraying on the inside and damaging the tube, then suddenly it would blow out.

I didn't carry many tools but I always had a shovel and an axe and a spare axle. I've been bogged more often than I can remember. Sometimes I'd be bogged and would dig out five or six times a day. One trip in the rainy season took 19 days from Alice Springs to Tennant Creek.

There's an often-told story of one carrier who ate 21 dozen eggs while in a boghole. It happened in 1936. After that episode Woodforde Swamp became known as Eggshell Flat.

Another hazard was the presence of ant hills on the track. With loads often stacked high on short trays, an ant hill, if struck at speed, could capsize a vehicle. Straying cattle and kangaroos took their toll of mudguards and radiators.

As time progressed and road gangs and graders began to make improvements to the track and relocate it in many places, dual wheels were introduced which allowed heavier loads to be carried and reduced tyre costs.

These improvements were followed by the introduction of semi-trailers, and in late 1930 ten-ton loads were transported frequently and successfully despite insufficient power to make the driving of such vehicles any pleasure. But competition brought rates down from £12 to £9 per tonne, although Dave still managed to obtain £12 for perishables. Fuel in those days was 2s 6d per gallon or about 8.5 cents per litre.

With war imminent grading and gravelling of the road was stepped up, but then came the dreaded corrugations which really played havoc with vehicles. Soon most mudguards and bonnets either fell off or were discarded; springs were being replaced continually and spring hangers were often welded straight on to the chassis.

After World War II when powerful defence force vehicles became available Dave Baldock purchased this Diamond T prime mover and set up his first road train, shown here consisting of seven unbraked trailers.

As his business grew Dave Baldock used various makes of vehicles. All-told he bought five Fords as replacements or additions, then a GMC. During the war he acquired a KS5 International with two-speed diff. He also at one stage had a Leyland with a Perkins P6 engine but it wasn't one of his most successful acquisitions. The improvement in truck technology that took place during World War II and the availability after the war of more powerful vehicles led Dave Baldock to change his modus operandi from semi-trailers to road trains:

I bought a couple of GMC 6 × 6s and we hauled two trailers behind each of them with 21- and 23-ton payloads. Twenty-six tons was as much as we could pull through the hills north of Alice Springs. We'd put the Aileron and Ti-Tree and Barrow Creek stuff on one trailer and drop it off and we'd pick it up on the way back. Those GMCs worked well; they had a petrol engine—a Buick-type engine, I think it was—and it was very reliable.

Then I got a Federal tank transporter with a Cummins diesel engine. I put a tray on the back of it and hauled three trailers with it. But it was underpowered. So I bought two Diamond Ts; they had Hercules diesel engines which did a good job. By that time I had quite a variety of vehicles, including small trucks which I used on the perishables because they were quicker.

I started actual road train operations about 12 months after the war. With the Diamond Ts we could pull seven trailers with 12 tons on each. The usual overall length was 186 feet. We once tried eight trailers which made the train 24 feet longer but we considered it to be a bit too much. Most of the time these outfits were handled by one man, even the hooking-up and unhooking of the trailers. That was where the clutch on the side of the Diamond Ts cab was handy. They were terrific vehicles; they had good steering, it was easy and accurate. They had two gearboxes, and you could 'two-stick' them easily. They could travel very slowly when you wanted them to; in fact you could walk around the train as it went along, checking that everything was okay. They had big tyres on them—1400 × 20—but if they blew out it was a big job repairing and refitting them.

I intended to go into livestock after the war but I got too busy on other work.

Freight rates dropped sharply after the war, when everybody seemed keen to run trucks which had been purchased cheap at disposals sales. Just before I started in 1936 the rate to Tennant Creek was £16; then it was £12, then £9. After the war it dropped to £6 a ton, but I kept going at my old price. I lost a bit of loading but gradually all the blokes running at £6 went broke.

In the early days I didn't get any back-loading; maybe there would be a few hundredweight to go back sometimes, but not very often. A couple of years after the war, I think it was, I began to haul south for Peko. Before that I would get an occasional load of wool from Wauchope and also got some copper from Barrow Creek (Home of Bullion mine). They used to send a fair bit of copper ore away at times; it was bagged, but the bags didn't last long. The ore contained a lot of sulphuric acid. On a hot day, after loading this stuff, by the time you got to Alice Springs your socks would fall off! They virtually rotted off; it was savage. In the summer the temperatures were very hot; we'd have it at 120°F for weeks on end; on the road it would be closer to 150°F.

The government started cracking down on axle loads and vehicle lengths about 1954. We made representations and got a two-year extension so that we could wear out our old vehicles and replace them with new ones that would comply with the new regulations. Actually the limit on trailer numbers was the hills out of Alice Springs; too many trailers would break drawbars and towing hooks. There were also problems with unbraked trailers, particularly at creek crossings, where they tended to bang into each other. By the time the last trailer reached the descent into the creek crossing, it would give quite a push to the prime mover but then there would be a drag back as it used up all the slack of the other trailers, and that was when couplings would snap.

I left the Territory in 1955 and didn't have much to do with the later developments; Jim and Harry McConville attended to most of that. I went back from time to time, of course.

From the 1937 Ford three-tonner the Baldock operation by 1962 had grown to six Leylands (three Hippos, two Super Hippos, one Buffalo) and four FG Fodens, plus 18 trailers with a total haul capacity of 380 tonnes. The trailers included one 16-wheel bogie-bogie, nine 12-wheelers, and eight 8-wheelers, all built by Freighters to the design of Jim McConville.

Jim and his brother Harry developed the Baldock operation and directed its fortunes in the expansive '50s and busy '60s. Records of Baldock tonnages show that in the 13 years to 1950 the total amount carted was 37,750 tonnes. In the next 12 years the figure grew by 114,358 tonnes.

Jim McConville's debut in transport took place in 1936 when he arrived in the Northern Territory from Quorn (S.A.), aged 26 looking for work. He was fortunate; he got a job as a mechanic with the Department of Interior at Alice Springs.

Jim McConville.

THE OLD AND THE BOLD

A Baldock road train with Diamond T prime mover and five trailers. The vehicle being 'piggy backed' is a Federal, also belonging to Baldock's. Top speed was around 22 mph but 15 mph was more usual in order to prevent trailer 'whip'.

He worked on the department's vehicles which, in addition to the famous AEC road train, included AEC Matadors and a Mammoth Major which were also used on road-rail freight transport throughout the Territory, and smaller vehicles such as Leyland Cubs, Dodge and Maple Leaf tippers, plus utilities which were used by the resident engineer and the deputy administrator.

In time he rose to the position of superintendent of workshops in the Northern Territory, based at Adelaide River during the war, not long after which he left the public service to join Dave Baldock in a partnership involving motor repairs and general engineering in Alice Springs. In 1954 he bought into the transport business of D. R. Baldock & Co., in which his brother Harry already had a financial interest, as did a fourth person, Milton Owen. Another brother, Len, was in charge of bore maintenance on the Barkly stock route from 1937 to 1946. He then went into the earthmoving business for a few years and later became the owner of Kulgera station, near the South Australia–Northern Territory border. He sold this property in 1964.

In the early 1950s, Baldock's saw the phasing-out of the ex-disposals Federal and Diamond Ts for Fodens with six- and eight-cylinder Gardner diesel engines and later Leylands, hauling trailers designed by Jim to carry 30-ton payloads:

Just after the war, *said Jim,* Baldock's were running some really long—in fact, the longest—road trains in the Territory. They were pulling seven trailers, none of which had any brakes!

They were mainly single-axle types; some were ex-army and some were built locally. They were supposed to carry seven tons but we used to put 10 or 12 tons on them. The overall length was about 148 paces! You just about needed a pushbike to ride from one end to the other! There was no trouble going

up through the hills with the seven trailers if they were handled carefully. The only brakes were on the prime mover. The driver would keep the prime mover down in about second gear until the bottom of a hill was reached, and then give it the gun to get up the next one. By the time he reached the top the speed was down to about two or three miles an hour. . .and so it went on.

The Diamond T's top speed was only about 18 miles per hour, going to 20 downhill. It was governed to 1650 rpm. It was a tank transporter, and had a 4-speed main gearbox and a 3-speed auxiliary. It had a DJXC Hercules diesel engine. We got a helluva lot of work out of that DJXC, but from time to time it used to crack the cylinder block on the right-hand side and allow water to leak into the lubricating system. That caused some bearing trouble but I put in a lot of work drilling the side and putting in a copper patch with a neoprene seal and we didn't have any more trouble after that.

The crack used to occur on the inside of a cover plate on the side of the motor; I don't know why they cracked there but I think it was probably something to do with headbolt tension. In those days nobody bothered much about tension wrenches and that was what I could see as being the most likely cause. The head gasket was solid copper; we used to anneal and soften them occasionally. When a head had to be tightened down they'd get a rod about three feet long and 'lay onto it' with plenty of muscle!

Talking of vehicles of the '50s, Jim McConville said:

We had a lot of rear-axle heating with the Fodens, but we partly overcame the trouble by carefully matching the dual tyres. We would check and match the tyres accurately about every fortnight or three weeks; we'd check each tyre circumferentially and match up carefully.

It was the leading differential on the Fodens that overheated, mainly because of bad tyre matching, in my opinion; also it was not a very good bearing set-up in those diffs. . .non-adjustable bearings weren't the best. Once we got on to the tyre measurement thing we found that you couldn't afford to have any great variation in tyres at all, otherwise

While one driver steered the other had plenty of time to walk alongside periodically to check the tyres for over-heating, punctures, etc. The box on top of the cab contained a stretcher on which the off-duty driver could rest.

there was 'fight' between the axles. If you had four pairs of tyres and two pairs were exactly the same diameter and the other two pairs were, say, an inch more in diameter but within the tolerance of about half an inch, we would put them diagonally opposite each other so that the differential would compensate for the difference in circumference.

We used a special synthetic oil in the diffs; it was a Shell product. The diffs were a worm drive. When climbing slowly up a long grade there was insufficient oil being fed to the overhead worm and consequently they tended to run dry and fail. I drilled the casings and fed more oil into the thrust bearing. The agents wouldn't believe that there was any trouble with these diffs so we simply had to do our own modifications.

We had very little trouble with engines overheating because the Gardners were very cool-running units and we always specified very large radiators.

We later switched to Leylands and had a good run from them. At first we had trouble with the Buffalos; we had to modify the clutch spigot bearing. The Leyland people simply didn't believe it could give trouble. However, once that was overcome the situation improved. When I left the company there were two cab-over Hippos, three Super Hippos, three Buffalos and the Foden with the Gardner 6LX. The oldest vehicle in the fleet was four years.

We didn't do much work into Darwin; we mainly serviced Tennant Creek, transporting ore southwards and general freight northbound. The ore was copper concentrate.

The biggest load we ever carried was over to Mt Isa. It was hauled on a special trailer that I got Freighters to make for us; it had three axles on the back and small 15-inch wheels on the front. The load was 38 tons. We also carried a small loco at one stage—about 28 tons. We hauled a Commonwealth Railways transporter on that job.

After a while regulations began to appear limiting loads—

cutting the seven trailers back to three! They began to tighten up in the '50s—about 1957 or '58. Our all-up allowable loads would be about 100 to 102 tons on the Buffalos.

By the 1960s axle loads had been limited to 8.5 tonnes on a dual-tyred axle and 16 on a bogie. Thus it was possible to haul gross train weights of up to 87 tonnes with a bogie-axled prime mover and two double-bogie trailers within an overall length limit of 145 feet (44 m). Double-bogie trailers could carry a payload of nearly 25.5 tonnes.

With gross train loads ranging from 60 to 87 tonnes, according to motive power, the safety factor became very important in Baldock's thinking. In management's view, at speeds over 55 km/h (35 mph) the margin of safety diminished markedly on heavily loaded road trains, so the company built its vehicle specifications and operating schedules around the 55 km/h factor and ordered rear axle ratios that would maintain that limit. Overdrive was locked out in boxes equipped with that ratio.

One immediately identifiable result of this policy, apart from the enhanced safety factor, was greatly increased tyre mileage. Bearing in mind that these were the days of rayon tyres, Baldock's tyre mileage figures make interesting reading for operators using today's greatly improved tyre technology.

Backed up by pressure checks before every trip, Baldock's were getting between 51,000 and 54,000 kilometres (32–34,000 miles) from cross-ribs on the bogie drive of the smaller Leylands, and around 43,000 kilometres on the Buffalos due to this model's higher

THE OLD AND THE BOLD

As the wartime equipment wore out Baldock's replaced it with heavy-duty Leyland Hippo (shown here) and Foden prime movers and specially built trailers designed by Jim McConville.

tractive effort and heavier loads. At this point tyres were transferred to trailer wheels where up to another 24,000 kilometres were obtained—on original rubber.

Baldock's did not rotate their tyres but changed them in pairs from one side to the other. Olympic tyres were used exclusively.

With the ratios specified the smaller Leylands and the Foden could cover the run to Tennant Creek in 12 hours, and the Buffalos did it in an hour less.

It was company policy to trade its vehicles when they reached the 200,000 mile (320,000 km) mark, although one Gardner-powered Foden was retained until it had clocked up 265,000 miles because of its unbeatable fuel economy—6.25 mpg with gross train loads of 60 tonnes. In modern parlance, this works out at 2.2 kilometres per litre of fuel, or 45 litres per 100 km.

By the mid-'60s declining prices of copper on world markets were causing cutbacks in production by Peko Mines at Tennant Creek and inflation was adding to the problems of running a business, so Jim and Harry McConville decided it was time to get out of the industry. They sold to Fleet Owners in June 1966 and although it was operated as a separate entity for a time D. R. Baldock & Co. eventually disappeared from the Territory transport scene.

End of the road for a Baldock Leyland Super Hippo in a yard at Alice Springs.

Early Days of Fuel Cartage

Like others who later became part of the Territory's transport scene, Len Kittle made his way to Tennant Creek seeking work during the Depression. But unlike others he stayed on and with his brother Geoff established Kittle Bros., which operated in the Tennant Creek area and then radiated from there to various parts of the Northern Territory. Len tells it this way:

I arrived in Tennant Creek in 1936 from Mount Oxide, northwest of Cloncurry, with an old Chev ute, looking for work. I was fortunate; I got work carting ore from mines around Tennant Creek into the government batteries. I bought a '34 Chev tipper and carted ore for the Central Mining Company, which was a division of Peko Mines. I also carted for private miners—there were about a hundred 'gougers' around the area at the time—and we'd get their ore to transport into the three government batteries which were scattered all round the field.

It was hard work; everything was loaded by hand shovel. At one stage we also had to shovel the ore off; that was at places where there was no weighbridge. We'd have to shovel it off into yard boxes so that they knew how many yards (or tons) you carried. From then on you got paid for that many yards for each load you brought in. And from then on there'd be arguments about whether the ore should be above or below the boards of the boxes.

The business grew; we bought a GMC T20, then a Ford, plus another Ford. At times we'd take a load of petrol from Alice Springs; the road was terrible. It was very sandy in parts; we'd have to follow the Overland Telegraph Line for much of the way; sometimes we'd be on the left of the line, at others we'd be on the right, and sometimes hundreds of yards away from it.

Len Kittle.

After World War II broke out and the Japs came into it I joined the Air Force and spent three and a half years as an engine fitter. My brother, who had ear trouble, didn't make the Army or the Air Force, so he stayed on at Tennant Creek and kept the business going. When the war finished we got the General Motors dealership for Tennant Creek; in fact, I was still in my RAAF uniform when I went along to apply for the dealership—I thought it might impress them! The South Australian manager for GM was an Air Force adjutant, so it went over all right.

Kittle Bros were early cattle haulers in the Northern Territory. An ex-military left-hand-drive GMC is the prime mover in this photo, pulling a bow-type semi-trailer modified to carry cattle, coupled to a two-axle bow trailer.

The brothers continued with their local cartage services but the changes the war had brought to road transport equipment led to their looking beyond Tennant Creek and expanding their operations. They had also acquired the BP fuel agency (in those days it was COR—Commonwealth Oil Refineries) in Tennant Creek and this added to the broadening of their horizons.

When the postwar disposals sales came on, *said Len*, we acquired three GMC 6 × 6s and a couple of K5 Internationals all with Army trailers. We got an Inter and semi-trailer for £180 and immediately went round to the COR depot at Darwin and picked up a load of fuel for Tennant Creek; we virtually got our money back with what we earned for that load!

There were some good buys in those days. At the sales, if you were a 'little' bloke bidding for something, the big dealers would let you get in to bid for the vehicle you wanted, then when you got it knocked down to you they would resume bidding among themselves for big lots. They were pretty good to work with.

We bought eight vehicles over a period at disposals sales. As well as the GMCs and Inters we bought a couple of Blitzes and a Blitz crane and a big Autocar which wasn't very successful; it had a petrol engine and was under-powered. We also bought a Cletrac front-end loader.

Arising out of the disposal sales at Darwin the Kittles got the job of carting 5,000 ex-army blankets to Sydney. They carried them on the two International tray-tops, one of which pulled a trailer. The blankets had been washed and cleaned but had not been pressed into bales; thus they were somewhat bulky and tended to cause the vehicles to sway, as Les recalls:

We hitched them as tightly as possible with ropes to reduce this movement but we couldn't eliminate it altogether. We also worried about the possibility of spontaneous combustion sending the whole lot up in smoke but fortunately nothing like this happened. Geoff and I brought the blankets from Darwin to Tennant Creek and then Geoff and another driver took them on to Sydney. They brought the trucks back empty.

They began to cart copper ore to Alice Springs and backloaded general freight and cars for their Tennant Creek General Motors agency. Then the fuel distribution business started to expand and they found themselves delivering fuel down the highway as far as Barrow Creek and up as far as Daly Waters and Elliott and other places along the road. This was in addition to hauling the fuel in bulk from the rail terminus at Larrimah down to their depot at The Tennant.

Len Kittle said that just after the war it was a case of 'anything goes' as far as the regulations were concerned:

With the GMC 6 × 6s we'd use them to pull a semi-trailer and we'd hook an ex-army trailer on behind. Sometimes we'd put another trailer on behind that! No brakes or lights on the trailers either!

We used to cart the fuel in cross-tanks. We could get four on the semi-trailer and two on the 'dog', plus a few drums of petrol and other packaged products. We had to mount them cross-wise because we could only get two tanks on the semi if they were mounted length-wise. The tanks were 9 foot 6 inches long, which meant that we had more than a foot hanging over the side. We had to put the tap on the inside of the tray so that it didn't get knocked off!

It used to take 24 hours for a round trip from Tennant Creek to Larrimah and back, a distance of about 600-odd miles. Each tank carried about 700 gallons so we had 2,800 gallons on the semi and another 1,400 on the dog trailer.

Those were the days of 900 × 20 tyres fitted to vehicles which were invariably overloaded. The best time to travel was at night so that the tyres wouldn't overheat and blow out. But that wasn't always possible, so if we were travelling during the heat of the day we'd pull up at the bore tanks and hose the tyres to cool them down.

Incidentally, we were one of the early cattle carters in the Territory. In 1946 we began to cart cattle from Banka Banka station for Ted Ward. We made up two cattle transporters from 22-foot ex-army semi-trailers and hauled them with the GMC 6 × 6s.

We built the semis so that there was space for a horse up

For a number of years Kittle Bros carried petroleum products in drums. Shown here is a K-series International with an ex-army bow-type semi-trailer and a trailer behind that—an early version of the modern 'doubles' combination.

As more powerful equipment became available, such as this Gardner-engined twin-steer Foden, Kittle Bros upgraded their fleet. They used this body truck and trailer combination hauling fuel from Larrimah to various destinations.

front and a compartment for petrol; we had to carry plenty of fuel because those GMCs chewed up the juice! We could carry 15 or 16 head of cattle in each vehicle, plus the horse which Ted Ward wanted with him so that he could round up the cattle in the event of their having to be unloaded en route for some reason or other. We also built a special tailgate which could be dropped right down to unload the cattle. It was so heavy that it took at least two blokes to lift it!

Later on Ted Ward built his own semi-trailer to cart Banka Banka cattle. He even built a passenger compartment up front, as there was no passenger service up that way.

The Kittle brothers eventually decided to delete cattle transport from their list of services and concentrate on fuel cartage as well as carrying copper ore to Alice Springs and back-loading with general freight for Tennant Creek.

As the wartime GMC 6 × 6s, Inter K6s and others reached the end of their useful lives, they were replaced with Inter K7s, a Diamond T which was purchased from Jim Crawford of Commercial Motor Vehicles Ltd, Adelaide, and similar heavier equipment.

Then, as the British and American manufacturers of such well-known makes as Foden, Leyland, Mack and International saw the opportunities that a rail-less Northern Territory offered to the road transport industry, they brought in what were then extra heavy duty models as prime movers for multi-unit operation. The Kittle brothers were among those who could see the economic advantages of larger and more powerful vehicles. In 1954 they bought their first two Fodens, then two more, all powered by Gardner diesel engines (three 6LWs and one 8LW). Later they acquired a Leyland Hippo and a Buffalo and in 1968 they purchased an Atkinson. But by the time they sold out to Fleet Owners in 1973 Mack was the favored brand in their four-vehicle tanker fleet which by then was hauling 3 million gallons (13.6 million litres) of petroleum products a year.

They operated the Macks as doubles—semi-trailers plus full trailer, each carrying a 7,000-gallon tank. The Atkinson was a bigger-capacity unit; it carried 5,000 gallons on its back and pulled two 7,000-gallon trailers.

Unfortunately the Atkinson and its two trailers were 'written off' 131 miles south of Darwin. The driver dozed off at the wheel and as he came to he put his foot on the brake instead of 'stretching out' the trailers with an application of throttle, and thus lost control.

In 1953 Len Kittle decided to get out of the general freight side of the operation and concentrate on fuel cartage. He sold his Co-Ord share to Stan Cawood who in turn sold it later to Fleet Owners. As mentioned earlier, he eventually sold the fuel haulage business to Fleet Owners who formed it into the well-known Red North tanker operation.

Len Kittle is one of the few transport pioneers of the Territory to have his name publicly commemorated. A street in Alice Springs has been named Len Kittle Drive, and there's a Kittle Street in Tennant Creek to perpetuate the name of the father of Len and Geoff.

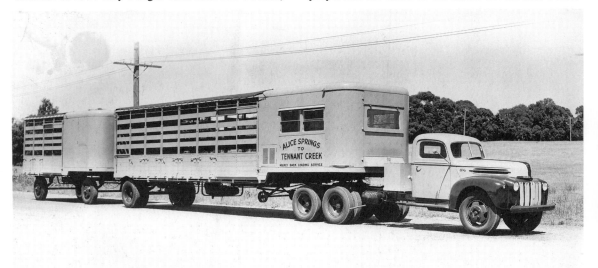

In 1945 Ted Ward of Banka Banka station put this McGrath-built combination in service between Alice Springs and Tennant Creek. The prime mover was a Ford-Thornton with V8 petrol engine; the leading section of the semi-trailer was fitted out to carry eight passengers and behind that there was accommodation for 14 bullocks. Between the two compartments was a small engine driving a compressor and pump to spray the animals with either anti-vermin solution or water to cool them. It could also be used to inflate tyres. The 20-ft 'dog' trailer had an insulated section for perishables and general freight at the leading end, and behind that seven bullocks or more freight could be carried.

THE OLD AND THE BOLD

From Trains to Tourists

Len Tuit began his transport career at the age of 19 when he established a truck service between Alice Springs and Darwin in the 1930s. Immediately after World War II he won the Alice Springs–Tennant Creek–Birdum mail contract and, as was customary then, he combined a passenger service with it. The vehicle he used on the operation was a K5 International pulling an ex-army 22-foot bow-type semi-trailer which was fitted with bench seats and a canvas canopy. Passenger amenities included a ladder to the trailer's deck.

As the passenger side of the business developed Len bought a K6 International and had it re-engined in Adelaide with a Gardner 5LW diesel. This unit towed a side-loading goosenecked trailer which accommodated mails, freight and luggage in the raised section over the turntable and over the rear wheels. The centre section or well deck was equipped with bench seats and side-loading doors fitted with detachable perspex windows. At the same time Len's freight service was being run with a Gardner-powered D-series International semi-trailer combination.

But there was also another operator with a keen eye for the Territory's tourist future in the person of A. G. (Bert) Bond who had been conducting excursions with a sedan car from Adelaide through the Territory to Darwin since 1926.

One of Bond's drivers in the Territory was Stan Cawood who first drove for him in 1927, running to Palm Valley and Arltunga. Cawood said that in the 1930s Bond and his wife and a girl would come up with a Big 6 Studebaker and would stay in Alice Springs for the winter, organising tours for parties arriving by the Ghan.

After World War II, when petrol rationing was lifted, Bond's Tours resumed operations in the Territory and by 1949 Bond and Tuit were competing vigorously for passenger traffic on the Alice Springs–Darwin route. The *Centralian Advocate* carried advertisements such as:

Going to Darwin? Then travel on Bond's weekly service.
Depart Alice Springs 6.30 p.m. Saturday, arrive Darwin 8 p.m. Monday.
Depart Darwin 7 a.m. Wednesday, arrive Alice Springs 1 p.m. Friday.
Single fare   £ 9/ 7/6 ($18.75)
Return   £17/12/6 ($35.25)

Travel by Parlour Coach on Tuit's Mail and Passenger Service, Alice Springs–Darwin. [Photo of single-deck semi-trailer coach with International K6 prime mover]
Departing Alice Springs 9 a.m. Sunday, arriving Darwin 8 p.m. Tuesday.
Departing Darwin 6 a.m. Thursday, arriving Alice Springs 9 p.m. Saturday.
Excellent meals and accommodation provided. Overnight stops at Tennant Creek and Daly Waters.

One of the Northern Territory's pioneer transport operators was the late Len Tuit. This early postwar 'triple' combination—semi-trailer and two trailers—had an International prime mover with a Gardner diesel engine. *(E. Marson, State Reference Library of the Northern Territory)*

Later that year each company was taking large display ads in the *Advocate* proclaiming the superiority of its services. Tuit's commenced a weekly front-page news column which gave details of passengers arriving in the Territory by TAA aircraft and then using Tuit's services. It was about this period that Len Tuit upgraded the passenger side of his business with a 1948 OB Bedford 26-seat coach powered by a Gardner 4LW diesel.

In 1950 he purchased the Tennant Creek–Mt Isa operation from Cavanagh's Motor Services and integrated it with his scheduled runs from Alice Springs and Darwin. The timetable was increased to a twice-weekly service using Cavanagh's Maple Leaf coach and two Gardner-powered ex-Pioneer International 25-seat coaches which carried the names of 'The Northerner' and the 'Barkly Belle'. The ex-Cavanagh vehicle was 'The Queenslander'.

Then in 1952 the 13 June issue of the *Centralian Advocate* carried the news of the death of Bert Bond's son, Max, in a plane accident at Broken Hill the previous week. Four months later, in the 28 November issue, it was announced that Tuit's and Bond's had amalgamated under the name of Alice Springs–Darwin Motor Service. But the 'marriage' didn't last long. In the following year the *Advocate* of 16 October announced that Bond's and Tuit's had parted company and would go their separate ways. Alice Springs–Darwin Motor Services was dissolved in December 1954 and once more Tuit and Bond were in competition.

Apparently everything went peacefully for a time. Then Bond's announced the introduction of a semi-trailer coach with toilet on the Alice Springs–Darwin service, adding that 'Bond's have been running tours from Adelaide to Darwin since 1926. In the last 12 months Bond's coaches have travelled 1¼ million miles and carried 200,000 passengers as far as Perth, Cairns, Darwin, etc.'

This was a bit much for Tuit who responded with a three-column, 40-cm advertisement thanking Territorians for their support for 'a passenger service born and bred in the Territory and which is 100% Territorian. I sincerely hope you will continue to support and patronise, as loyally as you have in the past, the Local Passenger Service. Signed L. R. Tuit, Tuit's Overland Passenger Service.' In a later advertisement, he said: 'We're glad we're on our own way again because once more we can give you that special courtesy and service you used to enjoy from Tuit's Coach Services'.

Bond's turned the other cheek by merely advertising their service, saying inter alia that Bond's Northern Territory Tours had commenced in 1926.

During 1955 Len Tuit decided to sell his share in the Territory Transport Association's Co-Ord road train operation to Fleet Owners Pty Ltd. He had played a leading role in the formation of the TTA and was a foundation member and shareholder in Co-Ord.

The proceeds of this share divestment went toward the purchase of a Foden 33-seat coach with Gardner engine for use on the Alice Springs–Darwin timetabled service pulling a 16-ton capacity four-wheel freight and mail van, giving the complete unit an overall length of 66 feet.

Although some desultory sparring between Tuit and Bond continued over the next 12 months, it would appear that the passenger appeal and the profitability of the passenger and mail operation (the mail contract would presumably meet all operating costs and the passengers' fares would be 'fruit on the sideboard') became a factor in Bert Bond's decision to sell to his competitor. And so the dust stirred up in a decade of skirmishing settled down at last.

To assist in the purchase of the Bond operation Len Tuit found it necessary to sell some land and buildings to Fleet Owners.

In addition to expanding the Alice Springs–Darwin–Mt Isa services Len Tuit had begun tours to Ayers Rock and Palm Valley using ex-army 4 × 4 vehicles equipped with passenger bodies as these were best suited to the rough bush tracks of those days. To accommodate his customers on these tours he established tent camps at Ayers Rock and Palm Valley and provided them with electric power, hot water and other amenities.

In the early days Len's wife Pearl worked as hard as he did on building the business and Stan Cawood recalled that Pearl would 'cook a week's tucker for the touring parties' that went out to Ayers Rock when Tuit's were the only operators visiting that world-famous attraction.

Then the *Centalian Advocate* of 6 June 1958 carried a public notice stating the L. R. Tuit had advised that his company was continuing its tourist, passenger-carrying, chalet and other activities in the Northern Territory, and that the business had not been sold to other interests, nor was it intended to be sold. The statement added that by arrangement with Pioneer Tours, that organisation had taken over the winter tours to Darwin and Mt Isa, with Tuit's as its booking agency. The usual passenger services were being continued by Tuits. Rumours often have some foundation in fact and in May the following year newspaper advertisements for Pioneer-Tuit began to appear, publicising weekly services to and from Darwin and Mt Isa. Ansett Pioneer had by that time acquired a major financial interest in the Tuit operations and AP's Dick Bennett was transferred from Tasmania to integrate the operations and supervise a £70,000 program aimed at doubling the company's tourist accommodation in time for the anticipated rush of visitors for the Territory's centenary year (1960).

THE OLD AND THE BOLD

Facilities which had been established some years previously by Len Tuit at various popular tourist spots were upgraded and extended. Rooms were added to the lodge at Serpentine Gorge and the sleeping tents at Palm Valley and Ayers Rock were replaced by more substantial buildings. In Alice Springs the first motel there, the Mt Gillen Chalet, had its bed capacity lifted to 100. It was originally part of an army staging camp which was acquired by Bert Bond shortly after World War II and converted for use as a tourist hotel. The twice-weekly Alice Springs–Darwin passenger and mail service was stepped up to three trips a week, and an Adelaide–Alice Springs express coach operation was introduced, coordinating with the Darwin service.

Two years later the oldest store in Alice Springs, Wallis Fogarty Ltd, was bought by the Ansett organisation and closed down. The site became Ansett's airline and coach terminal and offices, on the corner of Parsons and Todd Streets.

Len Tuit also established town and school bus services in Alice Springs but these were not acquired by Pioneer. Len transferred them to his son Malcolm who ran them for about five years. When Malcolm expressed a wish to leave the Territory and seek business opportunities elsewhere Len and his wife Pearl took over the services again for a couple of years and then appointed a manager. They moved to the Queensland Sunshine Coast in 1975 where Malcolm had bought a business. On 15 May 1976 Len went fishing in his small boat. Later that day the boat was washed up on the beach near Mudjimba, just north of Maroochydore. No trace was ever found of his body. He was 64 at the time of his death.

In April 1982 a block of town houses in Alice Springs was opened by the Housing Commission of the Northern Territory on what was formerly part of the Alice Springs racecourse. The block was named Len Tuit Court and a plaque on the wall of one of the buildings reads: 'This complex is named after Len Tuit, a major contributor to the transport industry in Central Australia. Opened 8th April 1982 by Mr Roger Vale, MLA.'

Recovery Expedition

Stan Cawood was the son of C. A. Cawood, the first Government Resident for Central Australia. The North Australia Act of 1926 divided the Territory at the 20th parallel of latitude into two regions—North Australia and Central Australia—each with a Government Resident for administrative control. C. A. Cawood's region extended from the South Australian border to a line just south of Tennant Creek. His term commenced in 1927 and he relinquished office in 1929. Only one other resident, V. G. Carrington, was appointed before the North Australia Act was repealed in 1930 and the Territory was reunited under a single administrator.

In 1926 when the Cawood family moved to Alice Springs—then known as Stuart—the town's population was about 40 white people. In the same year the Australian Inland Mission of the Presbyterian Church, under the leadership of Rev. John Flynn, opened a hospital-cum-hostel in Todd Street. Adelaide House, as it is known nowadays, met the nursing needs for the area until the first section of the present government hospital was opened in 1938. The AIM building then became a hostel for bush mothers and children.

Stan Cawood.

In 1929 Stan Cawood was a member of the party which retrieved the bodies of Keith Anderson and Bob Hitchcock, who had died of thirst when their aircraft, the *Kookaburra*, was forced through engine failure to land in wild country between Powell Creek and Wave Hill.

Anderson had decided in a spirit of sympathy and fellowship to help in a search for the crew of the *Southern Cross* which was flown by the famous Charles Kingsford Smith and Charles Ulm. *Southern Cross* had gone missing in remote country in the north-west of the continent on the first leg of what was to have been an historic journey to England, and four days later Anderson and his mechanic friend Hitchcock set off from Sydney in the *Kookaburra*. They were seriously ill-equipped; there were no emergency rations, Hitchcock's tool kit had allegedly been stolen in Sydney, and the aircraft's compass was unreliable.

Anderson decided to fly direct from Alice Springs to Wyndham over some of the most inhospitable, arid and sparsely settled country in Australia. The aircraft was overloaded; rations consisted of four bottles of water and a couple of loaves of bread cut into sandwiches; there were a few tools which Hitchcock had obtained to deal with engine problems which had manifested themselves several times after leaving Sydney; but no implements such as axes or spades were carried for use in an emergency landing.

Well off-course, at a point approximately 128 km south-east of Wave Hill Station, the engine 'played up' once again and they were forced to land. Hitchcock rectified the trouble but thick turpentine scrub and bullwaddy prevented a take-off. They cleared a short runway as best they could, using only their bare hands and a two-bladed penknife, but the plane's small narrow tyres were unable to cope with the sandy soil and one was staked by scrub roots.

The forced landing had taken place on 10 April and Anderson and Hitchcock probably died two or three days later. Unbeknown to them the *Southern Cross* and its crew were located, safe and well, on 12 April. An aerial search for Anderson and Hitchcock resulted in the *Kookaburra* being sighted on 21 April.

A land party set out on 24 April from the big Vestey station, Wave Hill, to either recover the bodies or bury them. As events turned out the party had great difficulty in finding the dead airmen and their plane, food and water ran dangerously low so it was decided to bury the bodies on the spot and return to Wave Hill, leaving the *Kookaburra* to the elements.

But the prime minister, Mr S. M. (later Lord) Bruce decided that the Commonwealth would reclaim the bodies. The responsibility for this operation was given to the Minister for Home Affairs and Territories, Mr C. L. A. Abbott, who later was appointed Admin-istrator of the Northern Territory (1937–46). When the decision was announced, Mr J. O. Anderson of Thornycroft Australia contacted Abbott with an offer to provide at no cost to the government a brand new Thornycroft A3 truck to assist in the recovery mission.

Designed and built in Britain, Thornycroft vehicles were renowned for their ruggedness and 'go anywhere' ability and their transmission componentry was second to none. The three-tonne capacity model loaned for the expedition had bogie-drive rear axles—a rarity in those days—and an auxiliary low-range gearbox in addition to a sturdy main box. These features made it particularly appropriate in difficult terrain. Modifications carried out for the trip included removing the front mudguards to prevent their being ripped off in the thick scrub, discarding the bonnet cowling to assist engine cooling, and fitting a mesh screen in front of the radiator and a heavy bumper to bash down scrub.

The Thornycroft was transported by rail to Alice Springs from Adelaide, together with two coffins which consisted of pine boxes sealed in special lead casings with ornamental outer caskets.

The party which left Alice Springs on 31 May comprised Thornycroft's South Australian manager Frank Nottle, driver-mechanic Les Miles from Sydney, reporter-photographer William Berg from the *Guardian* newspaper in Sydney, Mounted Constable George Murray of the Northern Territory Mounted Police, and Stan Cawood, who had offered to act as cook and relief driver.

At Newcastle Waters supplies of food, fuel, water and oil were loaded on the truck and four Aboriginal trackers joined the group. In all, the truck was carrying well over three tonnes plus the members of the party.

Stan Cawood said that it took five days to reach Newcastle Waters using the road that followed the Overland Telegraph Line. From Newcastle Waters they followed the Murranji Track in a north-westerly direction until they came to a partly obliterated railway survey line running south-west which they then followed. Progress was slow through the sandy semi-desert country but despite having to travel in first gear for hours the Thornycroft didn't overheat or falter. The only times the engine had a rest was when the vehicle stopped while punctured tyres were mended. Most of the punctures were caused by 'staking' on turpentine scrub. Fortunately the vehicle had an engine-driven air pump for inflating the repaired tyres.

For five days the truck bashed its way through heavy scrub. The Aborigines walked ahead trying to find the marker pegs of the survey line. Then suddenly their uncannily keen eyes spotted the almost invisible tracks made by the horses of the land party which had come down from Wave Hill Station about six weeks previously to try to retrieve the bodies.

THE OLD AND THE BOLD

A youthful Stan Cawood (second from right) alongside the stranded aircraft *Kookaburra* at the site where Anderson and Hitchcock lost their lives. Others in the photo are (left to right) Les Miles, Frank Nottle and Constable George Murray. *(From* Kookaburra *by Pedr Davis and Dick Smith)*

Loading the lead-lined coffins containing the airmen's bodies on the Thornycroft truck for the journey back to Alice Springs. Stan Cawood accompanied the party as relief driver and cook. *(From* Kookaburra *by Pedr Davis and Dick Smith)*

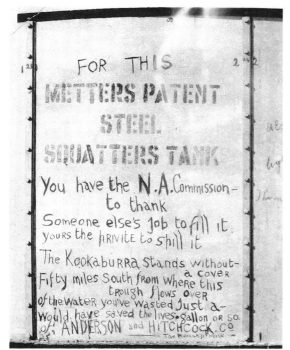

A reminder of the essentiality of conserving water in arid, remote areas was this inscription on a government tank along the Murranji Track.

After following one 'branch' trail which proved to be abortive but which cost the party valuable time and fuel, the Thornycroft's crew arrived at the fire-blackened area where Anderson and Hitchcock had lit the scrub in a vain effort to clear it. It took another day's searching to find the *Kookaburra*, and fuel was beginning to run so short that the expedition was near to giving up when the Aborigines, riding on top of the truck, yelled out that they'd seen the aircraft's wings shining in the sun. It was 13 June 1929.

The bodies were exhumed and placed in the coffins which were sealed in the lead casing. It had also been planned to tow the aircraft back to Newcastle Waters, but Constable Murray decided that this would be impossible so the aircraft's wings were folded back along the fuselage to reduce the risk of it being over-turned by wind, and all members of the party joined in the task of clearing a rough strip about 300 metres long and 50 metres wide so the aircraft could be flown out at some later date. (As it happened the aircraft was never flown out. It was virtually 'lost' for nearly 50 years, despite a number of attempts to relocate it. A successful search party in 1978 found the derelict remains which were removed to Alice Springs.)

The Thornycroft party then began its return journey with the coffins. Early on the third day it reached the Murranji Track where for the first time in ten days the Thornycroft was able to travel in top gear. Fuel consumption had been at the rate of three and a half miles per gallon.

The Aborigines left the party at Newcastle Waters and five days later the Thornycroft reached Alice Springs where the coffins and the rugged and reliable vehicle were loaded on the train for Adelaide. The expedition had lasted three weeks.

Born in Bellingen (N.S.W.) in 1907, Stan Cawood went jackerooing on Lake Nash Station for a couple of years before moving down to Alice Springs to rejoin the family when his father was appointed Government Resident.

For a time Stan drove occasionally for Bert Bond (Bond's Tours) who brought touring parties up from Adelaide in winter. Stan would take the tourists to such places as Arltunga and Palm Valley on excursions lasting several days. He also worked from time to time for Gerhardt Johannsen on various tasks.

Another job he had was operating the film projector at Joe Kilgariff's open-air Capital cinema in Todd Street, Alice Springs. Joe also owned the Stuart Arms hotel opposite the cinema and when it came time to change over reels on the projector, Stan recalled that Joe would tell him to take his time so that the patrons who had adjourned to the pub would have more time drinking. Later Stan was appointed manager of the cinema and the cafe.

Stan Cawood got into the transport business in 1942. The management of the Home of Bullion copper mine, about 32 kilometres north-east of Barrow Creek wanted ore carted to Alice Springs and offered Stan financial assistance to purchase an International KR 11 which in those days was a rather massive vehicle—the biggest in the Territory, according to Stan. He recalled that it had a 'Red 460' petrol engine which developed 143 bhp (107 kW) and a David Brown gearbox which had covered 800,000 miles without any failure when he sold the vehicle. The petrol engine was replaced with a Gardner 6LW diesel when a con rod went through the crankcase. The Gardner was an 8.3 litre engine with a rating of 117 bhp (87 kW).

The copper ore was carried in 44-gallon drums, each weighing 13 hundredweight when filled. The loaded drums were lined up on their sides down a gentle slope leading to the loading 'dock'. The truck tray accommodated 20 drums side-by-side and the dog trailer could carry another 16. 'You had to be accurate in rolling these drums on to the tray,' said Stan, 'because if you missed placing one in its exact position it was a helluva job moving it.'

Later he began carting ore from Harts Range. A big problem encountered on this route was the wide sandy crossing at Plenty River, where the tyres had to be

THE OLD AND THE BOLD

deflated to prevent them sinking into the soft sand, and then pumped up again with a hand pump.

The International was eventually converted to operate as a semi-trailer combination and with this he carted beer, 60 wooden kegs per load, from Alice Springs to Darwin, in the days when the Territory's beer requirements were supplied by Adelaide breweries. Jack Litchfield also had a semi on the beer run to Darwin at the time.

In 1949 Stan was one of the founding members of the Territory Transport Association (see Chapter, Organising the Unorganised) and became a shareholder and a director of Co-Ord, which was TTA's operating arm and contractor for the road-rail freight service. He built his operating interest in the Co-Ord to four vehicles—three of his own and one operated under contract by Don Tottey who made a specialty of carrying cars. Encouraged by the reliability of the Gardner engine in his International he purchased a Foden with a similar power unit. In time he bought two more, and each of these vehicles pulled two or three trailers grossing up to 60 tonnes, according to what loading was available.

Between 1953 and 1957 he was chairman of directors of the TTA and was regarded as the organisation's 'Mr Fixit'. Stan's pleasant and courteous manner served him and Co-Ord well in dealing with customers and handling tough negotiations with Comrails—in particular Commissioner Pat Hannaberry and the commercial manager, Norm Brearly.

It was Stan who managed to talk Peko into sharing out the copper ore traffic between Tennant Creek and Alice Springs which had been the exclusive business of D. R. Baldock & Co. He went to Melbourne to discuss this with Comrails but they weren't interested in who carted it by road because it all ended up in rail trucks anyway for movement south for smelting. Baldock's were carting about 500 tonnes a week; suddenly this increased and Baldock's began to farm out the surplus loading to Co-Ord.

Baldock's at this stage were not members of Co-Ord; Dave Baldock had been a founding member of TTA and took out a shareholding in Co-Ord but did not use it as he was fully occupied with the Peko traffic southbound and general Tennant Creek freight northbound, so he sold his share to Allan Allwright.

Stan Cawood ascertained that Baldock's did not have a contract with Peko, so while he was in Melbourne he conferred with company officials and came away with a verbal agreement that they would give half the tonnage to Co-Ord and the other half to Baldock's. This resulted in Baldock's buying back into Co-Ord to get some 'say' in its affairs.

In 1957 Stan relinquished the chairmanship of TTA/Co-Ord and John Ryan who had been the organisation's secretary took over. Like Len Tuit, Stan could see a bright future for tourism in the Territory and he began to diversify his interests. His Co-Ord share was operating satisfactorily with sons Greville and Ian looking after the day-to-day freight-handling and driving requirements, so he established a company which he named Alice Springs Tours and bought out Jack Cotterill's small tourist business when Cotterill intimated that he wished to devote his energies to developing King's Canyon as a tourist attraction, in association with an accommodation project that he was planning at Wallara, south-west of Alice Springs. Cotterill had built up a small fleet of passenger vehicles

An unusual consignment for S. Cawood & Sons was this rail motor destined for service on the North Australia Railway. Cawood's Gardner-powered K-series International hauled it to Larrimah where it was put on rail.

The Cawood fleet built up to three Fodens plus a couple of Bedfords for lighter work than that of road train operations.

to carry tourists between Alice Springs and Ayers Rock where Mrs Daisy Underdown, licensee of the Hotel Alice Springs, had built The Chalet. Len Tuit was already at The Rock with his tent accommodation. Eventually Stan took over The Chalet and combined it in his Alice Springs Tours operation.

The sale of Len Tuit's business to Ansett Pioneer put that organisation in a dominant position in the Territory's tourist trade. Early in the 1960s the Ansett airline and the company's express and tour coaches began to bring droves of tourists to the area where they were catered for in Ansett-owned accommodation and were taken on a variety of trips ranging from half-day local itineraries to extended tours to Ayers Rock in various types of Ansett vehicles such as the then-fashionable Flexible Clippers and specially-built four-wheel-drive buses designed to travel to remote places.

Naturally Trans Australia Airlines couldn't stand by idly watching all this 'packaged' traffic boosting its competitor's revenue so it decided to break into this growing tourism business and TAA's general manager Reg Rechner contacted Stan Cawood with the idea of setting up a local tour organisation which could offer a variety of tours radiating from Alice Springs as well as accommodation.

Having spent nearly 20 years in freight transport, Stan sold his Co-Ord share to Fleet Owners in 1961 and helped form the Central Australian Tours Association,

becoming CATA's first chairman. Foundation members were King's Canyon Tours, Legion Tours, Boomerang Tours (Lance Rust), Ross River Tours (Green Bros) and his own Alice Springs Tours. These companies could provide schedules ranging from local town sights to four-wheel-drive excursions.

An early move by CATA was to widen its ambit by including motels and hotels in its membership so that fully accommodated tours could be packaged by TAA. Members could also operate in their own right.

After operating The Chalet for nearly 20 years Stan Cawood sold it to the government which in turn acquired Ansett's Red Sands Motel as well as the Inland and the Uluru before completely reorganising Ayers Rock accommodation into one area at Yulara about 20 kilometres away.

In the late '70s CATA was sold to Australian Associated Tours (AAT) which was jointly owned by TAA and Mayne Nickless. In 1983 when AAT was acquired by Australian Pacific Tours, CATA also became a subsidiary of that big national coach tour operation.

Stan Cawood retired to Cairns, North Queensland, with his wife Ethel, who was a daughter of Mrs Daisy Underdown. A wing of the new Yulara complex at Ayers Rock was named after him in acknowledgment of his contribution to tourism and to transport generally in the Northern Territory.

Snapshot taken by a keen amateur photographer lopped off the Foden prime motor but captured the heavy loading on a Cawood road train bound for Darwin.

THE OLD AND THE BOLD

The Co-Ord: Organising the Unorganised

Before World War II and before the reconstruction and sealing of the Stuart Highway between Alice Springs and Darwin, the preponderance of freight consigned to Darwin and the Top End was handled by ship and the North Australia Railway moved any freight that required further transport south. A few truck operators offered services over various sections of the Darwin–Alice Springs route and a handful of these even covered the full length of the 954-mile run.

From the south the volume of freight, passengers and mail entering the Territory by the Central Australia Railway was less than that coming in through Darwin. From Alice Springs, where the CAR terminated, road trains and other vehicles in the government fleet moved materials to remote stations and a few individual carriers took general consignments and perishables up the Track. Mail contractors provided transport for any passengers.

After World War II the pattern of freight movement underwent major change. Shipping services to Darwin were reduced, although the Western Australian Government's Stateships and some others continued to call at Darwin it was at a reduced frequency. As a consequence there was a complete reversal of direction of freight flow into the Territory. It began to move in increasing volume from the south, to Alice Springs by rail with on-forwarding to Darwin and intermediate points by road. The road hauliers ignored the North Australia Railway's Larrimah–Darwin service as they were able to cover that sector quicker than the train and also avoid having to tranship at Larrimah the freight which had already undergone transfer at Port Augusta and Marree at railway break-of-gauge points and at Alice Springs from rail to road.

Naturally the parent of the NAR, Commonwealth Railways, was displeased with this rival freight development and went as far as making representations to the Northern Territory administration to restrict competition to its NAR by hauliers, as was the code of operation in all states at that time. But apparently this was legislatively impossible.

Comrails' dissatisfaction with the situation was shared by many of the users of road freight services, but for different reasons. Users contended that hauliers had tended to 'pick the eyes' out of the consignments, giving preference to carting heavy and compact items and deferring the handling of bulky and awkward goods.

So, to protect its NAR and enhance its commercial fortunes at the same time, Comrails came up with the idea of a coordinated road–rail service bridging the rail-less gap between Alice Springs and Larrimah.

But the idea and its implementation were two entirely different matters. Getting the hauliers together was almost impossible. They were individuals, unorganised, some of them pioneers in their own right, their spirit of competitiveness sharpened by the influx of demobilised defence-force personnel keen to carve their own niches in the new era that was dawning. Alice Springs was a microcosm of the situation that was spreading throughout the world.

Typical of the advertisements appearing in the *Centralian Advocate* (Alice Springs) in 1949 were these:

Overland Transport (Martin Bros.) (ex-A.I.F.) Carriers and Contractors. Diesel haulage service. Alice to all points on Stuart Highway and Darwin. Livestock and station carrying a specialty. Receiving, forwarding and commission agents. Mobile cranes and breakdown service.

J. H. Butler, Carrier. Alice Springs–Darwin. Station and mining people specially catered for.

Don Thomas and Lou Miller, general carriers.

Jim Clark, general carrier, Hartley Street. Heavy cartage by semi-trailer a feature.

Lackman Agencies, Railway Terrace. Transport and forwarding service. Speedy weekly motor truck service Alice Springs–Darwin. Agents for Vaccuum Oil Co. Pty. Ltd. Austin dealership.

For that carrying job, contact Mick Costello.

As one observer of the transport scene in the late 40s and early 50s put it:

There were a lot of small carriers running between Alice Springs and Darwin with Inters, Fords, Chevs and small stuff; they were disunited, disjointed; one-truck and two-truck men, all battlers, good blokes, but all battlers. So you might have one, Bill's Transport, up in Darwin broken down and he's got a load of beer in the Alice Springs railway shed. I'm just a mate of his so he says: 'Charlie, hey listen, will you bring the beer up to Newcastle Waters pub this week because I look like I'm stuck up here, I'm waiting for a new crankshaft.' So I say, 'Rightoh'.

They used to work in together but some loads got pinched from time to time. I might go down next week and I'd say, 'Listen, Bill said it was all right for me to pick the beer up,' but it wasn't at all, he had only given me authority for one week. There were occasional instances of pinching each other's loads and so on, but they were all friendly enemies really.

Eventually some of them got together and formed the Territory Transport Association and secured a contract with

Comrails to haul freight from Alice Springs to Larrimah. They lifted their game; in due course the economic potential of train-type vehicles became apparent, and 'big iron' like Fodens, Macks, Leylands and Internationals began to appear.

Whilst this was a simplification of what occurred it was indicative of the lead-up to the formation of a well-organised and profitable freight haulage operation which had no equal anywhere else in Australia and which in turn led to that unique vehicle combination, the road train.

Pat Hannaberry, the tough-talking and determined Commissioner of the Commonwealth Railways system which incorporated the Central Australia Railway (Port Augusta–Alice Springs), the North Australia Railway (Larrimah–Darwin), and the Transcontinental Railway (Port Augusta–Kalgoorlie), saw the situation this way:

They were a bunch of blokes with small trucks and no money, all competing with each other and cutting rates. We'd take the freight to Alice Springs but from there on we'd be entirely in their hands. Nobody seemed to care a hoot. In the Alice Springs shed there'd be goods which had laid untouched for goodness-knows how long. Nobody would want to cart them up. They'd pick over the freight that suited them best and carry that and leave the rest. They had no agents in the main cities like Sydney and Melbourne; in fact they had no organisation whatsoever.

The Commonwealth Government's Works Department had a transport service which worked out of Alice Springs and other places serving remote places and they wanted me to take it over and run it in conjunction with the rail freight service. But it was losing money and was very costly to run. I told them that if they couldn't make money with it, how could we? To my way of thinking they didn't have the right equipment. I approached the hauliers in Alice Springs and told them that the situation was intolerable and that I'd put my own road equipment on and send them all broke.

In September 1949 Hannaberry fired a salvo: 'It is my aim to bring transport under unified control even to places along the [Alice Springs–Darwin] route which are not served by any railway,' he told a *Centralian Advocate* reporter. He added that he intended calling tenders for the operation of a road service coordinating with the Central Australia and North Australia rail services. In other words, he intended chanelling all freight to the railways, using road services under contract to haul between the rail heads at Alice Springs and Larrimah.

No doubt the NAR's wartime volume of 147 trains a week was an indication to Hannaberry that the line could handle whatever traffic that could be directed to it. The words 'sole right' appeared in the tender specification, and to put further heat on the locals Hannaberry indicated that tenders would close in three weeks' time.

Pat Hannaberry.

Necessity or an emergency often throws people into each other's arms and a leader quickly comes to the top to marshal and organise strengths and special attributes.

Early in November a number of carriers from Alice Springs, Tennant Creek and Darwin quickly got together to form an association. They were: Len Tuit, Dave Baldock, Martin Bros, Overland Transport, F. Rowell, Costello & McArthur, Stan Cawood, and Litchfield's (all based in Alice Springs); H. Williams & Co., and Kittle Bros, (Tennant Creek); Alan Allwright, Sweetman & Co., H. Johnson, and G. Robinson (Darwin). They voted to 'go to court' if necessary to test the powers of the Commissioner for Railways to compel traders to consign their goods through the railways' contractor (if any) and if need be to finance legal action against such a move. They had a feeling that the whole thing was already cut-and-dried and that 'outside interests with far larger capital than any individual Territorian at present operating' were about to step in and take over.

The Territory Transport Association (TTA), as it was named, decided that despite the possibility of a fait accompli, it would send chairman Len Tuit to interview Pat Hannaberry at his headquarters in Melbourne. On his return to Alice Springs accompanied by Adelaide solicitor Mr S. Melville, Tuit brought the news that the closing date for tenders for the coordinated road-rail service had been deferred until 7 January.

As things turned out, the closing date was postponed several times and three years later—in November 1953—a contract between TTA and Comrails was finally signed and the defacto service was formalised.

Ironically, and as if to underline the interdependence of road and rail on each other in the outback, Kurt Johannsen was busy hauling railway rolling stock on his specialised equipment from Larrimah to Alice Springs to meet a shortage which the Commonwealth Railways were experiencing on the Central Australia operation. He'd been engaged to move four locomotives and tenders, plus about 30 trucks and some brake vans.

THE OLD AND THE BOLD

Kurt had always kept away from general freight operations, preferring to work in specialist fields such as heavy haulage and cattle transport.

In an apparent effort to stabilise their rates whilst tendering for the road-rail contract, the Territory Transport Association inserted the following Public Notice in the Centralian Advocate on 9 June 1950:

Allan C. Allwright, David Roy Baldock, James Henry Butler, Harry Byrnes, Stanley Walter Cawood, Harry A. Johnson, Kittle Bros, Arthur John Litchfield, Martin Bros, Janet H. McArthur, Lackman's Agencies, Gordon Robinson, Harold Williams, Jack B. Sweetman, Leonard R. Tuit, Karl L. Zahmeller, being members of the above association (TTA) wish to inform the public generally that owing to abnormal rises in operating costs they are compelled to charge the following rates per ton for cartage from Alice Springs:
1. Alice Springs–Darwin £25 per ton.
2. Cartage from Alice Springs to intermediate points north-bound at 6½d per ton mile.
3. All cartage from Darwin to Alice Springs and intermediate points at a similar rate.
4. Returned empties for clients at agreed prices between the carter and the client.
The above rates apply from July 1, 1950 until further notice.
P.J. COLSON, Secretary
Hartley Street, Alice Springs

Percy Colson, the TTA's first secretary, was an accountant, tax agent and auditor.

The Colson name was a respected one in The Centre. A tablet on a cairn at Birdsville, (Qld) provides the following record:

E. A. (Ted) Colson with Aboriginal companion Peter crossed the Simpson Desert, 1936.

On May 24, 1936, Ted, Peter and 5 camels left Blood's Creek, South Australia, and on June 11, 1936 arrived at Birdsville via Poeppel's Corner. The southerly return completed a journey of 600 miles in 40 days.

This monument was dedicated by W. F. Brook chairman, Diamantina Shire Council, September 1973.

The crossing of the desert by Colson was made three years before Dr Cecil Madigan on his well-equipped and well-publicised expedition crossed from Andado to Birdsville in 1939.

John Ryan took over from Percy Colson as secretary of the TTA about eight months after it was formed. Colson was in ill health and did not wish to continue.

Ryan went to the Territory shortly after he was demobilised from the Army at the end of World War II. He travelled to Alice Springs by the Ghan and then rode in the cab of one of Baldock's trucks which was driven by Alf Price, son of one of the original telegraphists on the Overland Telegraph Line, and he paid £2 10s. for the trip to Tennant Creek where he obtained a job shortly after with the Mines Branch. After about 18

John Ryan.

months he opened a mining equipment agency but the business didn't prosper so he went down to Alice Springs and once more obtained employment with the Mines Branch.

Following a couple more years' service with the government, he again went into the agency business, this time with Noel Buntine, who had arrived in the Territory in August 1950. They sold jackhammers, compressors, rock drills, etc., to mine owners and took on agencies for Tolley's Wines, Michelin Tyres, New Zealand Insurance and others, and at the same time offered bookkeeping services for local firms and individuals.

One of the first clients was the Territory Transport Association, whose secretarial requirements were provided on a part-time basis. 'We were all pretty inexperienced,' John said, recalling the formative days of Co-Ord, which was the name bestowed on the operating arm of the association:

I didn't know much about transport and they didn't have the right trucks. There were petty jealousies between some operators. But the catalyst was the Commonwealth Railway's determination to make the North Australia Railway pay its way, and the Commissioner, Pat Hannaberry, told us that if we didn't get ourselves organised he'd give the contract to another group or to an individual company. No doubt he had his eye on the O'Neils with their strong financial resources and organisational expertise. (See Chapter, And Then There Was One.)

John Ryan said that initial talks on freight rates weren't so much a matter of negotiation as they were of being dictated to and told what price Comrails would pay. In addition the standard of service that Hannaberry demanded meant that better and bigger vehicles had to be acquired and this forced operators to turn to hire purchase. In other words, they had to get bigger and think bigger.

The road rate between Alice Springs and Larrimah (623 miles) that was agreed upon by Comrails and the TTA was £16 a ton, with a lower rate for beer and some heavy goods. Ice-cooled containers carrying perishables (average load four and a half tons) were paid for by Comrails at £117 per container, including unloading, checking and delivery. Ten years later these rates were still in force, despite increases in operating costs.

In retrospect, John said, hauling to Larrimah was not a good idea. Co-Ord vehicles should have gone all the way to Darwin as the independents were doing, but Hannaberry insisted on shoring up the NAR and Co-Ord carriers simply had to make the best of the situation. At various times they were allowed to take perishables right through and that was a sound operation.

At first there was no firm contract between the TTA and Comrails. Then on 9 February 1951 a news item in the *Centralian Advocate* said that talks on the road–rail service had resumed. Mr G. Hudson, representing the Comrails commissioner, had just visited Alice Springs and discussed various aspects of the proposed coordinated road–rail service with members of the TTA, and he was quoted as saying that he thought the coordinated service—in a form acceptable to all concerned—would be implemented before many months passed.

Three months later Comrails were calling tenders for local pick-up and delivery in Darwin, to operate in conjunction with the proposed coordinated road–rail service. In his annual report for 1950/51 Pat Hannaberry forthrightly stated: 'The charge quoted for this service by local carriers is exorbitant and would not be accepted. It is hoped these difficulties will be overcome shortly and the co-ordinated services [come into] full operation in 1952.' But there were problems still. In his 1952/53 report Hannaberry noted:

The Co-Ord rail service between Alice Springs and Darwin introduced in 1950 did not function as intended. This was not due to shortcomings on the part of the contractors but almost wholly through railway staff shortage at Larrimah and Darwin and the difficulty of arranging suitable delivery and pick-up service in Darwin. The current contract terminates on August 31, 1953...tenders [have been] called...the most suitable was that of TTA and a contract operating from November 1 will be entered into with that company.

On 13 November 1953 a spokesman for the TTA announced that its contract with the Commonwealth Railways would commence the following day. His statement said:

The association was not formed with the idea of establishing a monopoly, but should provide faster and cheaper service to the people in the north.

A number of incorrect reports on proposed activities have been getting about and it is felt advisable to issue a statement. The association was formed nearly three years ago and carriers operating were invited to join.

Carriers of the association are Martin Bros, L. R. Tuit, Territory Transport Service (P. Colson), Kittle Bros, Lackman Agencies, G. Robinson, A. Allwright and S. Cawood. Mr D. R. Baldock is also a member.

A social gathering of operators and suppliers in the early 1960s included (left to right) Bob Fleming, Shell agent, Mt Isa; Des Jury, Shell agent, Alice Springs; Don Tottey, operator; Tom Cory, Jury's partner; Walter Allwright, Co-Ord traffic manager (carving pig in photo); Les Loy, Co-Ord secretary; Fleming's partner; and John Ryan, Co-Ord chairman (partly obscured).

THE OLD AND THE BOLD

In the early days of the coordinated road-rail service individual owners provided a varying range of equipment for hauling freight between Alice Springs and Larrimah. In the upper photo, taken about 1955, the Foden body truck and trailer were owned by Overland Transport. Below, Alan Allwright's Foden prime mover with semi-trailer and dog trailer is carrying 40 tons. *(Photos, John Ryan)*

About this time John Ryan and Noel Buntine got into the operating side of TTA by buying Martin's Overland Transport which gave them a share in Co-Ord. Later they acquired the share of Gordon Robinson (Darwin) which hadn't been actively used for some time and they built up the business with Ryan looking after the management as well as tending to TTAs requirements, and Buntine on the road plus an employed driver.

The TTA spokesman's statement continued: 'We will cart to Larrimah for £16/18/- per ton and it is anticipated that with the NAR charges customers will pay about £23 per ton to Darwin as against £25 the carriers charged when operating as independents.' He added that under the previous system delays in delivery of goods were unavoidable. Individual carriers had sole rights to handle certain customers' goods and quite often a carrier might have left for Darwin and a few hours afterward another consignment might arrive by rail at Alice. The consignment would then remain at Alice until the carrier returned:

Under the coordinated service any member of the Territory Transport Association may be rostered to take immediate delivery of goods the minute they are unloaded at Alice. The North Australia Railway system is ready to cope with the volume of work. At Darwin the association will operate a delivery service to clients.

Two weeks later a news item headed 'ROAD RAIL SERVICE STARTS SMOOTHLY' appeared quoting TTA secretary John Ryan as saying that the coordinated service 'shifted 60 tons from Alice Springs in its first week of operation. The first load, taken by Dale Colson got through to Larrimah in plenty of time and the system ran smoothly from the railways this end.'

Eleven years later tonnages hauled in the 12 months to 30 June 1964 by Co-Ord were:

Perishables:

Alice Springs–Darwin and intermediate points	804

General Freight:

Alice Springs via Larrimah to Darwin	5 053
Darwin, Katherine via Larrimah to Alice Springs	1 221
Alice Springs–Mt Isa	777
Mt Isa–Alice Springs	Nil
Mt Isa–Larrimah	939
Darwin via Larrimah to Mt Isa	259
Alice Springs–Tennant Creek and other points south of Larrimah	3 159
Tennant Creek and other points south of Larrimah to Alice Springs (includes copper ore)	33 299
	45 511

Needless to say, though, there were plenty of problems. Shortly after John Ryan announced the commencement of operations a story which appeared in the *Centralian Advocate* of 4 December 1953 was headed 'CO-ORDINATED SERVICE WILL WORK WELL' and John Ryan was quoted as saying: 'There have been some teething troubles but a few minor improvements to the railways facilities at Larrimah and Darwin will have the service running smoothly'. He admitted that the TTA and Comrails had agreed that perishables should go all the way by road from Alice Springs to Darwin pending the upgrading of facilities at Larrimah. There was a 'lack of facilities at Larrimah and understaffing at Larrimah... There are no sheds for sorting, there is no ramp for loading and unloading motor cars and there are no lights for the men to work under at night.' He added that the situation was the same at Darwin and 'there are bound to be delays until proper sorting sheds are established'. He praised the manner in which railway employees at Alice Springs had handled the matters. 'This end, things have gone smoothly and efficiently,' he added.

In 1953 the rail service from Port Augusta to Alice Springs consisted of one mixed goods and passenger train (the Ghan) and one goods train each week, with additional trains put on as required, such as special livestock trains during the cattle season. With the introduction of the coordinated road–rail service trains on the North Australia Railway we changed from one mixed and one rail car weekly, to two mixed trains.

In January 1954 the North Australia Railway introduced a 'cool van' and once again perishables were transhipped at Larrimah. But apparently the NAR fell down on the job because in July there was an announce-ement that perishables arriving in Alice Springs consigned to Darwin would go direct by road until diesel electric locomotives were introduced. The perishables train would be scheduled to arrive in Alice Springs at noon on Saturdays, which would enable fast trucks to reach Darwin on Monday morning.

About this time Comrails began trial runs with diesel electric locomotives on the mixed goods/passenger train and this led to a subsequent announcement that these new locos were expected to cut eight hours off the running time for the 800-mile journey, but 'due to the condition of the track they will be restricted to 30 miles per hour'.

As if to keep the road operators on their toes, Commissioner Hannaberry was quoted in the same issue of the *Centralian Advocate* as saying: 'We have no intention of competing with the Territory carriers or of giving the contract to a southern concern. Provided the TTA continues to give satisfactory service and doesn't increase freight charges they can be assured of an extension of contract.' This statement was made in rebuttal of a 'red hot rumour' that Comrails intended to 'wipe out the TTA by putting on its own diesel trucks to operate the coordinated service'.

Competition is the soul of trade, some say, and there's also the contention that it keeps people honest. Be that as it may, competition was certainly a feature of the haulage scene up and down the Stuart Highway as Comrails endeavoured to stabilise its service by means of its road–rail coordination scheme and independent hauliers offered faster transit times, less handling and delivery to door.

To keep the heat on the Co-Ord service the independents from time to time accused it of 'stealing' consignments from them.

In December 1954 the *Northern Territory News* published a statement by Ted Stiles, the proprietor of Outback Transport, who claimed that the Alice Springs stationmaster had been phoning and sending telegrams to independent operators' customers telling them that their goods had been in the Alice Springs goods shed for a considerable time, but that there was no independent truck near Alice Springs. He suggested that TTA should collect the goods.

Stiles denied that customers' goods had been left any length of time; independent trucks collected promptly and delivered virtually to the door. Whenever the railways had told the independents' customers these stories, an independent truck was available at Alice Springs, Stiles said.

TTA secretary John Ryan replied by saying that

It should be known that Mr Stiles and his association (Independent Freighters) were not regular carriers on the Alice Springs run until the North Australia Railways suffered severe setbacks from washouts last year. As opportunists during that period of disorganisation they canvassed Darwin traders and secured many of the old regular carriers' customers.

If the independents are capable of conducting a better service than the Co-Ord they need not fear the loss of customers, as invariably the consignee gravitated to the safe, speedy and reliable carriers. If they were efficient there was no need for the dubious propaganda published to cover up the deficiencies of their operations.

Regarding railway action in advising consignees that goods are waiting at the railhead...we contend that any livewire stationmaster would adopt this principle to empty his trucks when the time lag in arrival of the carrier concerned is so great as to cause hold-ups... Independent carriers should be prepared by having trucks available for the loading and thus save the need for telegraphing to have the goods unloaded...

All was quiet for some months and then an attack came from another and unexpected quarter. Stan Martin, one of the founder members of TTA claimed the coordinated carriers were a 'creeping monopoly'. At this time Stan and his brother Jim were operating a service from Alice Springs to Victoria River Downs and Wave Hill via the Stuart Highway and the Murranji Track, and were not involved in the Co-Ord operation. Stan claimed that the Co-Ord had been whittled down from a representative group of carriers to a Big Three oligarchy. Five years ago transport operators had formed an association which was intended to be a solid bloc of carriers joined together to protect their livelihood from the big southern combines. Then, referring to the formation of Co-Ord as the business or operating arm of the TTA with ten of the founding members forming Co-Ord on a shareholder basis, Stan said that gradually these shareholders sold out—to other members, *not* to outside independent carriers:

This—their first vital mistake—came from lack of foresight and from the very human tendency to let clear thinking be clouded by greed. The association, by hogging shares and keeping other independent carriers on the outer, ceased to be a representative body and became a closed operation.

Overnight, independent carriers found that a large combine had been let into the association [an apparent reference to Fleet Owners, a company owned by the O'Neil family of Sydney who had large quarrying and transport interests and owned Diesel Motors, Australia-wide agents for Foden vehicles] and at the same time Rudders, another large combine, were granted certain concessional rates on all railways throughout the southern States and on Commonwealth lines providing that all goods must be carried by the association and placed on rail at Larrimah.

A few weeks later one of the Big Four sold out and now the one-time voice of the N.T. carriers is the Big Three—one big southern combine and two N.T. operators. These three carriers—due to the Commonwealth Railways' effort to make the Larrimah–Darwin line pay—control 80% of all goods from Alice to points north of Larrimah.

The powers that be have spoken, and the association would keep the franchise even if the independents cut cartage rates and travelling times by half.

In the past competition between Co-Ord and the independents has been keen but fair. It is fair no longer. A few weeks ago customers of independents were approached by a Co-Ord representative and told they would get a big freight cut if they consigned through Co-Ord. Independents have since lowered charges accordingly and announced this through N.T. newspapers.

Then came a second stab in the back. Goods from Adelaide to centres north of Alice Springs began to be consigned through Rudders without consent of the consignors, thus preventing the independents from receiving the goods at Alice, even though the railways at Alice Springs had written authority that Independent Freighters were to carry the goods.

As if that broadside wasn't enough, the *Northern Territory News* of 13 September 1955 ran a front-page story headed 'N.T. TRANSPORT BATTLE OPENS AGAIN', which reported 'A new carrier has entered the field and there has already been talk of a rate cutting battle'.

By way of background, the news item said that after months of strong competition the independent carriers had joined forces with the TTA, resulting in all freight carted from Alice Springs going by rail to Larrimah. Railway Commissioner Hannaberry had hailed the end of the 'hot war' as a step forward in the development of transport services. But, the item continued:

This week came the first indication that the battle for freight markets from Alice north was not over, and the 'cold war' state of affairs warmed up.

Into the field came southern carrier Don McMillan, in partnership with well known N.T. transport driver Ivan Wiese.

The first of their massive petrol-engine 24-ton capacity units captured a large share of the perishables freight for Darwin traders and made what is claimed to be the fastest single delivery yet. Leaving Alice at midnight Saturday, the truck arrived in Darwin with the perishables very early on Monday morning. The new carrier announced a reduction of £5 per ton on the coordinated service charges of £25 per ton and there was immediately talk of a rate-cutting war.

Stories came into the News office that the coordinated service countered the new rate by offering to cart for £18 per ton from Alice to Darwin.

Speaking from Alice Springs, Territory Transport Association secretary John Ryan denied stories of a rate cutting war. The coordinated service rate is £25 per ton and at this stage he did not believe it was economical to cart under that. He pointed out that the £25 rate dated back to 1949 when operating costs were considerably lower than at present.

Mr Ryan said that other N.T. carriers had tried running at £21 per ton but had found this uneconomical.

The opposition from one truck at present on the road was not considered a threat, Mr Ryan said.

A few months later Ted Stiles returned to the attack, claiming that Commissioner Hannaberry was using methods of unfair competition against independent carriers. He said he had seen a letter from the Commissioner's office telling businesses in Mt Isa they would get a 25 per cent rebate on goods on the Central Australia Railway only if they used the coordinated road–rail service from Alice Springs onward.

But the TTA refrained from replying. Instead a spokesman said that Mr Stiles had been brought into the TTA on his own terms but later he considered the association was not strong enough to control the trade and stated that he could do better outside and subsequently broke away from the association. The spokesman added that whilst he was in the association Stiles consistently broke the conditions of the contract with the Commonwealth Railways by running in opposition to the North Australia Railway.

About this time Reg La Fontaine was advertising in the *Centralian Advocate* that he was a forwarding agent for Independent Freighters who were operating a bi-weekly service between Alice Springs and Darwin, operating from a depot near Johannsen's garage.

In his 1956/57 report Commissioner Hannaberry drew this picture:

The north-bound traffic by coordinated services included general merchandise, heavy machinery, motor vehicles, perishables, (including perishables carried in ice coolers, lift-on refrigerated containers and beer from Victoria), [as well as] pre-fabricated materials for a brewery being erected by Southern Brewery Company. South-bound traffic consists almost entirely of empties, but there were some consignments of machinery and ores.

He also noted, however, that

the Co-Ord Service, although operating effectively and growing in popularity each year, has not reached its full development owing to severe competition from independent road operators who run through to Darwin and thus compete directly with the (North Australia) railway. On this account quite a substantial tonnage is lost to the railway which is well equipped to carry it.

In 1956 two developments took place. The first was the extension of the Co-Ord service to Mt Isa from Alice Springs (748 miles) where a considerable expansion of mining operations was in progress. The second was a controversial one: Co-Ord obtained a foothold in the big copper ore movement south from Tennant Creek to Alice Springs, which had been virtually the exclusive business of Baldock's. In addition, some copper concentrates traffic was diverted to the NAR for export to Darwin.

Dave Baldock was one of the original 10 shareholders in Co-Ord, but as he was not interested in carting to Larrimah and Darwin he sold his share to Alan Allwright for £1,000 and concentrated on hauling for Peko Mines, taking their materials and general freight from Alice Springs and back-loading with copper concentrates.

It was at this time that Jim McConville and his brother Harry, with Milton Owen, bought into Baldock's.

Somehow or other, *Jim said*, Co-Ord managed to get into the Peko loading and it looked as if we would be cut right out. But we dug our heels in and came to an agreement whereby we would carry 50 per cent of the copper southbound and all Peko loading northbound from Alice Springs. There was some pretty bad feeling about this in TTA but we weren't prepared to sit on our hands and watch our business being taken from us.

I managed to buy one of the shares in TTA from Stan Cawood. It cost me £7,000 which was a lot of money at that time but it got me in to the conference table and I could then keep tab on what was going on.

A brief item in the *Centralian Advocate* of 23 June 1961 stated that D. R. Baldock & Co., had bought a share in the other transport firm under contract to Peko (TTA).

Co-Ord's keenness to obtain some of this traffic can be appreciated when it is realised that Peko began to step up commercial production of copper concentrates in 1954, when 6,000 tons per annum were being moved, to around 34,000 tons 12 years later.

Whether Baldock's were in a position to handle the ever-increasing copper tonnage is a moot point. It would appear that Stan Cawood's expeditious success in obtaining a share of the Peko traffic (see chapter, Recovery Expedition), could be linked to urgings by Peko management to expand the number of vehicles in line with the rising volume of ore to be moved to the railhead. The rate charged by TTA was £5. 5s. per ton from Tennant Creek to Alice Springs.

Apart from the Peko episode there were other problems among Co-Ord operators.

According to one observer who was closely associated with the organisation from its inception, the operators 'jockeyed' for loads which suited them best and used all sorts of ruses to avoid carrying the types of freight which were difficult or unpleasant or less profitable to handle.

Nobody in TTA liked perishables. In the early days of the coordinated service these came in boxes and weighed about 11 kg. Due to the indifferent train service they could arrive at Alice Springs at any hour, which meant dropping everything and loading as quickly as possible to get on the road. The rail vans were loaded haphazardly; carriers had to 'hunt' up and down the rail platform looking for consignments for various towns en route.

All operators taking part in the service were supposed to accept whatever loadings were allocated to them by TTA management, but he mused that 'it was strange how often my vehicles had to take perishables because (a) someone had broken down or (b) it was my turn, which seemed to come round rather frequently! But this was a fairly general grouch among members.'

There were all sorts of trailer hooks and couplings and ringfeder pin sizes to contend with. At times an owner would be asked to pull another's trailer because of a prime mover breakdown, and then the fun would start. Often it was preferable to transfer the load from the incompatible trailer to one which would hook-up more readily and safely. There was everything from Commer 'knockers' to Fodens of all sizes, from small to big Internationals to Macks. Mixed in amongst it all would be ex-wartime GMCs, Diamond Ts and others.

It would have been preferable and more efficient, the critic noted, if a company had been formed with shareholder capital which could have been used to provide a standardised fleet of vehicles. This, of course, was said with the advantage of hindsight.

The O'Neils through their company, Diesel Motors, got operators thinking along the right lines about more appropriate gear for the job and sold a lot of Fodens

By the time Rudders introduced containerised freight in 1957 the Co-Ord operators and the Commonwealth Railways had upgraded their equipment considerably. Bigger and more powerful Gardner-engined Fodens had been placed in service and an overhead gantry had replaced mobile yard cranes. *(Ken Moody)*

In later years, while body trucks were still preferred as prime movers by operators, before the advent of the 'triple' combination, Mack was the favourite and by this time (early 1970s) British-origin vehicles had virtually disappeared from road train operations in the Northern Territory. *(Ken Moody)*

THE CO-ORD

which did good work. But not only were they keen to sell Fodens, they were also anxious to get into the operations side and the locals didn't want them as they feared an eventual take-over of their services by these 'outsiders'.

Ironically, that's precisely what happened in the long run.

Despite all the skirmishing and criticism, TTA steadily forged ahead as the Territory's transport requirements increased. Between 1955 and 1970 the Co-Ord service reached its peak. The operational fleet grew to 35 units, mostly road trains consisting of 'body' trucks pulling two and three trailers of varying length, usually with a single-axle dolly under the front end and either two or three axles at the rear, grossing up to 60 tons per train.

John Ryan continued his part-time secretarial functions until 1960 by which time Co-Ord's business had developed to a point where a full-time secretary–manager was needed. So, with the appointment of Les Loy, John, wearing his other hat as Overland Transport's owner, slipped into Stan Cawood's place as chairman when Stan decided to devote more time to developing his tourism interests and sold his Co-Ord share to Fleet Owners.

In 1964 John Ryan disposed of his transport interests. He sold his two Co-Ord shares covering Overland Transport and Robinson's Transport to Noel Buntine but he maintained an association with the transport industry through his agency for Michelin tyres and later the Bandag tyre recapping process which he eventually sold to Bell Bros, of Western Australia.

John Ryan these days is a member of the Territory Development Corporation which is a government body designed to assist the establishment of new industries by way of long-term loans. Noel Buntine is also a member.

Les Loy was secretary–manager of the TTA/Co-Ord organisation from 1960 to 1964. He had been with Ansett Freight Express in various positions in Melbourne, Adelaide and Perth and had learned much from that company's modern methods in the competitive world of interstate freight movement.

Individually, the TTA members were good operators, he said, but as individuals they also had their own particular methods and jealousies. He added that it was the most lucrative operation in Australia. (This was borne out by the fact that the contract rates which Comrails were paying Co-Ord were almost 50 per cent higher than those for comparable distances on interstate transport operations in the eastern and southern States.)

When Les Loy came on the scene containerisation was expanding because rising costs were compelling operators to look to more labour-efficient methods of freight handling. Yet despite the obvious benefits of container movement it wasn't regarded with favor by some Co-Ord operators because the contract between the TTA and the forwarders included bringing back empty containers free of charge, which interfered with their copper cartage. Output from Peko was booming and it was worth £5 5s. a ton, Tennant Creek–Alice Springs, but the copper couldn't be carried in the containers as the floors would not stand up to the deadweight loading. Copper was one of the few back-loads available and big tonnages were involved.

A way around the problem had to be found because it was feared that the container operators might introduce their own vehicles under a separate contract with Comrails.

Eventually compromises were worked out. Some carriers placed sheets of strong plywood on top of the bagged copper and carried the containers on these plywood 'plates'; some vehicles had frames fitted above the copper to accommodate the empty containers; and there was always the easy way out by reducing copper loadings.

Although Les' original contract was only for two years he ended up staying for four, and during that time the business nearly trebled. Co-Ord was carting just

Les Loy.

about all the Territory's beer requirements which were coming from Adelaide; it was moving cement to Mt Isa and drums of steel balls for a crushing process at the mines; on the way back loads of copper concentrate were picked up from Peko (Tennant Creek) which, although it was carted at a low rate, put the cream on the cake.

You name it, we were moving it somewhere—machinery, building materials, motor vehicles, station supplies, hardware, iron and steel, wire, corrugated iron, groceries, pipes, domestic goods and equipment, the lot.

We didn't handle fuel; we kept clear of that type of work. We had enough problems with perishables!

Container traffic grew to the point where between 30 and 40 containers a week were handled by Co-Ord vehicles for John Dring and Rudder's (later known as Cargo Distributors). Rudder's and John Dring did their own local delivery and pick-up in Alice Springs, in addition to supervising the movement of containers through The Alice to other places throughout the Territory.

There were big Territory developments at the time and projects such as Rum Jungle and Mary Kathleen (uranium mining), RAAF Tindal, Mt Isa Mines, Peko Mines and others brought big tonnages in their wake and broadened the outlook and managerial expertise of those involved.

The polyglot fleet of light and medium capacity ex-wartime prime movers as well as the later Commers, Bedfords, Fords, etc., in semi-trailer and truck-and-trailer form were shouldered out by Fodens, Leylands, Macks, AECs and upper range Internationals. These were bigger and more powerful than most vehicles operating on the interstate routes in the more populous regions.

The earlier load capacities of 10 and 12 tons grew to 50 and 60. To a minor extent the semi-trailer configuration was retained, mainly for specific requirements or conditions, and given bigger motive power, but it was in the truck-and-trailer area that the most notable advances took place. With the advent of more power a second trailer was added, then a third. Next the prime mover (or 'body truck' as it came to be known) was increased in length. Later the trailers were lengthened but reduced in number to two per road train and bogies replaced single axles at the front and rear of each trailer. Overall length of these combinations gradually increased, and there must have been a temptation to keep adding trailers, as Dave Baldock did in the early postwar years. But the practicalities of braking, power, component strength and the probability of legislative action on length and loads tempered the operators' thinking and they settled for a three-unit train (body truck and two trailers) within an overall length of 145 feet (44 m), thus establishing a type of operation which was unique in the world. (For subsequent role of Co-Ord see chapter, And Then There Was One.)

Co-Ord's Bête Noire

Ted Stiles, like many of his road transport contemporaries, found his way to Tennant Creek in search of work. He came from Big Bell, near Cue, in Western Australia, during the late '30s and although he intended continuing on to Mt Isa torrential rain knocked out the road so he was forced to stay at the Tennant. He'd brought his saxophone with him and was very quickly 'adopted'; as he put it, he was 'king' for a time. He got work as a general labourer at one of the mines but he quit after a few weeks and went to Alice Springs. He got a job with the Department of Works at a time when D. D. Smith was engineer in charge of the Central Australia region.

Ted was employed as a driver on the department's transport service to remote stations, and some of the people he recalled working with at the time were Jim, Harry and Len McConville, Spurge Nicholls, George Nichols, 'Shorty' Fulton and Ewan Clough. He drove the department's AEC Monarchs and Matadors but didn't get behind the wheel of the famous AEC road train which was Ewan Clough's responsibility. But he and Clough got together musically; Clough was a 'pretty good' banjo player and they frequently played at dances and balls at Alice Springs and Tennant Creek.

While he was with the department at Alice Springs, Ted Stiles drove many trips out along the Tanami Track to The Granites and via the Murranji Track to Wave Hill and Victoria River Downs which were over 1,000 kilometres from Alice Springs. These services were the only supply lines for stations in remote areas during the war.

When the war ended Ted decided to strike out on his own. At a disposal sale of surplus defence equipment he purchased a Canadian Maple Leaf truck for £10 ('I've still got the receipt'), and for a while he dismantled former army camps, buying the building materials which were in short supply and despatching them by rail to Adelaide and Melbourne or carting them to Darwin for shipping to Fremantle and Sydney.

Then for a time he drove for Jim Lackman carting perishables. The method of handling perishables in those times was primitive, to say the least. There was no refrigeration, not even ice. In Ted's words:

We'd get them off the train when it arrived on Saturday night—if it was on time, which wasn't very often—and we'd cover them with a tarpaulin and get on our way so that we travelled as far as possible by night. If the train had been delayed the consignment would 'go off' pretty quickly. Likewise if we had trouble on the road we'd lose the load.

The late Ted Stiles.

Then about 1950 Ted decided to start his own business and called it Outback Transport, based in Darwin. At first he concentrated on handling perishables between Alice Springs and Darwin, and then he began to carry general freight as well. He bought a petrol-engined Commer semi-trailer unit and then another as the business grew and he extended his perishables service to Mt Isa.

In time the Commers, including a 'knocker', were incapable of handling the volume of freight and he began to buy Fodens, with each of which he pulled two trailers. When Mack trucks came on the scene Ted was among the first in the Territory to acquire one (in 1956), and it was so reliable that he bought a second. They cost £10,000 each in those days.

He experienced considerable differential trouble with the Fodens, but he added with a wry smile that they were worked very hard, frequently pulling 80 tonnes all-up. He also found the same trouble with the Fodens that other operators discovered: the range-change could not be engaged to 'split' whilst climbing a hill. The technique was to engage the required range in the auxiliary at the foot of the hill and not alter it 'on the run', otherwise a snapped tailshaft or damage to both boxes could easily result. Many a tailshaft, axle or diff was smashed helping other transports which had stalled and jacknifed on hills.

Ted Stiles was the 'bete noire' of the Territory Transport Association. When it was formed he opted to stay out of it and continue carting for the clientele he'd built up rather than pooling his freight with the group.

TTA secretary John Ryan said that Stiles wasn't big

enough to compete with Co-Ord so Stiles gathered some others, including Stan Martin and Percy Lake, to form an independent group.

Comrails leaned hard on us to take them in with us, *said Ryan*. We conferred with the independents and they told us that they wanted a third of the traffic. Well, we reluctantly brought them in but it didn't last for more than about six months. We found Ted was approaching some Co-Ord customers direct to handle their freight, so we parted company.

Ted said that these were originally his customers and he kept the pressure on Co-Ord in numerous ways, including letters and advertisements in the local newspaper. For example, the *Centralian Advocate* in July 1955 carried an item headed 'COOL VAN FOR PERISHABLES' and went on to say:

Mr Ted Stiles, spokesman for Territory Independent Freighter Service (in opposition to Co-Ord) said he was prepared to buy a special cool van to haul perishables from Alice Springs to Darwin, straight through by road.

He was commenting on an announcement by the Territory Transport Association that the Commissioner of Railways had ordered that perishables be sent straight through by road instead of being transferred to rail at Larrimah.

Mr Stiles said that the move was made because it was well known that independents were doing a faster and better job taking freight straight through by road.

Ted Stiles claimed to have built up a lot of business which was taken from him by Co-Ord:

A lot of stuff was consigned through me but I didn't get it. Co-Ord said that I was pinching their freight but I wasn't. I used to get my customers to clearly mark their consignments 'for transport by Outback Transport' or by 'Independent Transport Association' but it didn't seem to make much difference, unless I or one of the other independents was around when the freight arrived and we could claim it.

For instance, I organised the South Australian beer traffic to Darwin and Mt Isa but overnight I lost it; the railways diverted it to Co-Ord and there was nothing I could do about it.

Claims and counter-claims proliferated. There were occasional skirmishes in the rail yards and the hapless police were called to prevent a fracas developing.

'I eventually got a good man down there,' said Ted. 'He was Reg Lafontaine. We had a depot near Kurt Johannsen's garage and Reg organised things very well for us. He made sure that we got the stuff that was consigned through us.'

Rate-cutting was also indulged in, sometimes to 'give a bit of stick' to Co-Ord and sometimes to make life hard for a newcomer from 'the south' who was trying to break into Territory transport.

In a letter to the writer who was editor of the national publication *Truck & Bus Transportation* at the time (1955) Ted said:

Price cutters at present are causing a bit of an upset but we all know they can't last. The schedule price for hauling between Alice Springs and Darwin has been £25 per ton for many years. Only a couple of months ago a Melbourne operator came through with a semi and, with the co-operation of a local driver, started up a big 'Trans-Australia Service', with Sydney, Melbourne, Adelaide, Alice Springs and Darwin painted along both sides of the vehicle. They chopped the price to £20 a ton. Well, by the time this letter reaches you their service will have folded up; their customers are already handing their business back to me.

A Foden with sleeper cab owned by Ted Stiles' Outback Transport about to depart from Darwin with a small load. Southbound back-loading has always been much lighter than north-bound freight in the Territory. *(Ron Knight)*

CO-ORD'S BÊTE NOIRE

These flash-in-the-pan operators don't realise the big overheads here in the Territory, where everything is so dear. Garages don't stock any parts you require for your trucks and that means trunk calls to Melbourne or Adelaide, then heavy air freight charges on the items you request. It costs me £240 to send a truck with two drivers to Alice Springs from Darwin, and that is not allowing anything for depreciation. Tyres only average 10,000 miles. It costs a lot to operate up here.

Various operators came and went but Co-Ord and Outback Transport and other independents kept going. Ted continued to feud with Co-Ord, and despite his criticisms of rate-cutting he lashed out at Co-Ord in 1958 with a reduction from £25 to £20 a ton between Alice Springs and Darwin and advertised 36-hour delivery to Darwin, as well as 'chaser truck deliveries to all points en route'.

In 1959 he announced that he had introduced a fridge van on the Alice Springs–Darwin run. Costing £8,000 the semi-trailer unit and its Leyland Hippo prime mover plus another trailer would form a 125-ft road train departing Alice Springs on Saturday nights. The fridge van was 35 feet long and provided 1450 cubic feet of refrigerated space.

Ted Stiles also built up services to the Kimberleys and Kununurra in Western Australia, as well as to a number of Vestey stations and others in the Top End, carting general freight, station supplies as well as perishables. Occasional trips were undertaken to Borroloola and to places in Queensland's Gulf Country.

But in 1968 at the age of 60 Ted Stiles decided to call it a day. He'd been a battler all his life and although he'd built a reasonably successful business he could see more battles ahead. On the horizon he could see a tightening of load limits and other regulations in the Territory; the unions were beginning to push hard for higher wages and changed conditions; and more interstate operators were coming into the Territory and cutting freight rates. In addition insurance cover was difficult to obtain and it was very expensive. There had been 28 crashes involving complete loss of equipment—six in one year—and as Ted said, 'the insurance people wouldn't even nod to me in the street much less cover my vehicles or their loads!'

He said that he felt the writing was on the wall for him, so he decided to get out while he had some assets to sell. He disposed of his vehicles and depots in Darwin (Bishop Street, Parap) and Alice Springs (Stuart Highway) and purchased an area of land at Howard Springs, about 30 kilometres from Darwin, with the intention of turning it into a caravan park. This didn't eventuate and Ted died in August 1986 at the age of 78.

Working Conditions

In the 1950s and 60s the Railway Terrace area was the busiest part of Alice Springs. Along the eastern side of the street were the offices of the Territory Transport Association and Cargo Distributors; further down the terrace was Baldock's depot which was later moved out to the north of the town where it became a neighbour of Allwright's Transport, Overland Transport and Fleet Owners, among others. Up on the corner of Todd Street and Wills Terrace where the Shell Service Station now stands was McConville Motors, the General Motors agents, later acquired by Len and Geoff Kittle and moved along Wills Terrace to its intersection with Railway Terrace.

The western side of Railway Terrace was occupied by the railway passenger station, Comrails offices and train crew quarters. A couple of hundred metres beyond the station and adjacent to the terrace there was a small siding where perishables were transferred to road vehicles upon arrival of trains. All other freight was handled in the goods yard. John Dring had an office over there. The goods sidings were some distance to the west of Railway Terrace, more or less on the edge of the present greatly enlarged road-rail freight transfer area. Here the road trains owned by the TTA's Co-Ord operators pulled alongside rail trucks and vans to take on consignments for Darwin via Larrimah, Mt Isa, Tennant Creek and numerous wayside towns and settlements.

Truck & Transportation reported in May 1963 that

there are approximately 75 people employed directly by Alice Springs-based transport on general freight movement to Tennant Creek, Darwin and Mt Isa. Ninety-five per cent of the vehicles operated in the over-25-ton class are of British manufacture. Largest vehicles have a payload haulage capacity of 58–60 tons with prime mover and three trailers. Rated horsepower of these units is around the 220/230 hp mark.

Medium-capacity vehicles (payload capacity of 38/40 tons) with prime mover and two trailers usually have 150/160 bhp units. Also in the medium-duty class are 150/160 bhp prime movers with double bogie trailers, providing a payload capacity of 35/37 tons. The advantage of the latter unit is its shorter overall length and trailer stability. Many of the trailers are convertible to semi-trailer operation.

Working conditions in the 1950s were tough, and mechanical handling aids were virtually non-existent. Peter Gunner, who drove for Kittle Bros, and later for Fleet Owners, said that just about every item of freight was transferred by hand from the railway trucks and vans to the road vehicles:

It didn't matter whether you were a driver, a loader or a foreman; you just got stuck into it. There was very little handling equipment. An ex-army 'blitz' with a jib rigged up in front was used to lift heavy items but it was incapable of lifting a car or caravan high enough to put it on top of the load. At Larrimah there was one little hand-operated slewing crane which was quite inadequate, but gradually the situation improved.

We'd take a trailer down to the rail yard and hump bags of flour and all sorts of other loading across to it and then when we couldn't get any more on it we'd bring another trailer in and then the body truck. When these had been loaded we'd probably go around to the fuel depot and put drums of oil and petrol and other products on the third trailer and maybe we'd top-up with a couple of cars. After a couple of days spent this way we'd head off up the track. We'd usually only go about 30 miles and then make camp. There was always plenty of firewood up there and it was on high ground and out of the frost area in winter.

Next day the long, steady grind to Larrimah or Mt Isa or wherever we had to go would begin. When we reached our destination we'd have to unload and then we'd head back, usually empty. We didn't have much time at home in those days!

The trailers we hauled were usually a mixture of Freighter and McGrath and later Haulmark. They were usually called 'dogs'—I don't know why. The small ones with the axle or axles in the middle were known as 'pigs'; again I don't have any idea why, unless it was because they always seemed intent on going straight ahead due to the solid drawbar with which they were fitted. They were certainly a pig of a thing to handle!

Peter Gunner was a stockman before he joined Len and Geoff Kittle as a driver in 1947. He carted ore from the mines to the battery, and water to the mines. At first the ore was loaded by hand and then tipped into the grid by means of a hand-operated hoist. He regarded the advent of the hydraulic hoist as 'a modern labour-saving marvel' at the time.

When on water carting duties he said that he would go out to the Seven Mile bore to fill up but sometimes he might have to wait nearly all night for enough water to build up to fill the water cart because the bore would have been sucked nearly dry by other water carriers during the day.

After these stints carting to and from the mines he graduated to highway work hauling fuel and general freight.

He left the Territory for a period, driving for companies on interstate routes but he returned and began working for the O'Neil interests, first on their cattle cartage operation and later (1964) with Fleet Owners on the Co-Ord service as a driver and subsequently in a managerial role until he left in 1977 to pursue other activities.

Ian Cawood, one of the sons in S. Cawood & Sons and nowadays chief district ranger (parks and wildlife) for the Conservation Commission of the Northern Territory, painted a similar picture to that outlined by Peter Gunner:

In the 50s we used to load every vehicle by hand. Co-Ord had the contract to cart all the beer to Mt Isa, in the days before the breweries were set up in the Territory. We had to load every carton of beer by hand because there were no pallets and no forklifts. Cartons of matches, cigarettes, foodstuffs—you name it—we humped it on to the trucks and the trailers while someone checked it against the paperwork. It was usually a case of loading all day and driving all night in those Fodens which had a top speed of about 30 miles an hour. We knew where every consignment was located on the vehicle.

Tyre troubles added to our difficulties. At one time we were using Olympics and over a period we blew 32 of them. The walls used to bulge and then blow. On some trips we'd even blow our spares.

Stan Cawood said that Olympic admitted they were a faulty batch and replaced them. He later fitted Michelins, with greatly improved results.

We rarely had to mend punctures on the road, *Ian added*. The only times we'd be involved in fitting tyres to rims would be if we were carrying unmounted tyres and had blown our spares—then we'd have to get the tyre levers out and remove the damaged cases and mount fresh ones.

Across the Barkly Tableland the highway was flat and straight; if there was a slight bend in the road we sure welcomed it to break the monotony! Despite the flatness of the road it was remarkable how hard we had to push those Fodens when they were heavily loaded. It seemed to be uphill all the way and we rarely got into top gear. We knew every pothole, every minor bend, every bit of badly cambered road from Tennant Creek to Mt Isa. After we left Frewena the long haul to Mt Isa seemed like heading toward the end of the earth. It was like a black ribbon stretching out straight ahead and reducing to a pencil line away in the distance. It had a sort of mesmerising effect and drowsiness had to be fought off as we trundled along at a steady 30 to 35 miles an hour. On the Barkly Tableland the country seems to melt into the horizon. It's possible to scan the entire 360 degrees of the horizon without seeing a solitary tree.

The last leg of that route, from Camooweal to Mt Isa, was always very rough and very narrow and quite difficult to drive on. It was a very unpleasant bit of road.

Unloading was always a chore because you'd have no sleep the night before and you'd feel drained. Then you'd have to turn round almost immediately to get back to Tennant Creek for a load of copper to go down to Alice Springs. And if you didn't make that on time you'd probably 'do in' your weekend and some rest because everything started again on Monday.

How did we stay awake? Well, a slosh of cool water on the face sometimes did the trick. But mostly we'd stop and rest, even if it was only for 10 or 20 minutes. But that wasn't always

Ian Cawood.

easy because we always seemed to have some deadline to meet and we'd have to 'make miles'.

One bloke I knew used to go slower and slower as he got more and more tired. He used to subconsciously change down, regardless of what load he was carrying, until he was down to second or even first, and at that point he would realise it was time to stop and take a break. Tiredness caused him to ease the pressure of his foot on the accelerator pedal and that made him change down as the vehicle seemed to be pulling badly!

When we'd do the occasional trip to Darwin we'd camp near Mindil Beach where the casino is now—Vestey's old meatworks was in that area. We'd park the trucks on the beach—they never got bogged—and enjoy the tropical nights with a pleasant sea breeze blowing across the bay. Nobody ever bothered us or told us to move on.

At other times we'd camp out at Ted Stiles' place near Howard Springs.

Ted kept a pet crocodile in his back yard and it used to bark at us all night. It was about 12 or 14 feet long; he'd raised it from young and he kept it in an enclosure which was fenced with chicken wire. We used to camp out the back of Ted's place and we often thought that darned croc would escape and do us in!

From the viewpoint of the operators there were preferences for loading. A consignment which was heavy and could be loaded quickly and topped up with something bulky such as a motor vehicle was favoured. For example, at one stage drums of steel balls were being transported to Mary Kathleen and Rum Jungle for use in ore processing; these could be quickly slung aboard by crane and the driver could be on his way without having to manually load every box, package, coil, etc.

Ken Moody, Northern Territory sales manager for Co-Ord (now wholly owned by Fleet Owners) has been in the thick of the action since 1955. Although at first employed as a road train driver he quickly discovered that that side of the operation had no attraction for him so he got a job in the rail yard transferring freight. He said that the amount of handling involved before containers came on the scene was 'incredible':

The freight would be loaded into wagons at, say, Adelaide, then changed across from one wagon to another at Port Augusta, then transferred again at Marree, and on arrival at Alice

Ken Moody.

Springs it would be taken out of the wagons, loaded on to our trailers, tarped and roped, then go to Larrimah where it was unloaded once more into railway wagons to go to Darwin where it was finally unloaded. Quite a lot of it didn't survive the journey, but that didn't seem to matter in those days.

There was only one general freight train a week out of Larrimah for Darwin. It departed every Thursday. Why Thursday nobody knew because that meant the freight reached Darwin on Friday and what could you do with it on Friday?

We used to start loading here at Alice Springs on Saturday and would work all day Saturday and all day Sunday and all day Monday. We might finish about 10 p.m. Monday and drivers would then jump in their trucks and head off for Larrimah. They'd have to be there in time for all this general freight to be unloaded into the NAR wagons. The Co-Ord management would have to ensure that there were sufficient rail wagons at Larrimah to meet requirements.

It would take about two days to load the stuff into the rail wagons at Larrimah. There never seemed to be enough time to stack the freight properly. The train had to get away on time even though it didn't always get to Darwin on time.

In the early days Co-Ord employed 14 people in the Alice Springs yard and six at Larrimah. The only railway employees

at Larrimah were the station master and some gangers looking after the track. At Darwin the unloading was done by railway employees.

Most of the freight was shifted by hand. We had a little Fowler crane and an International. There wasn't a crane big enough to handle caravans and cars so we used to get the Fowler and the International at either end and pick them up. It was all rather primitive. We had roller conveyors, of course, as well as hand trolleys and there was a gantry which was hand-operated. There was also block and tackle gear.

Then along came containers, and we reckoned we were home and hosed. The first containers that Rudders brought into the Territory were little four-footers. They used hundreds of them! I think they were mainly used for shipping in the first place and they sent them up here to see how they went. As far as we were concerned they were great; we'd pick them up with the Fowler crane and transfer them in next to no time.

Later they brought in 8 footers and then 16 footers, and finally 20 footers in accordance with international standards.

The 8 footers were plywood and metal. The plywood was three-quarter inch stuff. The door was a piece of 8×8 plywood with metal all round. You had to lift it up and then drop it down into a groove and a couple of clamps came across with seals or locks on them. There was many a busted finger or toe caused by these drop-down panels. Why they couldn't have just put a couple of doors that swung open and shut nobody ever knew. If they were down on the ground you had to get up on a trailer platform or someting to lift the door; if they were up on a trailer or rail wagon you had to get above that again. We often had to use crowbars and hammers and that didn't do the containers much good!

The first lot of containers for perishables were ice boxes. They were packed with ice when they were loaded at Adelaide or Port Augusta but they always needed re-icing by the time they got to Alice Springs. So we'd get the ice for them down at Heenan's on the corner of Gregory Terrace and Todd Street

Heavy consignments were handled by mobile crane; all other freight was manhandled from rail vans to road vehicles. Photo shows Alan Allwright's Foden being 'topped up' at Alice Springs. *(John Ryan)*

WORKING CONDITIONS

and pile it into the tops of the containers and ram it down as hard as we could. The ice would then last till they reached Darwin. We had to transfer them from the rail wagons to the road trains by means of the hand gantry or by block and tackle. We used to lift each container up, then move the rail truck from under it and back the trailer under and lower it down. The rail trucks had to be 'shunted' by means of crowbars under the wheels. Then we'd have to bring the rail wagon back to get another ice box off, and repeat the process until we'd transferred them all. Fortunately in those times there were only about five or six ice boxes at a time. It used to take about three hours to re-ice them. They were usually taken direct by road to Darwin, although for a while they were transferred to the train at Larrimah but this wasn't satisfactory so they reverted to direct road.

Eventually the ice boxes were replaced by mechanical refrigerators, or refrigerated containers, as they're known. They came on the scene at a good time because the old ice boxes had begun to rust out and I think the railways were worried that one day we'd pick one up with the gantry and lift the top but leave the bottom and the contents on the rail wagon!

Even the ice boxes were a big improvement on the early days when perishables in boxes were loaded on to open semi-trailers, packed with some ice and covered with a tarpaulin.

The perishables carried in the ice boxes were mainly potatoes, onions, cabbages, cauliflowers, oranges and sometimes apples. No stone fruit, lettuce, bananas or similar commodities were carried because they simply would not travel; they deteriorated rapidly. We tried various methods of carrying some products, even using dry containers, but once the doors were closed the containers became 'sweaty' because the fruit or vegetables created their own atmosphere and they'd quickly go 'off'.

After a while things looked up. Comical Railways, as we called them, provided an electric gantry which was quite marvellous. It was worked with two switches; it took all the sweat and toil out of gantry work. They also introduced a shunting tractor, but as railway shunters seemed to be always in short supply we did most of the shunting ourselves, particularly at night. Many a time we only just stopped a runaway truck from going out through the gate! Trying to get those old crank-type brakes to work on a moving truck wasn't always easy. We'd often have derailments and next morning

the railways blokes would come in and say: 'Okay, where are the derailments today?' They'd then fix them up; usually it was only a matter of getting a mobile crane to lift the wagons back on the rails.

In the 1960s there were about three trains a week coming into Alice Springs. The perishables used to come in on the Ghan on Friday night and we'd work from about 9 p.m. till about 2 a.m. transferring them, and the trucks would get away about 5 a.m. Saturday, to be in Larrimah by Sunday afternoon for transfer to the train which would get them to Darwin by Monday. We preferred to take them direct to Darwin by road, which we did from time to time if there was some hitch with the train service. We could get them there much quicker by road, with two drivers on the job.

When mechanically refrigerated containers were introduced the whole perishables scene changed rather dramatically. Eventually we were moving something like 26 or 27 refrigerated containers at a time. By about 1970 we were moving them from Alice Springs to Kununurra and Wyndham in Western Australia and to Mt Isa in Queensland as well as to various places throughout the Northern Territory in addition to Darwin. We were getting six trains a week, plus extras when required and plus cattle trains, of course.

But the whole pattern of things changed after Cyclone Tracy [December 1974]. It just cut out everything. There were relatively few people up there for quite a time and their requirements in perishables and other foodstuffs were flown in. Then as the population began to drift back it was found that companies had begun to make other arrangements and supplies began to come in through Queensland. Also a lot more traffic began to move in big refrigerated pantechnicons direct by road from Adelaide and so the 16 footers and 20 footers went out of fashion.

Today along Railway Terrace a row of blue-grey athol trees with their drooping foliage symbolising the hot, arid climate marks the site of the former Alice Springs rail station and the old rail freight yard. Beyond this tree line there's a four-lane segment of the Stuart Highway carrying traffic along the western edge of the town. The passenger terminal is now about one kilometre to the west of the old site and is adjacent to the big freight transfer yards with their network of tracks stretching

Although containers took much of the manual labour out of the freight transfer operation, many consignments still had to be manhandled, as can be seen in this photo. The plywood refrigerated containers shown here, introduced by Co-Ord, didn't prove successful and were scrapped.

THE OLD AND THE BOLD

Two mobile cranes were used to transfer larger items such as this caravan from road to rail and vice-versa. Motor cars were slung in a cradle arrangement so that only one mobile crane was required. *(Ken Moody)*

for a further one and a half kilometres alongside the town's industrial area with numerous streets providing quick and easy access for road vehicles.

Gone are the days of sweating bodies toiling to transfer freight from rail wagons to road vehicles. A huge travelling gantry, operated by one man, straddles the tracks in one section of the yard, lifting containerised freight to and from road and rail vehicles.

Until recently, in another section of the yard, the driver of a 'yard goat' prime mover fitted with hydraulic lifting turntable moved rows of pantechnicons and flat-tops off railway wagons and angle-parked them on the adjacent hard-standing area. Today huge mobile lifters known as 'piggypackers' raise loaded semi-trailers off the railway wagons and deposit them alongside; company-owned prime movers then reverse under them, haul them to depots and couple them into road train combinations destined for distant parts of the Territory as well as Western Australia and Queensland. Over on a separate siding rows of rail tankers are loaded with crude oil transported from the Mereenie field by road, 250 kilometres south-west of Alice Springs, for refining in Adelaide.

The hissing and wheezing and clanking of the steam engines which brought the Ghan and the 'mixed' to The

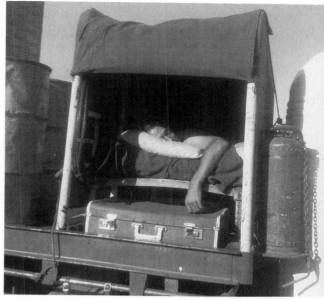

A 'sleeper cab' on an early model Mack was a far cry from today's standards but an improvement on the bunk on top of the cab of early postwar road trains. *(Peter Ritchie)*

Alice have been replaced by the throaty rumble of diesel locomotives with their five-note chiming horns sounding across the rail yards. Six 70-wagon freight trains a week—sometimes they're 80 wagons and 1,700 metres long—now come to Alice Springs and a similar number goes south. A few kilometres south of the town, through the Heavitree Gap, there are road trains unloading into the stock yards and cattle wagons on a siding ready to depart for the Adelaide markets.

The tedium of the break-of-gauge transfers of freight at Port Augusta and Marree has gone forever. The narrow-gauge (1.06 m) line which contributed to the frequently substandard performance of the former Central Australia Railway was replaced in 1980 by the new standard-gauge (1.43 m) line 150 kilometres to the west of the old route to avoid flood-prone regions. From Adelaide it shares the Transcontinental Line as far as Tarcoola and then comes up on an entirely new 831-kilometre track crossing 52 bridges and built to meet the latest standards of railway technology.

The Container Revolution

The amount of handling involved in getting freight to Darwin in the 1950s was almost unbelievable. From Adelaide it travelled on the South Australian Railways' broad gauge (1.6 m) system to Port Augusta where it was transferred to Comrails' 1.4-metre gauge trains which conveyed it to Marree where it again underwent transfer to the Central Australian 1.06-metre line which went to Alice Springs. It then had to be moved across to road vehicles for transport to Larrimah where once again it was put on rail for Darwin. Counting the loading and unloading operation all freight was handled six times; if it came from say, Sydney, it also underwent transfer at Albury and again at Melbourne before proceeding to Adelaide and thence to Port Augusta. The Melbourne–Port Augusta leg was all 1.6-metre gauge and did not require transfer at Adelaide.

This situation which bordered on the fantastic was a 'natural' for the introduction of containerised freight. Instead of manhandling every item at six points the transhipment became a simple gantry operation, picking up loaded containers and transferring them in a fraction of the time and at a fraction of the labour cost. The excessive labour cost was exacerbated by the pilferage rate which was 'unreal' according to one TTA member, who added that 'no insurance company would touch us'.

Two companies, Rudder's and Dring's, saw a textbook opportunity for the use of containers and in 1957 introduced this system to the Territory.

The big national firm of Rudder's Ltd, which had been in the freight forwarding business since the 1890s, had been sending freight to Darwin from other states for many years by sea but in the 1950s switched to the Commonwealth Railways' road and rail service for their Darwin consignments. In 1957 they began using containers for their Darwin and Tennant Creek traffic, thus providing virtually a door-to-door service to Territory destinations from all States, as well as a through-rate which included pickup and delivery charges.

Rudder's were very experienced in handling freight by containers, having used this method since before World War II, and announced the Container service in Alice Springs in February 1957. Rudder's managing director, Philip Rudder, summarised the advantages of containerised freight as being elimination of damage through multiple handling; prevention of pilferage; transit times comparable with passenger trains; twice-weekly dispatch; door-to-door delivery; fixed freight charges; and ease of handling by carriers.

A couple of months later Rudder's Alice Springs manager S. R. Hamilton was reported as saying that the new container service was proving very popular. Containers leaving Adelaide on Thursday night arrive in Alice Springs on Monday morning and are unloaded and delivered the same day. They are reloaded for the return trip on Monday night's train. Hamilton said that Rudder's would be extending the service to Tennant Creek in the next two weeks.

Next, Rudder's introduced a type of service which was proving very popular at that time in the eastern and southern States—the sealed rail van. Under this system

When the national freight forwarding company, Rudders Ltd, began its container service in 1957 in competition with other firms, labour-intensive transfer of freight at numerous interchange points, as well as pilferage, were greatly reduced. The Foden body truck shown here and its three trailers are carrying twelve containers. *(Ron Knight)*

the forwarder hired vans from the railways and filled them with freight, using their own employees to load and unload and process the paperwork. The railways' task was simply to haul the vans and rates quoted by Rudder's for this service between Adelaide and Alice Springs ranged from £15 to £46 per ton. Much of the materials and stores for the RAAF base which was being built at Tindal, near Katherine, was moved by rail van to Alice Springs and then transported by Co-Ord vehicles.

The first containers used by Rudder's were known as R-boxes. They were of steel construction, measured 7 × 5 × 5 feet 6 inches high (2.1 × 1.6 × 1.7 m), weighed about half a tonne and could carry three tonnes. They had been built originally for use in the coastal shipping trade and had proved very successful, but with the decline of this trade Rudder's had begun to re-deploy them on to rail services. In 1959, Rudder's announced that they were introducing 14-foot containers and that the weight/measurement ratio had been increased from 50 to 140 cubic feet (1.4 to 3.6 m³) to the tonne. These containers could carry 10 tonnes and their roofs were curved so that they could fit under rail tunnels.

Two years later Rudder's introduced a smaller and better constructed container of eight tonnes capacity but measuring 8 × 8 feet. A news item in the *Centralian Advocate* in April 1961 said that 'the new Cargotainers were proving very successful on the Adelaide–Darwin service. The initial consignment consisted of 31 tons enclosed in 10 Cargotainers containing 1548 articles.' The larger boxes were withdrawn and the 8 × 8s became the standard unit with Rudder's, supplemented by 16 footers which were coming into vogue as a nationally favoured size.

By this time Rudder's were consigning big tonnages to Mt Isa for the copper mining venture which was being greatly expanded.

In the same year that Rudder's began using containers in the Northern Territory, the Adelaide-based firm of John Dring Pty Ltd, which was founded in 1889, expanded its operations by introducing van-load rail freight services between Adelaide and Alice Springs. Rail vans were loaded in Adelaide and unloaded in Alice Springs by Dring's employees.

The volume of business increased to such an extent that in 1960 the company built its own depot and office in the Alice Springs rail yards, with a Territorian, Ted Smith, as manager. In the same year they introduced 14-foot steel-framed plywood containers known as Safe-T-Freighters. These were so successful that they led to the introduction of 16-, 20- and eventually 40-foot modules in both container and open box form as well as 16 and 20 ft 'cargo trays', thus facilitating a mix of sizes which could be carried on 40-foot road train trailers in combinations of two 16s and an 8, or two 20s, and so on. Dring's soon assumed a dominant position in the Territory's container traffic and built its inventory

D. R. Baldock's Leylands which for many years carried most of the bagged copper from Tennant Creek to Alice Springs, also 'topped up' with containers which were loaded with copper. Note absence of restraints for the containers. *(Ken Moody)*

up to 350 units. In addition the company developed a refrigerated container service in conjunction with the Territory Transport Association whose Co-Ord fleet carried them to places as far apart as Kununurra, Darwin and Mt Isa. Each container had its own refrigeration plant and commodities carried included snap-frozen vegetables and pre-packed meat at temperatures ranging between 17 and 7°C according to requirements. Back-loadings included fish and buffalo meat.

Dring's promoted their container operations vigorously by emphasising that it was faster and cheaper to move freight into western Queensland, for example, via Tennant Creek (the 'back door', as they termed it) than it would be handling it through Queensland's transport system. Thus most of the original stores, plant and building materials for the Mary Kathleen Uranium venture were consigned through Dring's via Alice Springs. Likewise during the 1960s the bulk of Mt Isa Mines' supplies were redirected from the east coast to the route through the Centre via the Stuart and Barkly Highways. To accelerate journey times and reduce handling, John Dring Pty Ltd, used their own vehicles to move containers, flats, cargo trays, etc., from Adelaide by road to Port Augusta, and also handled all Alice Springs local deliveries with their own trucks. At The Alice the company also provided storage, fork lift and crane-hire facilities.

At the height of the Peko Mines expansion in Tennant Creek Dring's were transferring 800 tonnes of containerised freight per month to Co-Ord road trains and these vehicles were returning with loads of copper concentrate for shipment from Port Augusta to Japan.

In September 1981 Dring's sold their Northern Territory operations to the Mayne Nickless subsidiary Railex. At the time Dring's manager in the Territory was John Holyoak who returned to Adelaide to set up his own freight forwarding business. Railex appointed John Mahomet as their Alice Springs manager. John is the grandson of an Afghan cameleer whose camel team worked from Oodnadatta to Newcastle Waters.

The Vehicles They Drove (1)

It was an assorted fleet of vehicles which operators used in the immediate postwar years. Power and capacity were the prime requirements; big wasn't just beautiful, it was functional.

There was a handful of D-Series Internationals, some of which were produced in 1939 and some during the war, featuring a side-valve petrol engine. These were superseded after the war by the KB model which some operators repowered with the more powerful and always reliable Gardner diesel engine.

In turn these vehicles were either joined or replaced by an influx of ex-military vehicles which had been declared surplus to peacetime requirements and were auctioned at disposals sales. They included such makes as Diamond T, Federal, GMC, Chevrolet, Maple Leaf, Ford and even a stray Autocar, Marmon-Herrington and FWD.

But most things mechanical have a finite life; in other words, they wear out. In anticipation of getting some of the business of replacements, several Alice Springs firms took on agencies for various makes of vehicles.

In June 1949 the *Centralian Advocate* carried an announcement by Champions Ltd, Adelaide, that Martin Bros had been appointed local dealers for Mack trucks, as well as for Studebaker, Rover, Citroen and Fiat cars. In the same issue N. M. Loutit Ltd, advertised that they were agents for McGrath trailer equipment as well as for Leyland Comet, Super Beaver and Super Hippo models and AEC Monarch, Matador, Mammoth and Regal units. Three years later Loutit's took on the International Harvester Co. agency.

In 1959 the Adelaide firm, Commercial Motor Vehicles Ltd, was advertising Commer trucks, with Martin Bros as local agents. During the year Martin Bros also stated they were agents for ERF, 'The British Giant', in conjunction with CMV.

British and American manufacturers were alert to the potential of road transport in the Territory. The wartime movement of supplies and personnel by road had drawn early attention to it and the subsequent action of the Commonwealth government to link its two railways by a coordinated road service would have confirmed the market possibilities in this region. As the ex-wartime vehicles began to reach the end of their days, Foden, Leyland and International, and later on Mack, brought forth their heavy-duty models which they offered as prime movers for multi-unit operation.

It was Foden that made the biggest impression in the Territory in the '50s and '60s. Astute marketing by Diesel Motors, owned by the O'Neil family who also established Fleet Owners quickly put Foden in the lead in the 'big iron' stakes.

The Foden catalogue in the early 1950s consisted of

the FG series with either single or bogie-driven axles as well as eight-wheelers, all powered by Gardner engines (5, 6 and 8 cylinders) of 7-, 8- and 11-litre capacity conservatively rated at 94, 112 and 150 bhp (70, 83 and 112 kW) and producing their maximum torque down at a low 1300 rpm. By 1955 the standard 5-speed transmission had been superseded by a 12-speed epicyclic set-up which the factory representative and principal distributor, Diesel Motors, said was 'designed for simple operation. The auxiliary ranges are pre-selected and come into use automatically when the clutch is depressed for the main change'.

Diesel Motors quoted the following table of typical transmission combinations and road speeds for a Foden fitted with a 6.25:1 rear end and 1100 × 20 tyres.

Gear (Main Box)	Range	Gearbox Ratio	Road (mph) Speed	(km/h)
4	High	0.77:1	41.8	67.2
3	High	1.30:1	24.8	39.9
2	High	2.33:1	13.8	22.2
1	High	4.76:1	6.8	10.9
4	Direct	1.00:1	32.2	51.8
3	Direct	1.69:1	19.0	30.5
2	Direct	3.03:1	10.6	17
1	Direct	6.18:1	5.4	8.6
4	Low	3.29:1	10	16
3	Low	5.56:1	5.8	9.3
2	Low	10.0:1	3.2	5.1
1	Low	20.8:1	1.56	2.5
Reverse	High	4.17:1	7.7	4.7
	Direct	5.41:1	6.0	9.6
	Low	17.9:1	1.8	2.8

Fodens were offered with a choice of four other diff ratios: 5.2:1 producing 40 mph (64 km/h) in direct drive top; 5.75:1 for 36 mph (58 km/h); 7.5:1 for 28 mph (45 km/h) and a very low 8.33:1 resulting in 25 mph top speed (40 km/h). There was also an optional 2:1 hub reduction available which, according to Foden publicity at the time, could be 'brought into use by a selector on

International K-series trucks such as these two Kittle Bros vehicles were early arrivals on the postwar scene. Some had a two-speed rear axle and the ratio could be changed manually by lever.

the hub when required. It reduces road speed by half and takes the strain off the whole power and transmission system, from engine to differential'.

By 1959 Foden was enjoying pre-eminence in the road train business. The HG series had been introduced, featuring air brakes (in place of vacuum-assisted hydraulic), power steering, a re-styled cab and the choice of three engines—Gardner 6LX, Cummins NH 220 or Rolls-Royce C6T. The double-skinned cab roof and tropical radiator had been introduced a couple of years previously and were retained in the new HGs as standard equipment. Of the three engines, operators began to look closest at the Cummins because although the Gardner was a tremendously reliable unit its 150 hp (112 kW) was beginning to lag behind in the power race and the famous British firm was adamant that it would not do anything to up-rate it; and Vestey's disheartening experience with the Rolls-Royce units in its two Rotinoffs was beginning to filter through to other operators (see chapter, The Vestey Road Trains). The NH 220 was naturally aspirated but was a higher revving engine than the Gardner. Its maximum bhp of 220 (164

International KB models also appeared just after World War II. The ex-army bow-type trailer shown here was used as a concert party stage for troop entertainment at Banka Banka. In photo are Jack Cottis and Peter Waddick. *(George Maff)*

kW) was reached at 2100 rpm and its peak torque of 606 lb/ft (818 Nm) was achieved at 1500 rpm. Its capacity of 12.1 litres outstripped the Gardner 6LX's 10.4 litres, and with the Cummins engine the Foden people were able to offer 100 tons gross train weight, which was well ahead of anything that Mack, AEC, Leyland or International had in their inventory.

Comparable gross train weights in 1960 were:

AEC Mammoth Major 8	40 tons
International R-192	22.75 tons
International RD-212	29.5 tons
Leyland Buffalo	44.5 tons
Mack B613	32 tons

Little wonder, then, that Foden became 'king of the road' in the Territory. There was even a Foden bus in 1963, owned by Len Tuit, pulling a four-wheel parcel and mail van on the scheduled Alice Springs–Darwin run. This service was later acquired by Ansett–Pioneer.

In June 1961 the *Centralian Advocate* carried one of the very few advertisements that Diesel Motors used in the Territory to publicise its range of Foden vehicles. It could have been that the company was anticipating competition from other makes, but more likely it could feel the strengthening pulse of the cattle transport industry. With its usual marketing alertness it pitched its advertising toward cattle transport, showing a photo of a Cummins-powered Foden hauling two self-tracking trailers operating in the Gulf Country of Queensland. Using some quaint phraseology the advertisement said that Peninsular Freighters owned these 'radio-controlled Fodenised stock trains'.

In 1962 Fleet Owners acquired Nothern Territory distribution for International when they bought Centralian Truck & Tractor Co.

Over in the eastern States International's 192 Series enjoyed a successful run in the 1950s. The company brought in models which its parent had designed for line-haul semi-trailer operations in the U.S.A. But in the Territory at that stage International posed no threat to Foden.

In 1950 International Harvester began producing Australian-built models to replace the K-series and gave them the prefix L—L-160, L-162, etc. The Australian models were confined to the lower end of the power and weight scale; apart from cosmetic body changes the bigger units remained much the same as before except for changes in the prefix; the KB7 became the L-180 and L-182 with a 269 cubic inch (4.4 litre) petrol engine developing 100 bhp (74 kW) at 3000 rpm. The KB8 became the famous L-192 which had a larger (6.1 litre) petrol engine rated at 143 bhp (106 kW).

The AR series came into being in 1954 and in the higher capacity segment Harvester had the petrol-engined R192 in the 25,000 lb GVW (11,340 kg) area and the RF195 bogie-drive unit to handle 35,000 lb GVW (15,875 kg). The engines for these models were rated at 144 and 162 bhp respectively.

A year later, in the typical tradition of American-origin manufacturers the Australian models underwent another change, this time blossoming forth as the AS series. In addition the imported R192 became a bogie drive type in the 25,000 lb GVW category with a 22 bhp increase in power and the RF195 was up-rated to 38,000 GVW (17,240 kg) with a choice of petrol engine or a J-Series Cummins of 135 bhp (100 kW) output in a new model, the RDF195. Then in 1957 both the RF and the RDF were further up-rated to 40,000 GVW (18,140 kg).

There were more up-ratings of the 192s and 195s in 1959 when yet another series, the AAs came into being and in 1960 Harvester brought out the petrol-powered R212 with the famous Black Diamond engine and the Cummins-engined RD212, both of which were rated at 66,000 lb (about 30,000 kg) gross vehicle weight.

Although AEC had won a very favourable reputation with its heavy duty vehicles during the war and supplied a healthy percentage of the Australian market in the postwar period with line-haul and local versions of its Monarchs, Matadors, Mammoths and Mandators, it did not make any great inroads in the Territory.

Walter Allwright was the only operator in the Co-Ord to use this marque. He had a Mammoth Major 8 which was an eight-wheeler with an 11.3 litre engine, 6-speed gearbox and 10.3:1 differentials. In overdrive its top speed was 33 mph (53 km/h). Later it was fitted with a two-speed auxiliary box which had a 1.64:1 reduction and faster (7.74:1) diffs, and this combination enabled it to haul three trailers grossing 50 tons through the steep and winding hilly section north of Alice Springs. As with many British vehicles, overheating was a problem but this was beaten by fitting a Foden 'tropical' radiator.

Despite the fact that the original (Government) road train was an AEC product, the AEC marque made little impression among postwar operators in the Territory. Walter Allwright was the only Co-Ord operator to use an AEC. It was a bonneted Mammoth Major (left) with an 11.3 litre engine. *(Peter Ritchie)*

Allwright later acquired an AEC Mandator which also had an 11.3 litre diesel engine, 6-speed main box and 2-speed auxiliary. It was rated to haul 36 tons and with it he pulled a doubles combination—semi-trailer plus dog trailer.

In 1957 AEC was offering two models of the Mammoth Major with 11.3 litre engine rated to haul between 53,760 and 62,720 lb (24,385–28,450 kg). Then in the following year it added the Mammoth Major II to the list with an 80,640 lb (36,580 kg) gross vehicle mass and an increase in output from the 11.3 litre engine of 15 bhp—from 150 to 165 bhp (112 to 123 kW).

During the 1950s the Commonwealth Department of Works in the Territory was operating three AEC Marshal trucks which were powered by the AEC 470 engine of 7.75 litres. This department had been using AECs since the late 1930s, including the original road train.

A notable exception to the 'Fodens for road trains' school was Baldock's, who operated Fodens for a time and then moved very successfully to Leylands, using Hippos at first, then Super Hippos and Buffalos.

The Hippos in Baldock's fleet were cab-over-engine models featuring Leyland 680 cubic inch (11.1 litre) engine, 5-speed main box and 2-speed auxiliary (direct and underdrive) and a 7.74:1 worm differential. Its gross vehicle rating was 49,000 lb (22,226 kg) and its gross combination (train) rating was 71,680 lb (32,513 kg).

The Super Hippo had the same 150 bhp engine and transmission set-up but other componentry was beefed up to take care of an increase in allowable train weight.

The Leyland Buffalo came on the scene in 1960. It was, in reality, a Super Hippo with a big 14.2 litre Albion engine developing 230 bhp, a ZF splitter transmission with 12 ratios, overhead worm-drive diffs with 9 in. (228 mm) centres, and an air-operated diff lock, air power steering, Albion-designed heavy-duty rear bogie suspension and a manufacturer's gross train rating of 45 tons, with an extenuation that 'higher figures would be considered for special applications'. This specification gave the Leyland Buffalo an edge on Foden.

The grafting of Albion heavy-duty components on to the top-of-the-line Leyland models stemmed from the takeover of Albion by Leyland in 1951. Ten years later Thornycroft was acquired by Leyland and in 1962 AEC was merged into the Leyland group.

Although the famous NR Mack was a familiar sight in military convoys in the Territory in World War II, few of them found their way into Northern Territory operators' hands after the war. It would appear that they could have made an ideal body-truck prime mover for road train service. Elsewhere in Australia they were widely used for many years. They were succeeded by the EG and EH models (petrol and diesel, respectively) and these were followed in the early '50s by the A51 with an 8.3 litre Mack diesel engine putting out 138 bhp (102 kW) at 2400 rpm. Transmission was a 10-speed duplex arrangement (5-speed main box, 2-speed compound box) and bogie drive rear axles.

There were still no takers in the Territory. In 1955 the B43 came out with much the same transmission arrangement but with an increase in power to 150 bhp (112 kW). Ted Stiles purchased one of them.

Then in 1956 the first of the model which was to become famous throughout Australia—the B61—made its debut offering 15 gear ratios via what Mack called a triplex transmission: a 4-speed main box with 3-speed compound box tacked onto it. It also had bogie drive and it was offered with more power (170 bhp/127 kW) from the same 11 litre engine as was in the B43. Air brakes, which were a feature ignored by Foden until round 1959, were standard on the B61 as they had been on all Macks since the days of the NR models. And the B61 used air power for its engine starter, the sound of which earned the name of 'the old lady frightener'.

Eventually Mack got a toe in the Territory door. Buntine and Ryan (Overland Transport) bought a B61 and so did Ted Stiles. By 1960 Mack had increased the power from its 11 litre engine to 190 bhp for use in the bogie-drive B613s and in 1963 this renowned power unit was bored out from 123 mm to 127 mm to raise its output to 211 bhp. At the same time Mack introduced its quadruplex transmission, or 'quad box' as it became known. Coupled to the primary 5-speed gear set (with overdrive fifth) was a 4-speed compound box which had a direct, a high splitter, a low splitter and a 'deep south' low–low.

At the lighter end of the capacity scale the Commer 'knocker' became popular with semi-trailer operators in 1955 in the eastern States and 'down south', but it didn't take off to any major extent in the Territory. Noel Buntine had one for a time but later traded it on a Mack, as did Ted Stiles.

The name 'knocker' was appended to the Commer TS3 diesel because of its peculiar knocking sound when under power. It was quite revolutionary; it was a three-cylinder, six piston horizontally-opposed two-stroke engine. The two pistons in each cylinder actuated a single crankshaft through a system of rocker arms. Porting was based on the Kadency principle and scavenging was assisted by a Roots-type blower. The TS3 developed 105 bhp (78 kW) at 2400 rpm and 270 lb/ft (351 Newton metres) torque between 1200 and 1500 rpm. It was the power unit for Commer models rated at up to 24,000 lb (10,886 kg) gross vehicle mass in today's metric-speak.

For several years in the late '60s and early '70s Peko

Mines NL operated their own road trains within their mining property. The operation followed a decision in 1961 to haul ore from the Orlando mine 40 kilometres to a central mill which also served the Ivanhoe and Juno mines. The company constructed bitumen-sealed haul roads and thousands of tonnes of ore were successfully carried on specially-designed vehicles.

Initially the hauling was done by semi-trailer outfits handling up to 25 tonnes per load. Later two side-tipping road trains were purchased with Foden prime movers to pull two bogie-bogie trailers. Capacity of each trailer was in the vicinity of 80 tonnes, and the Fodens were powered by NH Cummins engines coupled to 12-speed underdrive boxes and double-reduction bogie drive.

In 1969 a Scammell Contractor with body-mounted side tipper pulling three side-tipping double-bogie trailers was put into service giving a haul capacity of 110/120 tonnes. The bonneted Contractor had a Cummins turbocharged NTC335 engine, semi-automatic transmission with eight speeds, and 30-tonne bogie drive with reduction hubs. Overall length of this road train was 120 feet (36.5 m) and it ran on 58 tyres.

The side-tipping principle was preferred because owing to limits on sub-surface bin storage at the mill it was at times necessary to stockpile at surface level and this could be carried out with a side-tipping unit without uncoupling.

The capital cost benefits of using a road train consisting of body prime mover and three trailers were demonstrated by the company at that time to be:

1 × 110/120 tonne road train	$ 72,000
1½ × 70/80 tonne road trains	$ 78,000
4½ × 22½/25 tonne road trains	$103,500

Tom Petters, transport officer for Peko at that time, said that even allowing for the cost of the provision of haul roads the transport of ore by road trains to a central mill was more economical than operating a series of mills near the mine sites. He said that under prevailing conditions side-tipping was preferred but if bigger tonnages had been envisaged bottom-dumping would have had to be adopted because of better tipping rates. However, the body prime mover would still have had to be a side-tipper, for obvious reasons.

It was during the 1960s that Foden's dominance began to slowly decline. The faster and more versatile Macks and Internationals were gaining wider acceptance among operators. Elsewhere in Australia these two marques were also making their presence felt; in the more populous states they competed strongly with Atkinson, ERF, Mercedes-Benz, Scammell, White and White Autocar, none of which made any impression in the Territory at that time. Neither did Deutz which Ramsay Bros, of Alice Springs were advertising in the *Centralian Advocate*. The name in the ads was mis-spelt Duetz—not that that made any difference to sales in the

As the famous Gardner diesel engine began to drop back in the power race the American-origin Cummins power unit took its place in heavy-duty Foden models. This four-axle Foden was powered by Cummins. Note the 'false roof' above the cab, designed to reduce heat from the sun. *(Ken Moody)*

THE OLD AND THE BOLD

Buntine & Ryan (Overland Transport) put this B61 Mack—'The High and the Mighty'—on the road and it proved to be the precursor to a trend away from British-built vehicles and a preference for American-origin units. *(John Ryan)*

NR Macks were a familiar sight along the Stuart Highway in World War II and although large numbers of them were bought and used in the eastern and southern States after the war, very few were used by Territory operators. *(Australian War Memorial)*

area for there simply weren't any, despite the fact that this German-origin vehicle with its air-cooled engine enjoyed considerable popularity in the hot climate of western New South Wales and south-western Queensland.

By the 1970s Mack had gained dominance in the Territory road train scene, with White, White Autocar and Kenworth also winning some operator acceptance. Kenworth was a relative latecomer on the Australian scene; it was introduced in 1962 by Australian Kenworth Truck Sales of Doncaster, Victoria. But it was eight years or so before the first Kenworths began to appear in the Territory.

The famous British marques were failing to keep up with the power race; British manufacturers for some time had been busily engaged in self-immolation in the form of company take-overs, mergers and the like, paying insufficient regard to what was happening in the outside world and thus opening the way for the astute Americans and later European manufacturers to figuratively drape the Union Jack over the coffin of the once-mighty British motor industry.

Baldock's stayed with the Leyland marque until they sold to Fleet Owners in 1966. Hippos, Super Hippos and Buffalos made up Baldock's inventory. *(Ken Moody)*

THE VEHICLES THEY DROVE

The Vehicles They Drove (2)

What were the vehicles of the '50s like to drive? How did they perform? What were their vices and virtues?

Heavy transport driving in the 1950s was no task for the weak or the hesitant, particularly in a region such as the Northern Territory and adjacent States. A driver had to be his own mentor, mechanic, loader and unloader, clerk, navigator (for those trips off the beaten track to remote stations) and survivor. It's tough country in which to work; much of it is arid and summer temperatures hover around 40°C for weeks at a time. No matter what else was carried on the vehicle, adequate water had number-one priority, and tools were next on the list.

How the early road train drivers acquired the experience to qualify them for handling their big rigs was a question which was not usually asked and therefore didn't require an answer. Their mechanical ability evolved as they learned by perception and deduction how to cope with Murphy's Law which postulates that what can go wrong will go wrong.

Ian Cawood began driving his father Stan's trucks in 1956.

He got his driving licence on a Foden. In those days driving tests were carried out by the police and he fronted at the Alice Springs police station in a Foden loaded with 35 tons of cement. He had to do a test drive through the streets of the town; what that policeman didn't know was that he had to depart for Mt Isa within the hour with that load. Fortunately he got the licence but of course he'd had quite a bit of experience off-siding with his brother Greville who also allowed him to drive at times when they were on the open road miles from anywhere.

'I guess driving just came naturally because it was a family business established by my father and we were keen to follow in his footsteps. We were involved in transport from a very early age,' Ian said.

That truck was one of the first Fodens in the Territory according to Ian, and anybody associated with the transport industry of the mid-'50s would remember it as 'Jezebel'. In fact the Mt Isa people got to know it very well and if ever he went over there in another truck they'd ask him what was wrong with Jezebel. He drove it for about four years:

I don't know how I came to give it that name. I suppose it was because it wasn't exactly my favourite friend, as it was associated with hard work and it used to give the odd bit of mechanical trouble. The engine gave no trouble; it was a Gardner six cylinder; marvellous motor.

The steering was the 'armstrong' type—you had to have strong arms to handle it. We didn't get power-assisted steering until we bought our third Foden, which was a six-wheeler with an eight-cylinder Gardner engine. They all had an epicyclic range-change or auxiliary box. This was quite a good feature but sometimes it would miss out on engaging, through no fault of the driver's, and it would go into neutral. Then you'd be hoping like mad that the brakes would hold to prevent the vehicle running backwards.

Ian recalled one particular trip to Mt Isa in Jezebel when he missed with the epicyclic and the brakes failed.

I had this magnificent crate on the back containing some very expensive gear which was worth about ten times the price of the truck. Well, with the broken brake hose there was no way of holding the Foden, so back down the hill it went and tipped over. Fortunately I didn't get hurt and the truck wasn't damaged very much. But the Mary Kathleen Uranium people were very, very upset. However, despite the roll-over their piece of equipment wasn't damaged. The only extra cost for that trip was the hire of a crane to put the truck back on its wheels; I drove it back to Alice Springs.

Later, when father Stan decided to sell the business to Fleet Owners and pursue other interests in the Territory, Ian Cawood drove for Baldock's:

Although the work was just as hard, I suppose you could say that I was 'up-graded' to driving Leyland Buffalos. They were a magnificent vehicle to handle in those days, with that double gear shift and power steering and a marvellous motor. I used to pull a hundred tons out of Peko with a body truck and two trailers; I mean, 100 tons all-up, including the weight of the road train. The trailers were eight-wheelers.

A Leyland Buffalo could round-up a Mack in those days. The Macks were highly geared; in some places they'd get along at 60 miles an hour but they were down to 20 or less on hills, whereas the Buffalo was geared to 34 miles an hour and they'd travel at that speed up hill and on the level.

Mind you, the Leyland Hippos which Baldock's also had weren't nearly as good as the Buffalos. The Hippo had the older Leyland 6-cylinder engine, it was geared to about 28 mph, it had no power steering, it was very noisy and hot, in fact it was not a very pleasant truck to drive. I drove both the bonneted and cab-over versions of the Hippo.

During my time on the road there was quite a mixture of truck marques trundling up and down The Bitumen. There were Internationals, Fodens, Macks, Leylands and a few AECs—and of course smaller stuff such as Commers, Fords and even Bedfords but they weren't used on road train work; they were mostly rigids or semi-trailer prime movers on short-distance work.

My father had a big International which was a rather awful thing to drive. It had been re-engined with a Gardner which was really too big for the truck and intruded into the cab—or rather, the cowling did—leaving very little room for the gear stick or the pedals. The cab on those Inters wasn't very big to start with, and by the time you shared it with a larger motor than the original one, the driver's space was extremely limited. Once you managed to get into the seat, that's where you stayed; you weren't able to move your legs or stretch out in any direction. You sat there like a dummy, and every muscle in your body got very taut. It was a sod of a thing, in my opinion, yet others like Norm Davies who drove for us thought it was a darling!

Greville Cawood said that his father's fleet comprised three Fodens and a KR11 International, all with Gardner six- or eight-cylinder engines. Ian's Jezebel was No. 5 in the Co-Ord fleet; it had a 6.25:1 diff ratio. Greville's 'Nellie', which was No. 7 in the Co-Ord operation had a 7.5:1 diff which, he said, was in most of the Territory Fodens. Its top speed was around 42 mph. Fleet Owners, he said, had an eight-wheeler with 8.33:1 rear end giving it a top speed of 36 mph (58 km/h). It was fitted with reduction hubs which, when engaged, reduced its top speed to 18 mph (39 km/h).

He explained the principles and operation of the Foden transmission this way:

The main gearbox had 'crash' gears; that is, there was no synchromesh and drivers had to match engine speed and road speed accurately when changing up or down. The gear lever moved in standard H-pattern, as in a four-on-the-floor family car. The 3-speed auxiliary box was an epicyclic type; it had planetary gears which were similar in principle to the modern automatic transmission.

The lever which was used to pre-select the range in the auxiliary box was separate from the main box's gear lever and it was moved by the driver into one of three positions: down near the floor for low range; mid-way up towards vertical for intermediate range; and nearly up to vertical for high range.

The driver could pre-select the range he would be requiring but no action took place in the epicyclic box until he 'threw' the clutch pedal out and back quickly; then it immediately came into effect.

There was nothing high-tech or sophisticated about the pre-select mechanism: as the pre-selector lever was moved up or down by the driver it compressed springs which held the change-speed rod 'in abeyance'. As the load came off the drive train when the driver pushed the clutch down the appropriate spring moved the rod into the desired position to change the epicyclic gears.

The ratios in the epicyclic box were designed to fill the gaps between the gears in the main box. Although in theory there were 12 ratios available to the driver, in practice it was found that there was some overlapping and only about eight combinations were used. One that was never used, said Greville, was high range with first

gear because the strong torque of first put too much strain on the epicyclic gears. Broadly speaking low range was only used with first and second in the main box, and so a typical gear change sequence was: low range in the auxiliary with first in the main box . . . low and second . . . intermediate with first . . . intermediate/second . . . high/second . . . intermediate/third . . . high/third . . . intermediate/fourth . . . high/fourth.

That was the arrangement for Fodens fitted with six-cylinder engines. Those fitted with 'eight-pot' motors had different ratios in the gearbox, and as high/third was almost identical with intermediate/fourth, the high/third change was eliminated and so the sequence became: low/first . . . low/second . . . low/third . . . intermediate/first . . . intermediate/second . . . high/second . . . intermediate/third . . . intermediate/fourth . . . high/fourth.

In the late '50s considerable confusion was caused when the Foden engineers reversed the epicyclic pre-select gear lever positions. High range was down on the floor, and low was up where high was previously.

Said Greville: 'This produced some strange results when you were tired and/or in a hurry!' And, summing up, he said:

The epicyclic box was extremely reliable, but it could miss occasionally. The box itself and the engine were flexibly mounted in the chassis, but the selector lever was a solid fixture, which meant that movement of the engine in the chassis changed the distance between the gear lever and the gearbox. Normal wear and tear of brake bands, spring, etc. also tended to cause problems and that explained why, when tackling a steep hill and changing down it was best to get down into low range before selecting first gear; in other words, the last available gear change should have been made in the main box, not in the auxiliary, so that the driver had positive control.

In Peter Gunner's opinion the Fodens were quality vehicles and did a very good job. The O'Neils, through their company Diesel Motors, which was the factory representative and agent for Fodens Ltd in Australia, did the transport industry in the Territory a real service when they guided operators' thinking toward heavy-duty vehicles as the most appropriate equipment for transport operations which were quite different from those elsewhere in Australia. Foden at that time was one of the few manufacturers who produced vehicles that could be accurately described as being in the heavy-duty category.

The O'Neils not only sold Fodens but also operated them on road train work in their company, Fleet Owners, which was a shareholder in the Co-Ord.

When the Fodens first came on the road, *Peter Gunner said*, they were a very big change from what had previously been used up and down The Bitumen. They were the 'big iron' of the day and for many years subsequently. They were 'civilised'

Peter Gunner.

in comparison with what had previously been used. Those Gardner motors, they were beautiful. Not a moment's trouble.

Unfortunately the early models had vacuum hydraulic brakes which were somewhat ineffective, but when the later models came in with Cummins engines they were fitted with air brakes which greatly improved their stoppability.

The Fodens with Cummins engines performed well but there was a compatability problem with them. Some of the engines were manufactured in America and some in Scotland. Some of the oil lines were internal and others external and if there were a couple of vehicles off the road with fuel trouble it wasn't possible to rob Peter to get Paul back on the road.

The Foden diffs didn't cause any trouble if care was taken to measure the circumference of tyres and make sure that matched pairs were put on the drive axles. Otherwise they'd 'fight' and cause overheating of the diff which was a worm drive type.

Peter Gunner said that the epicyclic range change was great in principle but there were problems associated with its operation:

You soon learned never to attempt to change it on a hill. You could change the main box and the epicyclic box at any time to suit engine speed whilst on normal undulating terrain but it was a no-no on a big hill; you simply had to stop and re-start when everything had been selected for the climb.

The epicyclic component was somewhat unusual. It was a planetary system which worked well if correctly handled. There were different types or models, such as underdrive-low-direct, and low-direct-overdrive. Thus the main 4-speed box could be multiplied to provide 12 ratios (four in each range).

The *modus operandi* was to pre-select the required range by moving a lever which was down near the floor on the driver's left. Then when you depressed the clutch to change a gear in the main box with the ordinary lever the pre-selector would also go into action and simultaneously change the range and thus you got the combination which you considered would best meet your needs.

But . . . you did not attempt to do the two changes together whilst going up a hill. When you came to a gradient which you considered would require more than a change in the main box, you stopped at the bottom and did your selecting. If you attempted to do otherwise you either tore the tailshaft out or the pre-selector section would fail—quite dramatically! In fact the planetary gears and needle bearings simply disintegrated and made one helluva mess. The impact of the drop down in the range and a lower gear was too much. Mind you, we were carrying some terrific weights; there were no weighbridges and no weight checks of any kind; we simply loaded until we couldn't get any more on.

The Macks Peter drove didn't suffer from this problem. The impact of the 210 bhp engine on the drive line was greatly eased by the availability of plenty of gears.

Fleet Owners moved out of Fodens in the '60s and began to use Internationals, then Macks, and ultimately Kenworths. Somewhere along the line, in between these changes, the 'Gunnerbilt' appeared. Peter cobbled together this prime mover after Fleet Owners had taken over the Baldock operation. He was limited in the amount of money budgeted for a replacement prime mover so he cut two chassis—a Mack and a Leyland Buffalo—and joined them. The front end was Leyland, complete with Leyland cab, Cummins engine, steering etc., plus a Road Ranger gearbox; the other half was Mack. It was used for a couple of years hauling copper from Peko to Alice Springs and eventually was retired to 'yard goat' duties, shuttling between the rail yards at Alice Springs and the company's depot on the Stuart Highway north of the town.

John Ryan's opinion of Fodens varied from that of Peter Gunner. John was a partner with Noel Buntine in Overland Transport which was one of the operators in the Co-Ord service and in his view, 'the Foden organisation should have paid us to run those early models. The Gardner engine was great but those drive shafts—they cost us real money in roadside failures and repairs. We should have been given medals for carrying out Foden's experiments and tests.'

Among the Fodens acquired by Overland Transport was a model with the ill-conceived two-stroke Foden engine which, as most purchasers found, was a failure and was quickly withdrawn from the range and replaced with Cummins.

Overland Transport later acquired one of the first Macks in the Territory. It was a B61. Ted Stiles, operating from the Top End, also bought one about the same time. Drivers who handled the Macks, Fodens and other marques for Overland Transport included Doug

Foster, Peter Ritchie and Ivan Wiese, of whom more is written elsewhere in this book.

The Mack B61 was the 'glamour rig' of the '60s. It had power and complexity—sufficient of the latter to set a Mack driver apart from the rest of the mob. The blokes who could two-stick a quad box—that is, could manipulate the two gear levers simultaneously without making gear-grating noises or selecting the wrong compound ratio—were accorded grudging respect by their road colleagues who were trundling along in less technically advanced examples of the automotive engineer's efforts.

Although in hypothesis the Mack B61's 'quad box' would provide a four times multiplication of the main box, resulting in 20 ratios being theoretically available to the driver, in practice 13 speeds were all that were used. The deep section of the compound box was rarely called up, particularly in the Territory where steep hills aren't prevalent.

Here's what was available:

Shift	High split	Main	Low split	Low-low
5th	0.70	0.84	1.01	2.13
4th	0.84	1.00	1.20	2.53
3rd	1.47	1.76	2.10	4.44
2nd	2.61	3.13	3.74	7.92
1st	4.55	5.45	6.52	13.80
Rev	3.91	4.69	5.60	11.86

The two boxes were bolted together side-by-side as one assembly, making it a very compact unit when compared with the length of a traditional gearbox plus auxiliary or splitter behind or in front of it. A shorter wheelbase was one of the benefits of the Mack arrangement.

To manipulate the boxes there were two gear levers mounted close alongside each other. The left-hand one did the splitting and the other operated the main box. Contrary to what some readers may be thinking, most of the changes—in fact, in the ratio of three to one—were carried out with the splitter lever. Some changes could be made one-handed by deft finger manipulation, others required two hands, and to do this the right arm was momentarily looped through the steering wheel, much to the consternation of safety regulation authorities who never did work out how to ban the practice.

The accompanying diagram shows the two-stick layout, and here's how the author described the shift pattern to get the vehicle rolling when writing a road test report in the national magazine *Truck & Bus*:

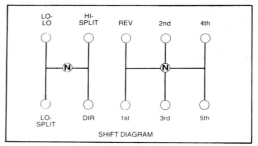

SHIFT DIAGRAM

Disregard the low-low position in the compound box. It's rarely needed. Select low split with the left-hand lever and 1st with the right. Once the vehicle is mobile move the left lever across to direct, gain speed and then move it up to high split.

Next, using both hands, move the left stick back to low split and the right stick up to 2nd. Leave the main box in 2nd and move the left stick to direct and high split, as speed dictates.

Using one hand this time, move both levers back toward the seat so that low split and 3rd are brought into action. Then do the next two changes with the left-hand lever.

These two Federals with J Series Cummins diesel engines were operated by Baldock's in the early postwar period. They were lighter and less powerful than Baldock's Diamond Ts. Peter Ritchie is seen alongside one of the Federals. *(Bob Dodd)*

THE VEHICLES THEY DROVE

Return the left-hand lever to low split and simultaneously push the main box stick up toward the dash to 4th, where it remains while the compound is put through the next two stages (direct and high split) to bring everything together in 0.84:1 overdrive. If a bit more speed is needed bring the right-hand (main box) lever back toward the seat to 5th position and the B61 should be moving along in 0.70:1 overdrive at 100 km/h with about 2100 rpm on the engine tachometer.

The procedure was reversed for changing down on hills.

It wasn't necessary to use every ratio; some of them were fairly close and didn't contribute a great deal to momentum. Thus drivers quickly learned how to skip-shift but it took quite a long time for even the best of them to get to the stage where they could two-stick a quad box and talk to a passenger at the same time.

Born in Barcaldine (Qld) in 1937, Doug Foster went to school in Winton and then with his family moved to Mt Gravatt, a Brisbane suburb, where he entered the motor trade via an automotive apprenticeship. He decided to have a look at the Territory for about six months and landed a job with Kittle Bros at Tennant Creek about mid-1955 in a dual capacity as mechanic-cum-driver.

Those were the days when the International K7 was a popular sight on the road. It had a six-cylinder petrol engine rated at 30.7 RAC horsepower and the unit that Doug drove pulled a semi-trailer.

Doug describes subsequent events this way:

I'd been with Kittle Bros for a period when Noel Buntine offered me a job. It was the first segment of a long association with Noel who then had three trucks—a bonneted Federal with a Gardner 5LW engine, an R182 International and a Commer 'knocker'.

I'd only been with Noel for about three months when he bought his first Mack and then a Foden eight-wheeler. This was in 1956, and these two bigger vehicles enabled him to cut his fleet to two and as I was last to join him I was first to go, which was fair enough. But he got me a job with Don Bale owner of Donald's Transport which was a Melbourne–Darwin operation.

Don drove a single-drive Mack which he bought from Champions of Adelaide about the same time as Noel bought his. Ross Snowdon drove a Mack B61 and I had a Ford F600 with petrol V8 engine. Our Melbourne agent was Martin's Overland Freighters.

The Ford was a single-drive type and it pulled a single-axle semi. It had vacuum brakes and vacuum two-speed axle change.

I worked for Don for about six months on the South Road. I was about 19 at the time. It was a strange job—a sort of do-it-yourself set-up. We'd pick up a load at one end and take it through, then pick up a back-load—possibly scrap metal at Mataranka and haul it south—and just drive. We mightn't see Don for six weeks and then we'd meet him somewhere along the road. We'd pull up at the nearest pub, he'd get out his wages book and write a cheque; he'd ask if you had any expenses and

you'd tell him if you'd had to buy a tyre or extra fuel, although there were special places where we could get our fuel, tyres, spares, etc. And then we'd be on our way again! It wasn't a bad life!

When I left Don I went to work for Fleet Owners; Denis O'Neil was running the show. I put in three years on the road driving Fodens and then went into the workshop at the end of 1959.

Fodens and Leylands were the tops in those days. There were other marques, of course, but those two seemed to predominate. Fleet Owners had Fodens and through a sister company named Diesel Motors the O'Neils did a good job of marketing the Fodens. Baldock's had Leylands, and 'Windy' Allwright had AECs. Mack drifted in rather slowly; I think Ted Stiles had the first Mack and Noel Buntine bought his famous High and Mighty. It was a B61 which seemed to be in and out of Mack's saleyard in Brisbane at various times. Noel worked a clever deal there; he'd work it hard for two or three years then trade it for say, £5,000 on a new one. Mack would then overhaul and recondition it and spend about £3,000 on it. Noel would buy it back later for about £6,000 or £7,000; work it for a couple more years and trade it on a new one for about £7,000. Once again Mack would do it up and later Noel would buy it back for possibly £8,000. That B61 was in and out of Noel's fleet for quite a long time!

Peter Ritchie's first driving job in the Territory was with Baldock's handling a Diamond T pulling seven ex-army bow-type trailers. It was powered by a Hercules diesel engine and was fitted with a 4-speed main gearbox and 3-speed under-and-overdrive auxiliary. It had served as a heavy duty tank transporter during World War II.

It did about 22 miles an hour flat out, fitted with 1100 × 20 tyres, *Peter recalled*. The rev counter had a tell-tale needle which the army had fitted so that if the engine was over-revved at any time the needle would stay at the high point.

The trailers were two-axle 24-footers equipped with 825 × 20 tyres which were smaller than those of the prime mover. We used to load nine tons of copper on the prime mover and ten tons on each trailer. The trailers had no brakes and only

Peter Ritchie.

THE OLD AND THE BOLD

basic electrical equipment. They had a ratchet-type handbrake for parking and the small side lights which were illuminated by batteries carried on every second trailer. It was a case of switching on each trailer's lights when darkness fell and turning them off at daybreak, and re-charging the batteries on return to Alice Springs.

Under heavy load conditions, such as when carting copper from Tennant Creek, road speed was kept to about 15 miles an hour to prevent the trailers from 'whipping'. If they did begin to whip the only method of counteracting it was to slow down to almost walking pace.

We usually had two drivers on a vehicle. One could have a sleep while the other drove. Our sleeping quarters, if you could call them that, consisted of an old army mattress mounted on top of the cab with a bit of three-ply over it as a sort of protection from the elements. In the event of rain we'd simply have to rest sitting up in the cab. One of the best places to have a snooze was up in the bow of the trailers, if there was room, because you'd be sheltered there. It was a bit hot up there in summer but at night it was good.

Another vehicle Peter drove for Baldock's was a Federal with a J-Series 150-bhp Cummins. It was a former tank transporter but it was smaller and faster than the Diamond T and didn't have to pull as many trailers.

For some months he handled an ex-World War II left-hand-drive NR Mack which Overland Transport owned for a short time. John Ryan of Overland said that Peter detested that vehicle and Peter's recollection of it was:

My legs would 'cook' in the heat that came through the firewall, and in rain it was better to get out and sit under the tray to stay dry because it only had a canvas hood over the cab and no side curtains. But it could work hard. I carted 40 tons of copper on it at times!

Two other NR Macks were used by Commonwealth Railways to move rolling stock between Alice Springs and Larrimah and vice versa.

Peter also drove for Kurt Johannsen; he started work

The two-lever set-up in the Fodens is shown here. The forward lever controlled the main box and the rearward one was used to pre-select the epicyclic range change.

with him just after he put GM 671s in his Diamond Ts which he said made quite a difference to their performance. He later went back to Baldock's when they had changed to Fodens:

The Fodens were king of the road in those days. Baldock's had six-cylinder and eight-cylinder Gardner engines in theirs. But the heat in those British cabs was unbelievable. The exhaust manifold was on the driver's side and in time the engine cover would simply burn away.

As has been mentioned previously, a feature of the Fodens was a pre-selective 3-speed auxiliary gearbox in addition to the conventional 4-speed main box. However, there were times when the pre-select didn't pre-select:

If you missed a change on a hill, *said Peter*, you were in trouble. Brakes in those days weren't anything like as efficient as they are now and they wouldn't hold if you started to run backwards. If you knew there was a long climb ahead, and even if it didn't get steep for some distance further on, the best technique was to get down in both boxes and simply be patient and crawl up in the gear you knew would do the job.

Peter said that the Gardner engine gave little trouble but if air got into a fuel line it caused problems. A couple of Foden 2-stroke engines were tried by operators but they were a failure, as was the experience elsewhere in Australia and overseas. Later Cummins 220 engines were fitted to Fodens and improved their performance:

The Fodens did a remarkable job. Many a time I've put 28 tons on the back of an eight-wheeler and pulled another 28 tons on a trailer. I've even carried a 30-ton bulldozer on a Foden. We used to have 30-foot trays on them, so we could really load them. I know one driver, Don Tuck, who brought 90 tons of copper down from The Tennant to Alice on a Foden and two 36-foot six-wheel trailers.

They were the biggest vehicles on the road in those days. They used to weigh about 12 or 13 tons empty.

Peter later worked for Noel Buntine and drove an International 180 and a Mack B61. He also worked for Ted Stiles, who, he said, brought the first Mack into the Territory—a 150 HP B43—and later he purchased a B61.

For ten years Peter drove for the Shell Company hauling petroleum products from Darwin to Alice Springs. He was one of the first drivers on the eight Atkinson tanker road trains which Shell put into service in 1970 hauling petroleum, aviation and diesel fuel, kerosene, etc., to airports, service stations, depots and industrial users south of Katherine.

The bogie-drive, four-axle Atkinson body-type prime movers had a wheelbase of nearly six metres (18 feet 10 inches to be exact) and were powered by Cummins NTC335 engines which were rated at 335 bhp (248 kW). Add-ons were a Jake brake and a compressor for cab air-conditioning. Each prime mover was fitted with a 15½-inch twin plate clutch and a 13-speed Fuller Road Ranger overdrive box.

Each prime mover carried twin 80-gallon (360 litre) fuel tanks and on the leading trailer there was another tank with 720 litres to ensure that there was sufficient fuel for the prime mover for the trip. The cab was double-skin reinforced fibreglass with sleeper bunk and air conditioning. The cab design incorporated intake vents above the windscreen to direct air into the cavity between the inner and outer roof skins to assist in reducing the interior temperature. Instrumentation was comprehensive and included temperature gauges for both axles of the rear bogie.

The single aluminium tank on the prime mover carried 4,500 gallons (20,450 litres) and on each double-bogie trailer there was a 7,500-gallon tank, making a total capacity for the train of over 19,500 gallons (86,400 litres).

Although they were hailed as the latest road transport technology at the time, Peter's experience with the Atkinsons was less than rapturous:

I don't know how Shell came to buy such vehicles. The first models that we drove overheated badly, and the gearboxes were a double overdrive affair which was not very practical.

And those cabs—they were hopeless. The way they were mounted resulted in them sloping down toward the front. You ended up with a sore neck from driving with your head forward and looking up under the top of the windscreen. The air conditioning was okay, it was about the best feature of that cab.

By the mid-'70s the move away from body prime movers had begun in earnest and Shell began replacing the Atkinsons with bogie-drive conventional prime movers such as Kenworth and Mack hauling doubles at first because of restrictions on road train lengths between Darwin and Katherine, due mainly to the twisting Pine Creek section of the highway before it was re-located and straightened, and then triples right through to Alice Springs once the road improvements were completed.

For almost 20 years the body truck ruled supreme as a road train prime mover in the Northern Territory. Obviously the AEC Government Road Train with its load-carrying power unit and the availability after World War II of heavy-duty ex-military vehicles which could carry a payload as well as pulling loaded trailers played a significant role in shaping operators' thinking, and this was continued through to the then-modern vehicles of the '50s and '60s such as Foden, Mack, Leyland, AEC and eventually Kenworth in the '70s. Powerful three- and four-axle body trucks and their trains of three trailers were unique; no other State—in fact, no other country in the world—had this distinctive 145 ft (44 m) configuration in its transport system. It was developed in the Australian outback and it served not only the Territory but remote areas of Queensland and Western Australia as well.

The Territory's regulations in those days were benign to the body truck combination and didn't favour variations or additions to the articulated configuration. In fact, for many years the Territory authorities would only permit a 20-foot two-axle dog trailer to be pulled behind a semi-trailer. The thinking of officialdom was that the semi-trailer kingpin was a potential Achilles heel, especially if additional loading (such as that of a trailer) was imposed on it. At that time, of course, turntables were mainly the plate type on a sub-frame bolted to the prime mover chassis; the quick-hitch kingpin and turntable with its stronger and more stable mounting was still around the corner. A further apprehension in the official mind was that the jackknifing

A 'Flintstone' Mack body truck with three trailers in the days before this configuration was replaced by the 'triple bottom' combination—prime mover, semi-trailer and two trailers *(Nick Struiksma)*

THE OLD AND THE BOLD

potential of the semi-trailer would be aggravated by trailer momentum.

But in the mid-'70s the first signs of change could be discerned. Full-length doubles—prime mover and semi-trailer, plus full-length multi-axle trailer—came on the scene, and the body-type prime mover began to lose support among some operators. Apart from the fact that the body truck was a special design more-or-less exclusive to the Territory and was a heavy unit with virtually no resale value beyond the Territory without extensive and costly modification, it also posed problems if it broke down on the road. If the mechanical failure couldn't be rectified on the spot, the vehicle would have to be unloaded and the freight would then have to be reloaded on to the replacement unit. But if, on the other hand, it was a conventional articulated prime mover pulling a doubles combination that was disabled, it was a much less complicated and cheaper exercise to lift the semi-trailer, remove the failed vehicle and back a replacement prime mover into position.

There seems little doubt that the recommendations arising from the Salter Report in Western Australia were the forerunner to triples being approved in the Northern Territory.

In 1969 a study group was set up in Western Australia to investigate 'ways and means of exploiting economies of scale in road transport vehicles for certain tasks in Western Australia'. It was headed by deputy police commissioner R. C. Salter who had had lengthy experience in traffic and transport technical matters in the state. Other members of the group were Mr W. F. Edgar, a Department of Main Roads engineer; Mr H. S. Gorham, transport consultant; and Mr W. Roots, who had had 32 years' experience in the transport industry with Mayne Nickless and Sweeny United Transport.

This group studied road train and other multi-unit operations in Western Australia, Queensland, the Northern Territory and western New South Wales.

Among Territory and Queensland operators the group found almost unanimous preference for articulated road trains, despite the long and traditional association with rigid prime movers and the report noted that

The only doubts expressed were in relation to the ability of the fifth wheel kingpin to stand the additional strain of a third trailer on a triple bottom operation. This opinion appears quite invalid in face of the strength of the certified kingpin as against many of the lighter and inferior trailer couplings used in road trains towed by rigid vehicles.

Moreover, kingpins are not subject to wear as are normal trailer couplings where the amount of play must allow wear to develop.

The study group found a strong body of opinion among Territory operators and drivers that, due to overhang, the tail end of rigid prime movers created sway, whereas semi-trailer prime movers towing from the fifth wheel (turntable) located over the centre of the drive axle(s) held the train in a better line and ensured better tracking and less swing.

'We found no evidence to suggest that doubles and triples are any less safe than conventional road trains—rather, the contrary may be the case,' said the study group in its report.

Whilst preference swung heavily in favour of articulated prime movers there were very experienced operators who favoured the use of body trucks in some areas of cattle transport. Doug Foster, who became the general manager of Australia's largest cattle road train operation, Buntine Roadways, said that on rough station roads and in jump-up country, diminished traction can be a problem for articulated prime movers:

If a driver gets caught on a steep jump-up out of a creek crossing with an articulated prime mover he's in real trouble. He can't reverse the trailers and have another run at it. The cattle begin to slide toward the rear and their weight comes off the drive axles and there's no traction. Unless there's another

Over 88,000 litres of fuel were carried in this Shell road train which went into service in 1970. The four-axle Atkinson prime mover had a Cummins engine and 13-speed Fuller box. The fibreglass cab was air conditioned.

THE VEHICLES THEY DROVE

vehicle in the vicinity which can uncouple its trailers temporarily and hook on the front of the stalled prime mover to help pull it out of trouble, there's nothing else for it but to unload, which means 'jumping' the cattle off the trailers, and the risks involved in that don't need to be spelt out.

Body trucks have been absolutely essential on some types of cattle operation because the weight of the beasts they carried helped provide traction. There'll always be situations where they are more efficient than the articulated prime mover.

Wayside Waterholes

Man's requirements for resting and eating are inexorable; they can be deferred but not eliminated. As motor transport developed drivers found themselves stopping by the roadside to refurbish their depleted bodies with food and rest. With the day-long roar of the engine gone the silence of the bush was like another world. Squatting around the fire, yarning, sometimes watching mice creep into the glow to steal scraps thrown their way, sometimes hearing the howl of the distant dingo—it was a denouement, a wind-down. Of course, for others the end of the day's work coincided with a stop at some convenient establishment for a re-charge of bodily needs and a bit of relaxation.

The nomadic life style of long-distance driving permits a man to be a loner and yet a member of an exclusive brotherhood; there's a fundamental satisfaction in improvising small comforts and contending with the elements and then discussing adversities and recoveries with understanding mates and acquaintances who speak the same language. Roadside eateries across the continent which are patronised by the trucking fraternity invariably have areas set aside and designated 'Truck Drivers Only'. These immutable itinerants prefer the company of their own select society.

In the early days of long-distance motor transport

in the Territory, the spacing between stops was longer than that of the camel and packhorse mail but much shorter than those of today. Mechanical behaviour and vehicle performance had—and still have—an influence on stage distances.

Heading north from Alice Springs in the 1950s, depending on how long it had taken to grind up through the Alice Hills and how late and how hot it was, the first stop would have most likely been Aileron, 82 miles up the road, and the Aileron pub was unofficially known as the First and Last. About an hour or so up the Track was Ti Tree, and between Ti Tree and Barrow Creek there was a popular 'camp site' at Central Mount Stuart where there was plenty of room for road trains to pull off the road while their drivers boiled the billy and yarned.

Central Mt Stuart, the geographic centre of the Australian continent, was originally named Mt Sturt by explorer John McDouall Stuart and his assistant William Kekwick in April 1860, to honour Stuart's close friend, Captain Charles Sturt. But an 'a' was later added to the name to commemorate the exploratory feats of Stuart in crossing the continent from south to north.

The pub at Barrow Creek was almost a compulsory stop. From Alice Springs it was 245 miles and the haul

A disused section of the highway makes a handy parking lot for road trains at Emerald Springs, north of Pine Creek, while drivers take a spell at the roadhouse.

THE OLD AND THE BOLD

would have been hot and hard. Hours of roaring and monotonous engine noise was replaced by the relatively genteel sound of a compressor motor putt-putting away as it powered the refrigeration plant, indicating the availability of a cool thirst quencher. Inside the temperature might not be much different from that outside, but there'd be refreshment and company, both of which were very welcome after hours at the wheel of the big rigs.

Adjacent to the pub the fortress-like Barrow Creek telegraph station, built long before the pub, was and still is a reminder of an earlier form of communication. It was one of a string of repeater stations spaced at approximately 250-miles intervals along the Overland Telegraph Line. Sitting close under a flat-topped hill the old buildings are surrounded by high stone walls, and two graves are a mute explanation of the reason for this protection; the graves are those of two telegraph officers who were speared by Aborigines soon after the station had been established. Other repeater stations were at Tennant Creek, Powell Creek, Daly Waters, Katherine and Yam Creek to the north, and at Alice Springs, Charlotte Waters, The Peake, Strangways Springs and Beltana to the south.

Just outside Barrow Creek there's the turn-off to the Home of Bullion mine, a few kilometres to the east through Neutral Junction cattle station and about 25 miles further on there was a large army staging camp during World War II. Another stopping place for many years has been Wauchope 66 miles north of Barrow Creek. The name, incidentally, is pronounced 'war-kup' whereas in New South Wales the north coast timber town of the same name is pronounced 'war-hope'. Its origin dates back to mining activities on the wolfram fields of Wauchope and Hatches Creek.

The Devil's Marbles on the edge of the Murchison Range are not far from Wauchope. Huge boulders of weathered granite lie in heaps or singly on each side of the highway for several miles and it was from here that the eight-tonne boulder for Rev. John Flynn's grave near Mt Gillen, Alice Springs, was obtained.

For the next couple of hours the road train driver of the '50s and '60s encountered undulating and twisting road conditions, necessitating plenty of work on the gear lever and steering wheel before arriving at Tennant Creek, 312 miles from Alice Springs.

At Tennant Creek there were a couple of cafés and a pub which found favour with drivers whose runs terminated or began at the mining town which grew from the discovery of gold by Malachi (Jack) Noble in the early 1930s. His name was perpetuated in the rich Noble's Nob mine, which has since been worked out.

But for drivers going on to Mt Isa or Larrimah or Darwin the pub at the Three Ways, where the Stuart and Barkly Highways meet 15 miles to the north of the Tennant, was a more popular meeting place. For drivers proceeding to Mt Isa it was the last refreshment stop before Camooweal, just over the Queensland border, 280 miles to the east, disregarding Frewena which was a mere 80 miles away.

North of Three Ways there were wayside places such as Banka Banka, Renner Springs, Elliott, Newcastle Waters, Dunmarra, Daly Waters and, as far as Co-Ord drivers were concerned, Larrimah, which was also the end of the run for them where freight was off-loaded on to North Australia Railways trucks and vans.

Banka Banka had been the site of a large military staging camp during World War II. Troops who were being moved north to combat a possible Japanese invasion were transported by road between the rail heads at Alice Springs and Birdum, just south of Larrimah. First stage was about 25 miles north of Barrow Creek; the second was at Banka Banka; and on the third day they reached Larrimah.

The derelict Dunmarra roadhouse which was run by Noel and Ma Healey for many years. A modern roadhouse and petrol station has replaced it.

In a corrugated iron building vacated by the army Mrs Mary Ward, wife of Philip Ward and partner in Banka Banka Station, set up a cafe shortly after the war, to serve travellers meals and tea. According to an advertisement in the *Centralian Advocate* of March 1949, it was then being operated by John and Dorothy Doyle who later established the Renner Springs roadhouse about 40 miles north. Renner Springs, incidentally, was named after Dr F. E. Renner who was the medical officer for the central sector of the Overland Telegraph Line; he drove by buggy between the construction workers' camps.

Sixty miles north of Renner Springs there was another wartime army establishment at Elliott, used principally for transport operation, and 15 miles further north at Newcastle Waters was the junction of the Stuart Highway and the famous Murranji Track which taps the equally famous Victoria River cattle country which once could boast of the world's biggest cattle station, Victoria River Downs. This has since been considerably reduced in size by sub-division.

From about Renner Springs northward the vegetation begins to change indicating transition from the arid to the sub-tropic zone. It was here that Henry Peckham, 'The Fizzer' in *We of the Never Never*, began as a stockman and in 1902 took over the packhorse mail contract from Katherine to Anthony Lagoon across the vast and at times dry Barkly Tableland. Later he was mailman on the Katherine to Wave Hill and Depot Landing track and lost his life in the flooded Victoria River. His grave is in the Elsey cemetery a few kilometres south of Mataranka.

Dunmarra, between Newcastle Waters and Daly Waters, is a short distance south of the junction of the Stuart and Buchanan Highways, and the Dunmarra roadhouse in the days of the Healeys was, like Barrow Creek, just about a required stop for road train drivers. There are stories galore about Noel and Ma Healey. Like many Territorians who claim to be the pioneer of something or other, Noel told the writer when he first called at Dunmarra in 1961 that he (Noel) had driven the first lot of solid-tyred trucks (Leylands, as it happened) from Queensland into the Territory in 1923. He also related how he had helped Bert Bond many years previously, when that well-known South Australian and Territory tourist coach operator had broken an axle in a vehicle he was driving with a load of passengers from Adelaide to Darwin. Noel apparently had a vehicle of the same model as Bond's coach so he whipped the axle out of it to get Bond back on the road.

From Dunmarra the distance to the railway terminal at Larrimah was 85 miles and this was the end of the trip for most road train drivers, particularly those on the co-ordinated road-rail service.

Beyond Larrimah those drivers hauling to Darwin

became aware of the change of surroundings. The vegetation seemed greener, the topography changed from plains with low surrounding hills to undulating country with many more bends in the roads, the termites' nests were taller and more numerous, and the crows and eagles which were noticeable further south were replaced by wheeling hawks and screeching flocks of parrakeets and other colorful birds.

For the remaining 300 miles there was a reasonable number of roadside facilities at Mataranka, Katherine, historic Pine Creek, Hayes Creek and Adelaide River. Northwards from Adelaide River there was abundant evidence of the heavy concentration of armed forces during World War II. Although no buildings were left, there were numerous airstrips beside the highway and hundreds of roads leading off into heavy jungle-like growth where Army and Air Force units had been stationed. For much of the time the road ran alongside the narrow-gauge railway line bedded on steel sleepers to overcome the problem of termite destruction.

Drivers who were on the road in the 1950s and 1960s were unanimous in their criticism of the inflexibility of cafe and pub meal hours along the road. Regardless of the reason for lateness, there was no chance of getting a meal if the driver didn't arrive within the prescribed hours. The chief exception to this rigidity was the Healeys' small pub at Dunmarra. But more about that later.

Doug Foster recalled the inventory of meal houses up The Bitumen from Alice Springs to Darwin in the late '50s.

After leaving Alice Springs there was a hotel at Aileron. At Ti Tree there was reputed to be an underground cafe up to about 1955 but when I was on the road, there was nothing there, just a store. At Barrow Creek there was a pub where you could get a meal if you were there at the prescribed time. Otherwise you missed out. The same applied at Wauchope.

At Tennant Creek you could get a meal at any hour at the Red Mill cafe which was run by Kay Woods who had a motherly affection for the young truck drivers of those days and made sure they were fed! Then up at Renner Springs there was a roadhouse where you could get a steak or whatever regardless of the time of day. I think Bob Lindon or Johnnie Doyle was there at the time.

Elliott had nothing at all by way of an eating place. Old Maxie Scheeber had the store there. He was a German and an irascible one at that. If you were friendly with Maxie he might take you out the back and cook up some stew or something like that. You always knew if Maxie was kindly disposed toward you if, when you walked in the door, he abused you. But if he just said G'day, whaddya want, you knew he was unfriendly that day. So there was no place to get a meal in Elliott.

Then along at Dunmarra there were Noel and Ma Healey who'd do anything for you but they really didn't have much in the way of facilities. There was no refrigeration, just a

Coolgardie safe; there was a wood stove; and the whole place consisted of a couple of Sidney Williams huts. It was best to eat tinned food there; the fresh stuff was a bit suspect!

On to Daly Waters pub and again it was a case of being there on time or forget about eating. It was off the road; quite a little village with about half a dozen houses. It seemed to be mainly a centre for people from surrounding stations. It also had an airstrip where the old DC3s used to land, as well as all manner of other aircraft. It was a well known landing ground in the early days of aviation where aircraft could be refuelled.

Next there was Larrimah and the Larrimah hotel. It was probably the worst of the lot as far as sticking to meal hours was concerned. An ex-policeman was the licensee; he and his wife ran a very clean house and Larrimah was always busy with trucks coming up on the coordinated service to unload onto rail. But if you were five minutes late for the evening meal, it wouldn't matter if you'd had a flat tyre or some other trouble, he would not give you a feed. You'd get a drink, but no meal. He was a hard man; good-hearted in some ways, I suppose, but as far as he was concerned a rule was a rule. Dinner was off at 7 o'clock; if you came in at five past seven—and you might have been patronising his pub for 12 months or more, eating his food and drinking his booze—his wife stopped serving. And that was that.

At Mataranka there was a hotel but no cafe. Katherine had two cafes, one run by Mrs Peterson and the other by Marsh Motors. North of Katherine there was the Pine Creek Hotel which was run by Bruce Cole when I was on the road. Bruce later set up a spare parts business in Alice Springs. Next door to his pub at Pine Creek was Jimmy Ah Toy's store.

Beyond Pine Creek there was the 133-Mile Cafe (133 miles from Darwin). That's the place which is now called Emerald Springs. In those days you'd never know if it was going to be open or shut down because there seemed to be a succession of owners trying to make a go of it and failing. Sometimes you'd get there and all you could buy was a packet of cold bacon and some stale bread; at other times there'd be no food at all because the proprietors had run out of money.

At Hayes Creek there was the Tank and Tummy Station where you could get a beer and a bite to eat, but the pub at Adelaide River was as hard as the rest of the wayside hotels; no meals between hours.

Despite its shortcomings Dunmarra was the best of them as far as hospitality was concerned. Moreoever it was completely unpredictable; you never knew what would happen next. I remember stopping there one time and my mate and I ordered a steak each. Mrs Healey went out the back and there was a helluva commotion; then, after a while she came in with two cooked steaks and muttering about the bloody cat which she'd found nibbling at one of the pieces. I still don't know which of us got the nibbled bit! After that I always ordered tinned stuff!

But I suppose in some ways the inflexible meal hours at most wayside eateries didn't really mean much more than temporary annoyance and inconvenience. If you knew you'd missed the meal time you wouldn't bother stopping; you'd go through until you met someone down the road and boil the billy with him or simply boil one on your own because sooner or later someone would turn up to join you for a cuppa and

a yarn and maybe share a tin of braised steak and onions. At least you knew what you were getting from the tin.

One much-used method of meal preparation was to put a can of beans, or tinned 'dog' or whatever it was you had in the box, somewhere on the engine to warm it up. On the Fodens the ideal place was near the epicyclic range-change lever; it could stay there all day without overheating. It would rattle around and the labels would wear off but when you opened it it was just at a good eating temperature.

You had to be careful, though. I tried it once on a petrol-engined 180 Inter. I was getting towards Larrimah and put a can of 'dog' of some sort on the exhaust manifold. About a quarter of an hour later it exploded and I had to drive hard to burn all the junk off the manifold! It was just a bit too hot for warming tinned food.

When I come to think of it we wasted quite a bit of time along the road, not so much at the wayside eateries but just 'camping' at the side of the road, boiling the billy and yarning. Back in the '50s you could drive five or six hours without seeing another vehicle and so it was a bit of an event when you met another truck.

Then, sometimes, we'd travel together and pull up together. For instance, you might meet a few other drivers at Mt Isa unloading and getting ready for the run back to The Alice or wherever. You'd plan to leave together and the bloke with the fastest truck would go ahead and boil the billy somewhere along the road while the rest of us caught up.

I recall spending one complete night just yarning and drinking tea. It was just outside Camooweal; four of us had been to Mt Isa and unloaded and were coming back empty. It was Norm Davey, I think, who had the fastest truck. It was an Inter KR11 with a Gardner Six in it; Stan Cawood owned it. Norm elected to go ahead and about 10 o'clock at night we reached the spot where he had a fire going. Well, we yarned away and next thing it was daylight. Of course we were buggered the next day but that didn't matter. There wasn't much pressure in those days to be at a certain point at a specified time. For instance, on the Co-Ord run, provided you made the train on time at Larrimah and stopped off for a load of copper on the way back to Tennant Creek, if you got back a bit early, there was no demand made for you to get going again and get another trip or half-trip done.

A truck was expected to do a trip a week to Larrimah and back and everyone was happy. Of course if you got back a day late that was a day less that you had off. Mind you in those days the economic return for the owners was better than it is today. Nowadays drivers are expected to do one and a half trips a week to Darwin to make it pay. Owners aren't enthusiastic about people spending hours at wayside stops or yarning while the billy boils.

Getting back to the wayside pubs and so on, I think the blokes that made them so colourful and entertaining were the ringers and bore-pumpers and dam sinkers and fencers and so on. They'd be out in the bush for weeks and then they'd come into civilisation and spend a week in the pub. They'd strike up a yarn with anyone who cared to listen and they'd tell you some marvellous tales. They were rough and ready blokes, and some of the people running the pubs were just as rough and ready too.

In time I moved up from driving to management and I

could appreciate what went on and what was a fair thing to expect.

But a humorous episode I'll never forget took place around 1968, I guess. It involved the bloke running the Three Ways pub. I was Noel Buntine's manager at Alice Springs then, and we used to buy fuel at the Three Ways. We knew the drivers were getting a few things put on the fuel bill; maybe they'd get $10 put down as fuel whereas it was the price of a feed and a packet of smokes or a bottle of beer. Although it wasn't the right thing it was accepted to a certain extent.

I was on a trip with one of our drivers one day when he said: 'Listen Doug, this bastard at the Three Ways is ripping us off—both of us, I mean.'

'What do you mean?'

'The other night I got fuel and he put $20 on the bill and he said I could get a hamburger, a packet of cigarettes and a bottle of beer. Then he made me pay for the beer. So, you paid $20 and all I got was a hamburger and some smokes. I tell you, he's a bloody thief!'

Ripping the boss off was one thing, but ripping the drivers off too was intolerable, according to my bloke's way of seeing things!

Ian Cawood, who began driving his father's trucks in 1958 at the age of 17, said that some of the wayside places haven't changed much except for some general refurbishing and improvements, but of course with faster vehicles capable of travelling further between stops, the same use is not made of places such as Aileron, Ti Tree, Barrow Creek and even Tennant Creek, which was superseded as a truck stop by the roadhouse at Three Ways, 24 kilometres further north.

The rigid meal times adhered to by many publicans and even some cafe proprietors were somewhat frustrating, but there were exceptions and among them Ian remembers publicans, Jim, Tom and Dennis (Bluey) Herreen who took over the Barrow Creek pub in the 1960s:

Just about every driver who was on the road when the Herreens were at Barrow Creek counted them as friends. They were first-rate hotel-keepers. Nothing was a trouble to them; they'd have a beer with you and talk to you as if they had all the time in the world. They were bushies, not strong on refinement but extra-strong on hospitality.

In the '50s there was a small pub at Three Ways, where the Stuart and Barkly Highways meet.

On a run to Mt Isa there wasn't much in the way of eateries along the Barkly Highway. There was a rough-and-ready sort of place at Frewena, about 80 miles east of Three Ways, then nothing till you reached Camooweal in Queensland, 200 miles away. Mt Isa was a further 120 miles.

Going north after leaving Three Ways there were the old-established wayside places such as Renner Springs and Dunmarra.

I was yarning with another driver outside the Healey's place at Dunmarra one day and we decided to see if Ma would knock up something for us. We were pretty tired and thought a beer and a feed would set us up for the remainder of the journey.

Noel and Ma had been away for a time and had only just arrived back. The place was a bit of a shambles and they weren't really organised for catering, but we knew they'd find something around the place that would go towards meeting our needs.

At Dunmarra you could always expect the unexpected. Occasionally there'd be a pet pig in the bar; there always seemed to be a few chooks walking in and out the front door and flying up on to the bar counter. And if you happened to go out to the dining room for a meal there'd always be a dog or two sprawled out under the tables.

Well, we asked if we could get something to eat and Ma said she could make a couple of hamburgers. We thought that sounded pretty good so we had a couple of beers while we waited. In came the hamburgers eventually and we sat down to devour them but we soon realised we weren't going to be able to eat them.

From the first mouthful it became evident that she didn't have any lettuce or cabbage so she'd done her best to oblige and had garnished them with grass! I don't know whether it was kikuyu or paspalum but whatever it was it was shredded amongst the meat and we just couldn't cope with those hamburgers! We offered them to the dogs but they turned up their noses at them.

I don't mean to denigrate Ma; I'm saying what a great and hospitable person she was—she'd do anything for you. It was no wonder that Dunmarra was a favourite spot for most of the drivers in the '50s and '60s.

Today at Dunmarra there's a new roadhouse adjacent to the Healeys' pub-cum-store which is now derelict. Noel Healey was badly beaten-up by a 22-year-old hoodlum and died of his injuries in Alice Springs Hospital in June 1970. The cryptic wording of a plaque outside the new premises falls a long way short of the many pleasant and sometimes hilarious memories that drivers have of the Dunmarra pub. It states simply: 'This plaque is erected in memory of Edgar Noel Healey 1892–1970. Pioneer.'

One driver who was on the road for many years said that it was easy to slip into a way of life that led to a dependency on liquor and pills. The sameness of the day-to-day driving routine and, in the summer months, the high temperatures—at times up to 48°C (120°F) for days at a time—were conducive to having a few beers and yarning with other drivers. These breaks from the monotony and heat would sometimes be extended for hours and then to make up for the lost time amphetamines would be swallowed to ward off sleep.

Sometimes I would drink all night and then hit the road. I always considered I wasn't drunk and that however much I drank I could always handle my rig competently. I never had an accident due to grog but I went very close to killing myself a few times. I gave myself quite a few frights.

The biggest fright I experienced didn't involve my vehicle or any other vehicle, and it led to my eventually giving the grog away. I was driving through the Devil's Marbles after a pretty heavy night on the booze and had helped myself to a couple of 'yippee beans' to keep me awake when suddenly I felt very sick—quite different from anything I'd ever experienced before. In fact I felt so crook I thought I was going to die. I thought I'd really overstepped it this time. I looked in the rear vision mirror and my face had gone blue, particularly around my nose and mouth. I thought I was about to have a heart attack. I pulled over to the side of the road and climbed into the sleeper bunk and stayed there for a couple of hours. When I'd recovered a little I got back behind the wheel and reckoned I was going to survive, but I got to wondering how many more times would I get away with it? Was this meant to be a warning? It wasn't long after that I stopped drinking. Unfortunately I'd lost my wife and family through drinking; I'd turned my back on them. I began to realise what a mess I'd made of my life and theirs and I stopped drinking. No, I didn't experience a 'bolt of lightning' or anything like that, but I became interested in the Christian way of life, and although it needed a determined effort on my part to quit drinking I don't think I should take all the credit; I'm sure the Lord Jesus Christ helped me change my life.

Drinking by road train drivers wasn't something that began in the post-war period. A friend of the author who was visiting Alice Springs in pre-war days said:

On one occasion I watched the departure of the Government road train; it was leaving on a three-month journey to outback stations carrying supplies. On top of the high load on the trailers were numerous Aborigines plus their bits and pieces, no doubt getting a free ride in return for loading and unloading help. The driver, full as a boot, was carried from the pub and bundled into the rather primitive open cab but like so many of those tough old-timers, once in command, his handling of the outfit gave no indication that he was drunk.

Drinking by drivers also caused problems for management. Jim Cooper (Gulf Transport) related some of his experiences with drivers who slaked their thirst somewhat more than circumspectly:

Like other companies we had troubles occasionally with drivers down the track thinking that once out of sight they were out of mind. I remember one night getting a phone call from the Frewena roadhouse on the Barkly Highway to tell me that one of my drivers was heading to Mt Isa with a load of cars that were consigned to Darwin. He had stopped at the Three Ways Hotel for too long and when he emerged from the bar he set off in the wrong direction. He got as far as Frewena where someone turned him around and pointed him in the direction of Darwin.

Another time I received a call from the police at an Aboriginal settlement below Wauchope. Apparently two policemen had been driving south from Tennant Creek when they came upon one of my road trains sitting in the middle of the Stuart Highway with its engine running and the bull lights on and the headlights on high beam. They stopped to investigate and found the driver completely out to it draped across the drawbar of the first trailer. They obviously couldn't leave the vehicle where it was so in an effort to do the right

thing they drove it into the nearby Aboriginal settlement for safekeeping. Needless to say that driver didn't work for me after that.

You'd send a driver off with a load to be at a certain place at a certain time. Next thing there'd be a phonecall from the other end saying the load hadn't arrived and when could they expect delivery. I'd then phone the road houses asking if one of my vehicles was there but they would assure me it wasn't. Yet I'd know darned well it was at one of them but as long as the driver was spending they'd cover up.

It's different now; drivers don't stop for very long at roadhouses and wayside pubs. They've got to keep moving. They stop for meals and to have a rest, of course, but that's about all. Time is money these days, and delays are costly.

John Frazer-Allen of Darwin began driving road trains in the '70s and found similarities and differences in conditions along the highway when making comparisons with earlier days. These were some of his impressions:

I suppose you could say that the 'downfall points' such as Wauchope, Three Ways and Dunmarra were still there when I started driving up and down The Bitumen. There used to be a sort of legend that 60 miles either side of these places you'd be sure to see some sort of disaster as the stimulus of the grog wore off and drowsiness took over. Be that as it may, I *do* remember a mate of mine rolling a trailer north of Dunmarra. He was surveying the scene when a tourist happened along and asked: 'Did you roll your trailer, feller?'

'No,' said my mate, 'every hundred thousand miles I do a wheel bearing inspection and I found this is the easiest way to do it.'

He'd stayed a bit longer than he should have at Dunmarra.

The bloke who had the Three Ways pub was quite a character. Truckies could get a meal there for a dollar. He is reputed to have had the highest sales of diesel fuel in Australia. He must have had a tremendous through-put of beer too. I've seen the parking area around his pub so crowded with road trains that it was damn-near impossible to get another rig in it. There always seemed to be hundreds of them there!

If you happened to pull in with a new rig and he heard about it, he'd make some excuse and sneak out and grab a badge or something off it and put it up in the bar. Had quite a collection! But it was all tossed out when the old bar was

John Frazer-Allen.

closed down and moved into the new roadhouse. That didn't do anything for good PR with the truckies, let me say.

Going north after leaving the Three Ways sometimes I'd call at Daly Waters. You'd have to serve yourself there because the publican was usually drunk.

I never called at the Larrimah pub; it was off the road and I preferred to go on to Mataranka where old Gool Mahomet was always good for a yarn. He'd been a cameleer in his day.

There were times when I'd give away the pubs and eateries and simply pull up along the road, light a fire and prepare a meal. It was something like the old drovers' camp; other blokes would pull up and soon we'd have the tea made and a few spuds on the way. Grab a shovel and throw a bit of steak on it; a shovel makes a good barbecue plate. All very simple.

But they don't seem to stop along the road as much as they used to. I guess it's because the trucks are faster and the roads are better and the tourist trade has made the owners of the wayside eateries lift their game and provide meals at any time.

In the 15 years that Nick Struiksma has been driving for Fleet Owners (now Co-Ord Transport) he has seen what he describes as 'a complete change of character' in road train operations.

Of Dutch origin, Nick began driving for Gerry Vaughan of Melbourne on interstate routes. Then he drove for Wright's of Mt Isa and later for Denis Buntine, before joining Co-Ord in the days when B-type Macks were being phased out in favor of Maxidynes. Nowadays

he pulls triples with a Kenworth powered by a 450 bhp Caterpillar engine, for the Co-Ord associate company Red North which hauls petroleum products such as distillate, avgas, petrol etc. He's known by his colleagues on the road as 'Spook':

We used to have time to stop along the road and have a yarn with our mates, but those days seem to have gone. Sometimes it seems that the only way to talk to other drivers is by radio. Some drivers use CBs to keep in touch with their mates; I don't have a CB in my truck. I prefer to use the two-way radio which the company has installed in all its road trains.

When I first came to Alice Springs things were pretty free and easy. When the perishables train came in there'd be a round-up of blokes from the pubs to load the trucks and get us on our way. We drove two-up, and had ten hours to get to the Three-Ways, which was no trouble for the Maxidynes. Today we do that leg in eight hours on our own and Darwin in 22 hours' driving time. At Darwin we've got air-conditioned sleeping quarters where we rest before heading south again.

I don't even have to stop to refuel because my prime mover carries 1,900 litres of distillate which gets me to my destination quite comfortably. Pulling a fully loaded train the Cat engine averages a bit over one kilometre per litre.

We don't have to carry log books in the Territory. The tacho chart can be consulted if there's any query about driving hours or vehicle performance.

A fairly typical trip for Red North tanker drivers would be, say, departure from Alice Springs at 3 p.m.

Nick Struiksma.

into Tennant Creek (500 km) about midnight, sleep in the bunk till 6 a.m. then back behind the wheel for the 1,480-kilometre leg to Darwin which would be reached early on the evening of the second day. After a night's sleep, depart Darwin with a full load in the morning of the third day, and with a rest en route during the next night, reach Alice Springs in the afternoon or evening of the fourth day. There would be a rest period of at least 24 hours, possibly 48, depending on loadings.

Up until 1976 the Co-Ord service only went as far as Larrimah and drivers found Elliott to be a pleasant stopping place when Bob and Betty Smith owned the premises there.

But at the old Dunmarra pub anything was likely to happen, *said Nick*. Sometimes there'd be fowls in the bar and it wasn't unknown for a brumby to come in and join the drinkers! Undoubtedly the most 'educated' horse was the brumby at Emerald Springs which would come into the bar with an old Holden hub cap clenched in its teeth. It would bang the hub cap on the bar counter until someone filled it with beer, which the brumby would then slurp down with great enthusiasm!

But some of the colour has gone out of many of the roadside stopping places. That home-away-from-home atmosphere is missing. Yet they still look after the truckies pretty well. You can always catch up on a bit of gossip at any of the stops.

I guess the whole scene has changed, really. Some drivers don't seem to have either the time or the urge to stop for a yarn. No longer does a company have to phone pubs along the way to find out where its drivers are; they simply get on the two-way radio and call 'em up!

Even at Alice Springs things have changed. The Alice Springs Hotel, which was owned by 'Uncle' Ly Underdown, used to be the truckies' pub. There'd be drivers and other employees from about four different companies, as well as blokes who did the loading and unloading of railway wagons and trucks—we used to call them 'desert wharfies'—and railway blokes and in fact just about anyone who had anything to do with transport. We used to go there in shorts and singlet and bare feet straight after work; sure, it was a bit rough and ready but it was a good place to meet your mates and have a yarn. Uncle Ly used to look after us well. When the transport union moved into the Territory and we had our first strike—it lasted for 11 days—Ly Underdown gave the truckies $1,000 credit across the bar while we were off the road.

Unfortunately the pub had a sad ending; it was burned down and Uncle Ly died the following day. Nowadays you've got to get dressed up to have a beer after work!

Mike Flynn is one who has been on both sides of the roadhouse scene—as a user and as an owner. In 1985 he opened the largest truck station in the Territory. Situated on the southern outskirts of Darwin it provides a full range of services for road trains as well as accommodation and food for drivers, and, of course, for motorists and the public in general. 'The colourful days of roadhouses seem to have passed,' says Mike, who in 1988 was president of the Northern Territory Road Transport Association:

Today it's a question of dollars and time. People are paid a lot more money per hour than they were in earlier times and drivers can't just stand around chatting. Once upon a time a driver could stop and have a few beers or park his vehicle for a couple of days and get on the booze but that's just not on these days because, (a) the roads are busy and traffic moves fast, and (b) the vehicles have to be kept moving because it's a competitive market and people don't want to be kept waiting for their freight to arrive.

In years gone by everybody knew everybody on the road and in the pubs the conversation was self-generating; a lot of 'do you remember' stuff and episodes such as the one when a well-known character was thrown out of one of the pubs and he came back with a chain-saw and cut all the verandah posts off the pub causing the verandah to collapse! Sure, they still stop to break the monotony of the road, but they don't stop for as long as they used to.

Although operating conditions have changed dramatically over the years drivers still find time to pull off the road at favoured truck stops or roadside camp sites to 'have a mag' about truck performance, loads, rates, transport inspectors, the boss, sub-contractors, company drivers, tourists and their antics in cars—in fact, virtually any subject that pertains to or even remotely impinges on their work.

In some places there are glamorous colour photos on the wall depicting some of the 'big iron' that graces the road these days; sometimes there are less flattering wall decorations in the shape of dishonoured cheques, displayed for all to see.

Walking into a roadside bar it's possible to see a row of backsides, broadened by the sedentary nature of driving, flowing over stools as their owners lean on the counter and swap yarns and experiences. It's also possible to catch snatches of conversation, such as. . . 'And I was goin' so bloody fast that the dog mascot out front had his paws over his eyes'. Or to hear a tall tale such as the one about a truckie who was sitting alone at a table in a roadside cafe when he was approached by three bikies who set about provoking him, but without success. He got up and left, and the bikies later sidled up to the cafe owner and said:

'What a mug! Left before his meal came. Said he didn't fight.'

'He can't drive either,' said the cafe owner. 'He's just backed over three bikes out the front!'

Mishaps and Mirth

The volume of freight being moved at any given time and the conditions under which drivers worked in the early days of multiple unit operation meant that it was inevitable that the occasional accident would take place.

From time to time the newspapers recorded incidents involving transport vehicles. On 23 January 1953 the *Centralian Advocate* reported:

Twenty bags of Darwin mail, a huge trailer, two reels of movie film for Alice Springs and thousands of pounds worth of welding equipment went up in flames when an Alice Springs–Darwin Motor Service vehicle burnt on the Stuart Highway last Saturday. Only the valiant efforts of drivers Ray Bell and Gordon Stanion saved the prime-mover from complete destruction. Exploding ammunition and the danger of a fuel blow up made the job of salvaging from the inferno extremely dangerous. Stanion and Bell managed to save four bags of mail.

The vehicle was cruising south about 24 miles below Wauchope when Gordon Stanion pulled up to investigate after hearing an explosion from the rear. Flames rushed towards the prime mover as soon as it stopped for the entire load of the trailer was an inferno.

The two men made frantic efforts to save the mail. For the next two and half hours they tried to stop the flames spreading to the prime mover.

At one stage exploding ammunition, which unknown to them had been loaded with the freight, forced them to lie flat. Two holes were punched in the prime mover cabin.

Gordon Stanion said that Ray Bell attempted to shake loose the blazing load on the trailer by driving the whole 'works' over rough ground beside the road.

'How it stayed on I'll never know, but it did,' said Gordon.

They then resorted to throwing sand over the fuel tank at the rear of the prime mover and were able to hold the fire back.

A brief item on 4 March 1956 said that one of Outback Transport's vehicles had overturned (no location mentioned) and that Kittle Bros were helping out with a loaned vehicle.

A couple of weeks later the following public notice appeared: 'The management of Outback Transport wishes to thank those who went out of their way to help us at the scene of our perishables smash last Sunday. Special mention to those who willingly forfeited their Sunday morning sleep to arrange cranes, oxy cutting plant and an ambulance to free our driver Willi who was badly injured and trapped in the wreckage. The offer of all assistance possible by our opposition in transport in Alice Springs reached our Darwin office very shortly after the accident occurred, something for which we give our special thanks once again.

E. J. STILES'

In the 1930s the 'highway' was a pair of wheel tracks which followed the Overland Telegraph Line. The Ford and the vehicle behind it were bogged for days, and had to be completely unloaded before they were extricated.

THE OLD AND THE BOLD

Another news item:

A series of truck accidents in the past couple of weeks culminated in a trailer catching fire and a large proportion of its goods were burned.

The mishap occurred about 60 miles north of Alice Springs. The rear trailer of an Overland Transport Co.'s two-trailer outfit caught fire. The cause was traced to a tyre blowout. Heat generated by the flat tyre set it alight and flames spread to the load. Transport driver Ivan Wiese was able to save part of the load and successfully unhitched the trailer from the rest of the unit. However, considerable damage was done to the unit and its load which included an aeroplane engine.

The following week there was an item relating to the destruction of 74 bags of mail when a trailer caught fire. The driver was Wally Truman.

'ALCOHOL BLAMED FOR DEATH OF ROAD TRAIN DRIVER' was the heading of an item in the *Centralian Advocate* of 8 August 1958. This related to an incident in which a Baldock's vehicle ran into the back of one owned by Fleet Owners. Evidence was given at the inquest by Jim McConville, a partner in Baldock's, who said that the driver of one of Baldock's Hippos had given the wheel to a passenger while he had a sleep and the passenger drove the vehicle into the rear of a Fleet Owners road train which was parked partly on the roadway. It was revealed in court that the drivers of both road trains had been drinking beforehand. The names of the drivers and passenger were not mentioned in the report.

Ted Stiles put the cause of many accidents on drinking and drivers going to sleep at the wheel. He said that it was extremely hot in the cabs of vehicles which had been designed and built in Britain. Add to that the monotony of the job and the fact that drivers were a long way from base, and the result was often a few too many beers at too many wayside stops.

He laughingly recalled a joke relating to drinking that backfired on him. A friend of his who didn't drink or smoke advertised for an employee who didn't drink, to work on a drilling plant. Mischievously Ted then advertised in the following week's paper for a mechanic who, if he drank, would be paid an extra £10 a week. Somehow or other the story became garbled and when it was later reported in a Territory newspaper that Ted Stiles of Outback Transport, Darwin, was looking for drivers who drank, he was almost inundated with replies from grog-loving hopefuls in every state and the story was repeated in a Californian newspaper!

Ian and Greville Cawood drove for their father for many years. Ian recalls an incident involving Greville, who lost most of a load of beer whilst driving to Mt Isa on one occasion:

It was raining at the time and although the load was tarped and roped, some water apparently got under the tarpaulins and wet the cartons. Normally we had racks or gates at the front and rear of the tray but this time they hadn't been put up and once the cartons got wet they began to collapse, the ropes came loose, and the bottles began to slide off. They were falling off for quite a distance and he didn't find out until he did a tyre check. We used to check tyres about every 50 or 60 miles during the day but at night when the temperatures were cooler and

A Kittle Bros Bedford was in dire trouble when the rear axle went down and the semi-trailer parted company with the prime mover. *(Peter Ritchie)*

MISHAPS AND MIRTH

if the truck was going well we'd go for 100 miles or more. Well, this particular night everything was fine—except the weather, of course—and Grev was batting along nicely, quite unaware that he was leaving a cascade of beer and broken glass behind him until he pulled up at Wonarah which is about 65 miles east of Frewena. That's where the awful truth was revealed! Norm Davies, who was driving the Inter about an hour behind him, reckoned he was picking glass out of his tyres for the next six months! He got to Mt Isa with about 160 dozen short.

Despite their seriousness, some accidents had a humorous side. A Darwin newspaper item related the following incident without comment:

A burning trailer from a heavy transport was unhitched from a truck carrying 3 tons of high octane petrol on the Stuart Highway last night. Driver Brian Morrissey used the big diesel transport moving to blow the flames to the rear while his mate, Keith Webb, threw 13 drums of fuel to the road and then uncoupled the trailer.

'It was sheer guts,' said Outback Transport proprietor, Ted Stiles.

The vehicle, valued at £14,000, was travelling along the Highway near Mataranka. At Warlock Ponds a drum of fuel fell off the truck, exploded under the trailer and set it and its load of timber alight, from end to end. Morrissey and Webb saw at once that if the flames bridged the narrow gap between the trailer and the truck, the load of fuel would explode. Morrissey, therefore, kept the transport moving slowly to fan the flames to the rear while Webb crawled out on the load and rolled drum after drum of petrol off the truck. A passing motorist had seen the flames roaring along through the darkness and then saw a man sitting on the load and a driver at the wheel. He raced to Mataranka Police Station and told Constable Peter Wilson that two madmen with a truck on fire were driving along the road.

After getting the last drum of petrol off, Webb tried to uncouple the blazing trailer. At the first attempt he fell off, he scrambled out of the way of the wheels and was helped by another passing motorist to separate the two vehicles, while Morrissey kept them moving slowly. The trailer was a total wreck.

Ted Stiles added: 'Apparently the car driver who reported the incident to the Mataranka police saw the silhouette of Taffy Webb against the flames, moving about the trailer as he tried to unload the drums but the motorist thought Taffy was actually building his own funeral pyre or doing a Joan of Arc or something!'

Ted Stiles employed a driver whom he called 'Willi the Wog' who was of German descent.

One of Willi's delights, *said Ted*, was to drive at speed through large pools of water lying on the road, soaking everything and everybody nearby. He was coming into Darwin one Sunday with a load of perishables and when he reached the Elizabeth River about 24 miles out, instead of slowing down like an ordinary person would and—probably because many Darwinites were picnicking at the old low level crossing which was running well over a foot of water from rains the previous

The poor condition of the highway in early postwar years often led to serious mishaps. In this instance the road shoulder near the Three Ways gave way and the entire road train slid sideways, rolling on its side. *(Bob Dodd)*

THE OLD AND THE BOLD

The result of a jack-knife south of Tennant Creek. The prime mover remained upright but the three trailers whipped around, one ending on its back. *(John Ryan)*

A Buntine & Ryan Mack with its load ablaze. The driver was able to uncouple the prime mover and drive it from under the semi-trailer. *(John Ryan)*

A devastating fire which completely reduced a tanker road train to molten metal. *(Geoff Bullen)*

MISHAPS AND MIRTH

A burnt-out Foden body truck and one trailer, victims of a fire in a load of drum fuel. The other two trailers were disconnected and pulled away by another road train. *(Peter Ritchie)*

day—Willi just hit that water so hard he nearly drained the crossing, according to a policeman who was drenched as he stood near one of the solid marker posts just out of the water level. Next day I got quite a roasting and a running commentary from that gendarme at my Darwin depot which was in Peel Street.

On another occasion Willi 'caught' a motor car and its occupants while they and he were crossing the Manton River. Ted said that there was water pouring from that car for the next 30 miles!

But Willi's fun with water brought him unstuck near the King River, south of Katherine. The approach to the old river crossing had a slight bend in it. According to Ted there was about a 40 metre stretch of water over the bend and Willi steamed into it at great speed, throwing water up over the cab and as Willi didn't have his wipers operating he went straight ahead and capsized, spilling the load. 'There was fibro and timber everywhere,' said Ted. 'When he rang me in Darwin to tell me of the accident he said: "And, Ted, there's 3 by 2 and 2 by 3 all over the place!" For years after I laughed when I saw a piece of timber and wondered if it was a piece of 3 by 2 or 2 by 3!'

A somewhat similar incident that occurred at Barrow Creek involved a driver nick-named 'Boots' who was at the wheel of a Mack B61 owned by Overland Transport. An eye-witness who viewed the episode from the Barrow Creek pub said:

He was coming down the long drag into Barrow Creek and he was making the most of that downhill run because there weren't many of them in that part of the Territory. Just before the turn-off to the pub there was the creek which most times was dry but it couldn't be seen until you were virtually right on it. Unknown to 'Boots' the creek was running fairly high. As it wasn't possible to stop in time Boots plunged the Mack into the torrent and went it emerged on the other side water had entered the air intake and wrecked the engine: two con rods were busted.

Roadside breakdowns, like accidents, often had their humorous side. Here are Peter Ritchie's recollections of a couple:

I was carrying a load of cement with some furniture stacked on top of it, and I broke an axle just west of Mt Isa so I had to unload the furniture and then the cement. I had the furniture stacked on the side of the road and the bags of cement nearby and I decided to have a spell. I was sitting up in a lounge chair under the shade of a tree when along came a party in a car. They must have thought I was some sort of looney who'd decided to build his house right alongside the road because they didn't stop; in fact they seemed to accelerate away!

On another occasion I was driving one of Windy Allwright's Fodens pulling a semi and a dog trailer. I had another bloke with me and we'd just rounded a bit of a bend in the road north of Barrow Creek when I saw in the mirror that one of the dual wheels had come off the trailer.

I pulled off the road and decided that the other driver should go into the Wauchope pub about 16 miles away and I'd stay with the outfit because I didn't want to leave it unattended as the trailer was carrying (among other things) about eight tons of gelignite. In those days 'geli' was worth its weight in gold, and all around that country there were tin mines, gold mines, copper mines, wolfram mines, etc., and most of them were one-man shows.

I told my offsider that when he got to Wauchope he was to send out something for me to eat, and in the meantime I'd walk back along the road to see if I could find the missing wheel.

I had walked two or three miles before I found the wheel and I was sitting down having a spell when along came a car from the direction of Wauchope. It stopped and the driver got out with my breakfast on a tray—sausages, eggs, toast etc.— all nice and hot and covered with a clean cloth.

The car went on its way so I sat down on the trailer wheel and started to eat my breakfast. There wasn't much traffic on the road in those days but soon I saw a car coming from the direction of Barrow Creek. When the driver saw me he slowed down and then stopped. He didn't come up close; he stayed about 50 feet away, wound down the window and asked me

THE OLD AND THE BOLD

if I was okay, to which I replied that I was. He then turned to his wife—they had a couple of children with them—and spoke to her. As they looked at me their eyes appeared to be as big as saucers; they just couldn't make it all out. I can imagine what was going on in their minds: they'd just driven 45 miles from Barrow Creek, the last 27 miles were dead straight through semi-desert country where you can see for miles. No houses, no vehicles in sight, and yet here's this bloke sitting on the side of the road with a properly prepared tray of food, having breakfast in the middle of nowhere! Nothing else was said. They simply wound up the windows, drove around me and headed north rather quickly!

Les Loy, secretary-manager of the TTA, 1960–1964, tells a story of Peter Ritchie which earned him the name of 'Pogo Pete'. At one time Peter carried a pogo stick with him in his road train, and had a lot of fun with it at the expense of tourists travelling up and down the highway. A typical episode was one in which Peter had parked his big vehicle out of sight in the Devil's Marbles area. He waited for a car to come along and then mounted his pogo stick. As he hopped along the road the car driver pulled up and asked him where he was going. 'I'm heading for Wauchope,' was the reply, 'but I'm buggered if I know how far it is but I've been hopping for two and a half hours and I don't seem to be getting anywhere.'

The bemused tourist and his passengers decided they couldn't be of much help to an eccentric like that so they went on their way, leaving Peter to wait and play the same trick on the next unsuspecting motorist!

Another prankster was Ron Dingwall, aka 'The Horse'. Driving one of the big lumbering Diamond Ts which trundled along at a gentle gait around 18 to 20 miles an hour he'd spot a stationary car up ahead with its party resting at the side of the road. He had a big black dog which travelled everywhere with him and as he approached the travellers he'd sit the dog up at the steering wheel, set the hand throttle to maintain a steady speed, and then duck down so that he could just see above the bottom of the windscreen. Seeing a dog at the wheel and nobody else in the cab must have been quite a sobering sight!

At one stage when Ron Dingwall was driving a semi-trailer rig on the Alice–Darwin mail run for Litchfield Transport he would poke a small hole through a newspaper and when a motor car approached from the

Stranded in floodwater at Newcastle Waters.

opposite direction he'd put the paper up in front of his face as though he was reading it as he drove along.

Playing jokes on motorists was about the only relief we had from the boredom and discomfort of driving those hot, slow vehicles in the '50s and early '60s, *said one driver*. But, at the same time no road train driver would see a motorist stranded. If a motorist was seen to be held up by a flooded creek or mechanical breakdown, he was soon on his way again if a road train driver came along, even if it meant hooking the car on to the rear trailer and towing it through the floodwater or along the road to the nearest town.

I never heard of anyone 'doing a perish' along the road, as has happened on the Birdsville Track, but I've met some travellers who've been horribly hungry and thirsty. They've been badly equipped and have been broken down on the road for a day or so, but I've never seen them at the stage of tearing their clothes off. They've been awfully glad to see me and get some water or soft drink and some help to get their vehicle on the move.

The Australian penchant for handing out nicknames found fertile ground among Territory drivers. In addition to such characters as Willi the Wog, Pogo Pete and others previously mentioned, there were Sandwich Sid, Soup Head, Bones, Bomb Head, Spooky, Spinifex, Drought Foal (the origin of this one is obscure) and, of course, the usual Mad Mick who in this case was described as 'a bloke with steel-rimmed glasses, a balding head, and protruding teeth which seemed to more rightly belong to a camel!'

MISHAPS AND MIRTH

Off the Beaten Track

The road train operations pioneered by Ivan Wiese (pronounced 'Weece') were different from most of the others. Instead of forming part of the supply line between Alice Springs and Darwin and places en route, the company founded by Wiese, Northern Transport, concentrated its business on providing a freight and perishables service to remote settlements and stations west and north-west of Alice Springs and into parts of Western Australia.

Unlike many of his contemporaries in the business, Ivan Wiese didn't start his Territory life in Tennant Creek. His introduction to line haul operations was as a driver on interstate routes in the eastern States. In Melbourne his contact point for loading and messages was the Caxton Hotel in Lygon Street, Carlton, where numerous other transport drivers and owner-operators gathered and talked shop and picked up instructions or information regarding available loads. On one of his visits to the Caxton Ivan met Len Tuit and Len persuaded him that the Territory was the place with the future.

So, when Ivan became one of the many victims of the States' road taxes which put his employer out of business, he took off for the Territory and got himself a job with Len. About six months later Ivan decided to return to the eastern States but a particularly cold Christmas in Melbourne a fortnight later saw him raking up his air fare to Alice Springs to rejoin Tuit and trundle up and down the Stuart Highway in one of three Internationals—a D60 with Gardner 6LW engine, or a D50 or a KB7, each fitted with a 5-cylinder Gardner.

The round trip to Darwin and back occupied a neat two weeks in those times.

After a couple of years with Len he took a job with Kurt Johannsen who at that stage was still running his ex-army Diamond T prime movers. Those were the days when a driver had to be his own mechanic. On one trip the engine 'threw' a con rod through the block near Wauchope. Kurt's response to Ivan's breakdown message was to send up another block, a piston and big end, and a small tripod to lift the engine. After removing the radiator and de-rigging the engine, he waited until

Ivan Wiese with friend, in front of an Autocar, which was used on Northern Transport's service westward from Alice Springs.

one of Baldock's road trains came along. It hitched on to the rear of the Diamond T and moved it back a few feet so that the faulty engine could be lowered to the ground where Ivan could work on it. A week later another Baldock vehicle came along and shunted the Diamond T sufficiently far forward for the engine to be dropped back into the chassis. After spending another day on reassembling and reconnecting the ancillary bits and pieces, Ivan got on his way once more.

'You had to be able to do more than just steer 'em and swap gears in those days,' said Ivan in a model of understatement.

Next he did a stint with Overland Transport (Ryan & Buntine) and in 1955, after a brief period with a southern operator who started hauling perishables but didn't last long, Ivan went into business on his own, carting perishables with an International 190 semi-trailer outfit. Trade built up and he acquired a second 190 which he operated as a small road train (body truck and one trailer). Then he bought a second-hand Foden which pulled two trailers. In 1960 he formed his business, which he'd named Northern Transport, into a partnership with Ralph Smith and Ian Lovegrove as co-directors. Ian, who was born in the Territory—his father was a sergeant in the Northern Territory Mounted Police—was a fully qualified diesel mechanic and welder, and he looked after the workshop side of things while Ivan organised the freight operation.

After about five years of head-on competition with Co-Ord the partners could see that it would make more sense to develop the business along different lines. So they moved into local cartage and crane hire and purchased the business of Ralph Smith who was handling John Dring Ltd's Alice Spring requirements. At the same time they began a line haul operation to and from Adelaide. Bedfords and Chevrolets were used on the local scene and the highway work was handled by a mixed fleet of Commer 'knockers' with semi-trailers and Mack and Foden body trucks hauling trailers. In all the business owned 22 units.

Recalling his experience with the Foden 2-stroke engine, Ivan said:

We must have been the only idiots in Australia who bought two of those things in one hit. We were operating to Adelaide at the time, doing three services a week. They would not do a trip to Adelaide without breaking down, nor would they get back to Alice Springs without failing somewhere along the road.

But the Fodens brought an innovative twist to the operation. As both Ian and Ivan were enthusiastic aviators they decided to buy an aeroplane with which they could fly to a Foden failure and land nearby with parts and tools to get the show moving again. Ivan, incidentally, was a foundation member of the aero and

the gliding clubs at Alice Springs and a news items in the *Centralian Advocate* of 17 November 1961 mentioned that he had gained his Gold 'C' for a 6 hour 40 minute flight in a glider at heights of up to 14,000 feet.

In the face of increasing competition and rate-cutting by 'southern' operators whose numbers were increasing, Northern Transport backed away from the Adelaide–Alice Springs run and looked around for other avenues of business. Fortuitously this was about the time that the search for oil and gas was being stepped up and Northern Transport began hauling drilling equipment to various places in the Northern Territory and in the north of South Australia.

Venturing into remote areas carrying plant and supplies for oil exploration companies gave Ivan the idea that there was considerable potential for hauling general freight and fuel to isolated stations and Aboriginal settlements and so Northern Transport built up a series of regular runs to places which were generally regarded as 'the back of beyond'.

Services were established to Aboriginal settlements at Yuendumu (294 km from Alice Springs), Hermannsburg, Haast's Bluff and Papunya (296 km). The Ayers Rock run (422 km) which had been developed some time previously was extended to Docker River (a further 230 km) and eventually to Giles Weather Station and settlement 103 kilometres inside the Western Australian border, making a total of 755 kilometres for this route.

The longest run pioneered by Northern Transport was from Alice Springs to Warburton (W.A.) via Curtin Springs, Mulga Park, Amata, Pipalyatjara (the last three in S.A.), Mt Aloysius and Blackstone (W.A.), covering a total distance of 1,159 kilometres.

The Warburton road train took a week to reach its destination and a week to return—if the roads were dry, added Ivan—and it passed through some of the most desolate and arid regions in Australia. Both Giles and Warburton are on the fringe of the Gibson Desert in Western Australia; Giles was named after explorer Ernest Giles who traversed the area, 1872–76, and Warburton got its name from another explorer, Major Peter Warburton, who earlier crossed the continent from the vicinity of Alice Springs to the Oakover River, in the general region of Port Hedland.

The company also had other (shorter) runs to the south-east (Santa Teresa Mission) and north-east of Alice Springs, carrying fuel supplies only.

Complementing the company's road train operations the two aviation-minded partners commenced a small air service to carry perishables and packages to the isolated communities and stations on their regular road train runs. In time they acquired a second aircraft and this was used (among other duties) to bring fish from the Borroloola region to Alice Springs. For the most part Northern Transport's operations were on roads which were well below highway standards and as a consequence Ivan Wiese used vehicles with plenty of power, robust construction and shorter length—two trailers instead of the usual three.

Although Fodens were the 'big iron' of the 1960s Ivan found that they fell short of his requirements in the 70s so he decided to import a long-bonnet Peterbilt.

When I went down to Sydney to pick up the Peterbilt there was a wharfies' strike and we couldn't get it off the boat. Laurie O'Neil by that time was selling Peterbilts as well as Fodens, and while the strike lasted he'd take me down to the docks each day to show it to me. It had a big placard on it: 'THIS TRUCK HAS BEEN CUSTOM-BUILT FOR NORTHERN TRANS-PORT, ALICE SPRINGS, AUSTRALIA'.

It had a 250 Cummins motor. We eventually got the truck out and put it to work straight away. Everyone in the Territory said I was crazy paying £16,500 for a truck because in those days that was a lot of money. But it just went to work and stayed working and for three years everybody watched that truck's performance over some of the roughest roads and toughest conditions imaginable.

We tried running an Oshkosh for about 12 months but we could hardly keep the fuel up to it. Running empty to Adelaide and coming back loaded it would average 1.78 miles per gallon [about 140 km per 100 litres]; it was costing us more to run than a vehicle with a 250 Cummins which was pulling bigger loads. So we sold it and began to buy Kenworths with Cummins 350 power. Then we brought an Autocar with a Cummins 400 which did a great job for us, and then a White Road Boss with a 350. We got good results from all of these because they had the power and the transmission that stood up to our operating conditions. They could lug down to about 900 revs in sandhill country and save changing gears which can be fatal when climbing over a sand ridge.

Likewise the trailer equipment used by Northern Transport was stronger and heavier than that of many other operators.

It had to be, said Ivan, considering the roads and the general terrain. You've probably never seen anything built as strong in your life. We couldn't afford to have equipment failure nearly a thousand kilometres from base and sometimes a hundred kilometres or so from the nearest human habitation. It's in the equipment area that blokes who've tried to 'knock us off' have fallen on their face; their gear just couldn't stand up to the road conditions.

Northern Transport confined its road trains to two trailers, partly because of the heaviness of its units and partly because pulling three trailers was very difficult in the bush: 'With two trailers you're all right; with three you can get into all sorts of troubles, particularly in sandhill country. The prime movers don't get knocked about so much either.'

Ivan Wiese had a sound schooling in multiple-trailer

operation in the days when he drove for Kurt Johannsen:

There were times when we used to pull four 36 ft self-tracking trailers from Jervois to Mt Isa. If we only had three trailers behind the body truck we'd have to unhitch at some creek crossings and pull them one at a time up over the bank. But with four trailers it was easier; we'd keep up our momentum and drop down into the creek bed and then begin to climb out. There'd be one trailer up out of the creek, another coming up the bank, the third in the creek and just when you thought everything would stall, number four trailer would come down and give us that push which put all three up on the top and it was easy then to get the last one up and resume normal speed.

It goes without saying that as Ivan Wiese's operations were mainly away from highway-standard roads he had encountered plenty of troubles stemming from weather and Murphy's Law.

On more than one occasion he was caught by rain out near the Gibson Desert. In one instance that he recalled, he and an offsider were marooned by incessant rain:

It rained like hell for about four days. We just could not get out of the truck cab. When we did we found ourselves in the middle of a sea of water with no hope of moving until the water dispersed and the ground dried out. Into the bargain we were bogged to our backsides. When the rain eventually stopped we set about building a small levee bank around the road train and for some distance beyond, and then we pumped out the water with transfer pumps which we carried to discharge fuel into storage tanks at various places on our delivery runs.

Having got rid of most of the water we then set about digging the prime mover and the trailers out of the mud. If you like hard and monotonous work, that's it. First you use small shovels to get the muck out that's covering the diffs and front axle and you heap it alongside. Having cleared the prime mover you crawl out and get into the mudheap with long-handled shovels and clear it right out of the way. Then you slide in under the trailers and give them the same treatment. It can take days to get a road train out of a bog. Still, you've got nothing else to do while the place dries out.

An episode of a different kind concerned the transporting of temporary school buildings from Alice Springs to Mudginberri in Arnhem Land. Three trailers carried a 16-metre portable classroom, a six-metre kitchen and a six-metre ablutions block, a 27,000-litre tank, plus sundry equipment on the body truck, which, incidentally, was one of the wartime Diamond T prime movers that Kurt Johannsen had used and which had been re-engined with a Caterpillar motor.

Our problems started, said Ivan, when the Department of Works insisted that from Pine Creek we had to use the road through Goodparla to Jim Jim, instead of allowing us to go to Batchelor and out across through Marrakai to the Arnhem Highway.

Well, it took us six weeks to do the 68 miles from Goodparla

THE OLD AND THE BOLD

to Jim Jim—six weeks of chopping trees down. We were away from home about nine or ten weeks altogether on that job. The track simply wasn't wide enough, so each morning my offsider and I had to get our axes out and clear the path ahead. Sometimes we could use the truck to bash down scrub and small saplings and other stuff up to about six inches thick. For a while we counted the trees we chopped down but after a while we got sick of that; we had cut down 1,100 when we gave up the tally. But that wasn't the only trouble; crossing some of the rivers gave us a mighty headache. The banks were often very steep and sometimes the track down to the river and up out of it involved sharp turns. We'd have to unhitch the trailers and bring them across one at a time. The schoolroom caused big problems and at times we had to lay out cable and winch the back of the trailer around so that it could negotiate the bend. Fortunately we had a winch set-up on that Diamond T which we'd used on oil rig work and it was an enormous help.

In 1982 Northern Transport was sold to Tony Richards of N.T. Fuels. At that time the company was operating two Kenworth 924 prime movers, a White and an Autocar. Ivan left the road transport industry and moved up to Boroloola where he went into partnership in a boat hire and fishing charter business.

A Moving Business

One of the facts of life in the transport industry is that furniture removers have almost invariably preferred to use their own vehicles and equipment rather than entrust their clients' goods and chattels to the sometimes not-so-tender handling of general carriers. One such selective company was the old-established removals firm of Richard Mitchell & Co. of Adelaide. Founded in 1876, Mitchells became the largest privately-owned furniture removals business in Australia, operating 40 vehicles as well as owning substantial storage and terminal buildings in the South Australian capital.

The company first entered the Territory transport scene in 1952 by successfully tendering to move furniture from Adelaide to Darwin for the Hotel Darwin. Two trips that year by company pantechnicons carrying furniture and some general freight all the way by road generated a number of inquiries which in turn resulted in a moderate volume of freight and furniture becoming available and this in turn led to trip frequency being increased to one every six weeks.

Next Orlando Wines (Gramps) consigned a large quantity of a new product, a sparkling wine, known as Barossa Pearl, to Darwin via the Mitchell service and the load arrived undamaged, despite the 'goat track' condition of the Stuart Highway north of Port Augusta. Then other wine companies began sending their products in Richard Mitchell vans and the South Australian Brewing Company followed suit with consignments of West End beer. By 1956 business had built up to a van a week carrying 80 per cent general freight and 20 per cent furniture. Twelve years later

A Richard Mitchell container en route to Darwin on a Kittle Bros Dodge truck pulling a dog trailer with a motor car as payload.

In the 1970s Richard Mitchell & Co used doubles pulled by a sub-contractor.

Mitchells were loading daily for Alice Springs and Darwin.

About the same time that Richard Mitchell & Co. began operating in the Territory the big national removals firm of Wridgways also extended its activities into the Territory, followed some time later by another 'national', Grace Bros. Wridgways and Grace Bros concentrated exclusively on furniture.

Business continued to boom for Mitchells, with the result that the company opened its own branch offices in Darwin in 1959 and Alice Springs in 1960.

For the first eight years the company's semi-trailer and three-axle rigid vans went by road from Adelaide to Darwin, taking between three and four weeks for each return trip. Then in 1960 the decision was made to use Commonwealth Railways' 'piggyback' service from Port Augusta to Alice Springs. The vans were carried on railway flat-top wagons and the drivers travelled on the trains.

There must have been times when Mitchell's management wondered if they'd done the right thing in deciding to send their vans by rail. The founder's grandson, Richard Mitchell, who was managing director of the company at the time, said that there were innumerable delays, mostly the result of floods, washouts and derailments along the line. One interruption to the company's Northern Territory service lasted 13 weeks.

We had ten vans operating on that service at the time, *Richard said.* Some were caught in Darwin because the Stuart Highway was also cut, and some were in Alice Springs. Eventually we flew all our drivers back to Adelaide and sat it out.

For the first few weeks we continued to accept freight at our Adelaide depot but we had to call a halt because the store was overflowing with goods. When the wheels began to turn again it took several weeks to catch up with the backlog.

Our experience with damage to freight was that it was caused in the main by railway accidents. The worst occurrence I can recall happened at Marree. One of our vehicles—it was a brand new semi-trailer pantechnicon on its first trip—had just been transferred across to the narrow-gauge flat-top which was then shunted. During the shunting operation the rail wagon ran off the track and toppled down an embankment. You can imagine the scene, with beer, wine, new refrigerators and washing machines, all mixed up with smashed household furniture and personal goods. It was a debacle!

In 1969 Richard Mitchell & Co. was taken over by Wridgways but both companies continued to operate separately. At times some furniture consigned through Mitchells would be sent in Wridgway 'home packs' which were containers specially designed for household removals. In the Territory, the 'home packs' were carried on Co-Ord road trains beyond Alice Springs, but Mitchells continued to move all their consignments in their own vehicles between Alice Springs and Darwin. The Mitchell operation was expanded by Wridgways in 1970 to provide a weekly Darwin-Brisbane–Darwin general freight and containerised furniture service, using two semi-trailer units.

In 1973 Wridgways was taken over by Ansett Transport Industries and Richard Mitchell & Co. was merged into Ansett-Wridgways. Then in 1984 the Mitchell name reappeared in the removals industry when the founder's grandson formed a company in Adelaide, Arem Pty Ltd, which operates as Richard Mitchell Removals.

THE OLD AND THE BOLD

Record Heavy Haul

By 1958 the indications were plain that the '60s would be boom years for transport in the Territory. In addition to the steadily growing freight requirements of Darwin, Tennant Creek and Alice Springs, in line with the general development of the Territory as well as the expansion of mining activities and tourism, there were big projects coming 'on line' just over the border in Queensland by way of a uranium mining venture at Mary Kathleen (60 km east of Mt Isa) and at Mt Isa itself as the copper mines there geared up for a big increase in their smelting operations.

As part of the Mt Isa expansion considerable quantities of very heavy electrical equipment, manufactured in Britain, had to be moved in by road transport, including a 62-tonne stator for the new power station. In 1959 the handling of the stator was the longest heavy haul to have been undertaken in Australia up to that time and was the forerunner of many more such movements into Mt Isa through the Territory over a period of nearly two years.

In planning the task, rail movement from Brisbane or Townsville was ruled out because the dimensions of the loading were out-of-gauge for the 3 foot 6 inch (1.06 m) rail line and Queensland Railways rolling stock did not have the necessary weight capacity.

After rejecting Darwin and other ports for various reasons, including inadequate handling gear, it was eventually decided to bring the equipment into Port Adelaide, take it by road to Port Augusta, put it on rail for Alice Springs, and then transport it by road to Mt Isa. Total distance, Adelaide–Mt Isa, was calculated as 1,758 miles.

The specialist heavy haulage firm of R. H. O'Regan (Carriers) Ltd, a Sydney-based company, won the contract. Although Territory operators such as Johannsen and Cawood had hauled locomotives weighing up to 25 tonnes and other items of railway rolling stock, none was equipped to handle loads such as those that had to be moved into Mt Isa.

Mr Harley O'Regan, managing director of the firm founded by his father in the days when horse teams hauled generators over rough bush tracks to new power stations on the outskirts of the Sydney metropolitan area, designed an ingenious double-gooseneck well-deck transporter for the Mt Isa contract, capable of being used on road and rail. Fitted up for road operation it had eight axles in two groups of 16-tyred bogies (64 wheels). When converted to rail operation the road wheels were replaced by rail bogies. Both types of undercarriage (road and rail) had common or matching turntables where they were attached to the transporter frame. The rear dolly assembly had power-assisted steering with a small Deutz diesel engine supplying power to a Vickers Detroit hydraulic pump. This engine also drove a compressor which provided additional air for the transporter's brakes.

Two Mack B633SX turbo-charged prime movers were purchased from Champions of Adelaide for £11,500 each. This model developed 205 nett bhp (153 kW) and 560 lbs/ft (756 Nm) torque, and its power was transmitted through a 14-inch (355 mm) clutch to a 20-speed 'quad box' and thence to a 9.02:1 double reduction rear bogie giving a total drive reduction of 124:1 in low–low.

One Mack was used for pulling the transporter, and the other was a pusher.

The 62-tonne stator destined for Mt Isa arrives at Marree on rail bogies prior to being transferred to road wheels for the remainder of the journey. *(Harley O'Regan)*

Two Macks, one pulling and one pushing, are shown as they were about to negotiate the hilly section on the old highway north of Alice Springs. *(Harley O'Regan)*

Upon reaching Alice Springs after the rail journey from Port Augusta, the transporter and its payload were jacked up, the rail bogies removed and replaced by road dollies, and the two Macks took over the haul to Mt Isa.

Despite predictions that the 62-ton stator would take about 12 hours to move through the hilly 13-mile section of the old highway north of Alice Springs, this was accomplished in 65 minutes. And although the schedule set by O'Regans estimated 60 miles a day, the Mack drivers Jack Sutton and Fred Britten achieved more than twice this.

The two drivers swapped positions morning and afternoon. The pusher driver was under considerable strain because he was driving 'blind'; the load was 11 feet 3 inches (3.43 m) wide and he was unable to see round it. As a consequence he had to do much of the driving by 'feel'.

The prime movers were fitted with two-way radio. The driving technique which was adopted involved the pusher operating one gear higher than the front prime mover. When it came to changing down the lead driver changed first and having settled down in that gear he instructed the pusher driver by radio to change down also. When changing up the lead driver instructed the pusher driver to change first and then the leading vehicle followed.

This technique was designed to prevent strain on the draft gear, pivot pins, etc., and to ensure continuous momentum. The drivers kept in touch with each other through chest-type microphones and ear phones.

For much of the time along the Stuart and Barkly Highways one prime mover was sufficient to keep the unit moving. It was able to travel along the level in third direct. When the two prime movers were involved fourth direct was the more usual gear. When a rise was encountered the pusher was quickly attached to the rear to keep the outfit rolling.

Altogether, nine moves were undertaken with the special transport in a total of 1,000 tonnes of equipment moved by O'Regan's into Mt Isa via Alice Springs.

THE OLD AND THE BOLD

PART TWO

Cattle Transport

Man of Many Parts

'On Sunday afternoon the family gathered in the dining room and after a short service little Kurt Gerhardt was solemnly baptised, to the joy of his parents...'

Thus Rev. Bruce Plowman wrote of a call he made as a patrol padre on camel back to Deep Well in his book *The Man From Oodnadatta*, which covers the period 1913–1918. The boy was Kurt Gerhardt Johannsen, born at Deep Well on 11 January 1915, who became one of the Northern Territory's most renowned road transport operators and the first to operate road trains in the immediate post-World War II period.

Around 1929, when the railway line was being constructed through Heavitree Gap, the Johannsen family moved up to Alice Springs from Deep Well, 47 miles to the south. Kurt's father, a Danish stonemason who had erected buildings at Hermannsburg Mission as well as police stations and other structures for the government, had contracted poliomyelitis. This disabling illness came on top of seven years of drought at Deep Well which led to the family walking off the property and taking their few possessions to Alice Springs.

At that time, apart from a few government-built houses, Alice Springs consisted mainly of timber shanties. The government buildings were constructed of concrete blocks, and although there was plenty of

Kurt Johannsen.

sand available every bag of cement had to be brought in by camel train and later by light trucks from Oodnadatta, 300 miles south. The cartage cost was as much as the materials and labour, thus putting the price of reasonable quality houses beyond the pocket of the average citizen who settled for bush timber with iron, or even thatched roofs.

It fell to the lot of young Kurt to earn what he could to support the family. Although only 14 years of age, he was a tall, strong fellow with lots of energy and a very bright intellect:

I started in transport right at the bottom, you might say; I ran the first night cart and garbage collection service in Alice Springs with a Dodge 4 truck. Dad had got the contract but he was still too weak to work, so I became the family breadwinner. I carted firewood for the bakery and the hotel and I learned to carry out repairs to windmills and pumps. At a later stage I acquired an old motor car engine and a generator with which I charged batteries for those people who owned radios in the town. I earned two shillings a battery.

In those days the population of Alice Springs, or Stuart as it was known until 1930, was only about 200 and as the sanitary and garbage requirements didn't take up a great deal of time the Johannsens cast around for other avenues of income. They became interested in mail contracting and took over the mail run east of Alice Springs to Arltunga, Winnecke, Mount Riddock and McDonald Downs. But as this was only a fortnightly service young Kurt still had time to take parties of anthropologists to remote place such as Mt Liebig, west of Alice Springs, and Docker River, on the Western Australian border. Occasionally he assisted Sam Irvine on the Alice Springs–Tennant Creek–Birdum mail run.

Sam Irvine was a pioneer of the motor mail era in the north of South Australia and in the Northern Territory. In 1925 he won the contract for the Oodnadatta–Alice Springs and Alice Springs–Arltunga mail

Pioneer mail contractor Sam Irvine, from whom the Johannsens (father and son) acquired mail runs at Alice Springs, is shown leaning on the mudguard of his Reo truck outside the original Alice Springs post and telegraph office in the early 1920s. Others in the photo include Frank Pearce (centre) and Laurie Wutke (right). *(Wutke Collection, courtesy of the Conservation Commission of the Northern Territory)*

runs, reducing the camel train time of four weeks to four days. As the railway line pushed northwards Sam Irvine's mail services were adapted to the changing needs of the area. He relinquished the Arltunga run which was taken over by the Johannsens and he became the contractor on the Alice Springs–Tennant Creek service which was later extended to Newcastle Waters and Birdum. Sam and his old Reo and GMC trucks were the subjects of many a story of perseverence, courage and heroism that have been related down the years.

The small gold mining settlement of Arltunga had its heyday in the 1890s. Although it was not a rich field its existence led to the establishment of a mail service from Alice Springs Telegraph Station long before Alice Springs township came into being.

Winnecke was another small goldfield north-west of Arltunga. It is mentioned in association with the Johannsen name in Ernestine Hill's, *The Great Australian Loneliness*, first published in 1940 and later reprinted several times. In it she wrote of a trip to Winnecke: 'I rattled through those ranges for five days in a little prairie-schooner of a mail truck with the Danish driver, Mr Johannsen. . . I met many wonderful characters out east of Alice Springs.'

The first vehicle which young Kurt used around Alice Springs and later on the Arltunga mail run was the Dodge 4 with 24-inch wheels which provided plenty of 'belly' clearance in the scrub and when negotiating stretches of sand and mud. But the Dodge wasn't big enough or sufficiently robust for the Tennant Creek–Birdum leg of the mail service which was acquired from Sam Irvine, so the inventive young Johannsen put together a 'bitzer' consisting of a Dodge G-Boy rear axle under a Willys Knight chassis which had been extended with a Studebaker gearbox and Buick motor. And on this contrivance loads of up to eight tonnes were carried.

Eventually the Johannsens acquired the full Alice Springs–Tennant Creek–Birdum mail contract. The service was weekly to Tennant Creek but monthly to Birdum. During the Wet season the mail truck terminated at Newcastle Waters and the mails were taken further north on horseback.

During the record floods of 1938 Kurt ran into some serious trouble. The packhorse mailman demanded double rates for the run from Newcastle Waters to Roderick Bore and threatened a shoot-out if he didn't get them. Kurt refused, and decided to complete the run himself with the bitzer. He fitted a box on the back to carry the mails, a swag and rations; he 'snorkelled' the air intake with some canvas sheeting and waterproofed the magneto and spark plugs with hose and a paste made from local black soil; and, of course, he disconnected the fanbelt. As he approached Lake Woods the water had spread out over 10 miles and he had to skirt around the lake and over ridges to get back to the Overland Telegraph Line which was hanging in the water in some places. He finally made it to Newcastle

Waters aerodrome where he borrowed 12 fuel drums and made a raft from lancewood rails lashed together with wire from the aerodrome fence. He crossed Newcastle Waters Creek by tying a rope to the raft on which the truck was being carried and then swimming from tree to tree, securing the floating vehicle as he progressed. He was eventually swept to the far bank where he drove the truck off the raft.

However, his troubles weren't over even then. He was again confronted by the packhorse mailman who tried to prevent the mail going any further. Kurt disposed of this problem by 'dropping' the mailman with a well-aimed punch and headed off across Stuart Plain which at this stage was a huge, shallow lake about 12 miles wide. With Kurt standing on the seat and the accelerator jammed open with a piece of timber, the bitzer, fitted with improvised chains on the rear wheels, pushed its way steadily across the flood plain. Twenty-four hours later he arrived at Roderick Bore where he had another lot of packhorses available to take the mail on to Birdum.

Kurt said that the only witness to this part of the episode was a Qantas pilot, flying from Daly Waters across to Queensland, who saw the wide bow wave created by the vehicle as it made its way through the floodwaters. He radioed back to Daly Waters that the mail was on its way.

There were many other times during the monsoon season when Kurt's bitzer with its 24-inch wheels proved its worth in areas that were inundated, particularly in the troublesome Newcastle Waters region. But even the bitzer couldn't cope on occasions, as these entries in a Postmaster-General's file show:

21.11.39 *Telegram* 'Wet season setting in early up here. Horses can only carry light mails.
Regards   Johannsen, Mail Contractor'
Some mail sent by boat from Fremantle to Darwin, for places north of Birdum. This enabled him to continue using pack-horses.
28.12.39 Johannsen used motor transport.

5.1.40   330 points rain recorded Powell Creek this morning. Southbound Overland mail held up here.
6th Jan. Overland mail still in bog mile south of Powell.
8th Jan. Johannsen still at Powell Creek.
9th Jan. Left Powell Creek 1.55 p.m.
26.1.40   Mail Contractor Johannsen sought permission to fly overland mail Newcastle to Daly and Daly to Newcastle (Creek uncrossable without soaking mails as boat not available). Johannsen to pay costs and arrange horsemen to pick up Dunmarra road mail if any. Permission granted.
1.2.40   Overland mail arrived at Powell Creek per truck. Johannsen said he had to swim Newcastle Creek with the mail, as the boat was not serviceable. He swam the river, pushing the mails ahead on a camp sheet.

As if the episode mentioned in the note dated February 1940 wasn't enough, Kurt Johannsen ran into further trouble, this time by way of an official report which led to a reprimand. The report, from the Acting Superintendent of Postal Services, directed to the Deputy Director, stated:

1. On or about 1.2.40 Mail Contractor K. G. Johannsen, of the Alice Springs–Birdum mail service, while in the course of conveying the mails, opened the Newcastle Waters-to-Alice Springs mail bag. The mail Contractor reported his action upon arrival at Powell Creek and has since submitted a report in which he stated that, owing to floods, and the fact that the boat at Newcastle River was in bad repair, he was obliged to swim the Newcastle River, and, in order to have the whole of the mails in one parcel, so as to facilitate a safe crossing, he opened the mail bag for Alice Springs and enclosed therein all the other mail bags and floated the one bag containing all the mails over the river on a raft to which he had fitted a camp sheet.

2. The Postmaster, Alice Springs, in forwarding the Mail Contractor's report, advised that his enquiries from the Police Constable at Newcastle Waters elicit that the boat was in good order and was actually used by the Mail Contractor.

Mr Johannsen, however, maintains that the boat was not serviceable and among other defects there was only one oar available and he did not use the boat but had to swim the river.

Soon after he commenced road train operations Kurt Johannsen won a contract to pick up, clean and transport 63,000 40-gallon drums left behind by the defence forces throughout the Northern Territory. There are 1,150 drums in this photo. *(Denis Buntine)*

3. Paragraph 28 of the General Conditions of Mail Contracts provide that any Contractor or Mail Driver who, contrary to his duty, opens or tampers with any mail or postal article is guilty of an indictable offence and liable to a penalty not exceeding £100 or imprisonment for not exceeding two years, vide Section 115 of the Posts & Telegraph Act.

4. There is no reason to suppose that the Mail Contractor opened the mail bag for any dishonest motive. His action, however, was most irregular and I am much concerned regarding the serious error committed by him. There are, however, some extenuating circumstances in that torrential rains had fallen and the country was flooded and the mail route almost impossible, in fact, at this particular time on the Northbound trip, the Mail Contractor found it impossible to proceed further than Newcastle Waters by road and with the concurrence of this Office conveyed the mails at his expense thereon to Daly Waters and return to Newcastle Waters by air and it was immediately after this incident that he found it necessary to swim the mails across the river and committed the serious irregularity of opening the Alice Springs mail bag to enclose all the other mail bags therein.

5. In view of the peculiar set of circumstances and the trying time experienced by the Contractor and his special efforts to maintain the service, it is thought this is a case where the infliction of a fine or more serious action might be waived and it is proposed, subject to your convenience, to specially draw the Contractor's attention to Clause 28 of the General Conditions of Contract and issue a severe reprimand to the Mail Contractor and to inform him that he must not open a mail bag in future under any conditions.

Gerhardt Johannsen's health and strength were improving all the time and with an eye to increasing their earnings he established a passenger service which operated in tandem with the mail runs.

Every Sunday the mail coach, which was a Studebaker President 6 (an eight-seater car) departed Alice Springs at noon and five hours later it arrived at Aileron, 138 km (86 miles), where the passengers had a meal before pushing on to a point between Ti Tree Well and Barrow Creek, where they camped for the night. Continuing on through Barrow Creek and calling in at the Wauchope wolfram mining field, they made camp for a second night between Wauchope and Tennant Creek. Arrival at Tennant Creek (315 miles/506 km) was scheduled for 11 a.m. on the third day.

On the monthly run to Birdum, the passengers spent the third night at Banka Banka and the fourth at the pub at Newcastle Waters. Arrival time at Birdum was 5 p.m. on Thursday, and the return journey commenced one week later. This gave Darwin people time to reply to their mail.

Southbound passengers from Birdum overnighted at hotels at Daly Waters and Tennant Creek, and camped in tents provided by the operator at the same spots as those used on the northbound run. The journey took from the Thursday evening to the following Monday afternoon.

The fare schedule was uncomplicated. From Alice Springs to Aileron it was 30 shillings; to Ti Tree Well £2; to Tennant Creek £5; to Powell Creek £7; to Newcastle Waters £7 10s.; to Daly Waters £9; and to Birdum £10. The fares included meals throughout, whether taken at hotels or provided by the contractor.

By comparison, 1988 fares on express buses are: Alice Springs to Ti Tree Well, $16; to Tennant Creek, $59; to Daly Waters, $87; to Birdum, $88. These fares do not include meals.

Luggage limit on the mail run was 224 pounds per passenger (about 100 kg). Today's coach operators allow each passenger two pieces of luggage free of charge, within certain overall dimensions.

By way of interest, the first-class rail fare from Adelaide to Alice Springs in 1939 was around £7, and second class was £4 15s. 6d., plus meals and sleeping berths. For the 330-mile (525 km) rail trip from Birdum to Darwin, the passenger in 1939 paid £3 16s. first class and £2 4s. second class. The train in those days stayed overnight at Pine Creek, and a local pub charged about 10s. for dinner, bed and breakfast. The hotel at Birdum charged a similar rate for the stopover before the train left on the following morning.

In between operating the Tennant Creek–Birdum section of the mail run once a month and sharing with his father the driving on the weekly Alice Springs–Tennant Creek service, Kurt began a small sideline at Tennant Creek in mechanical repairs for locals' motor cars and lighting plants. At the same time he worked on developing a wood-burning gas producer which could provide an alternate source of power for petrol engines. He had a hunch that in the event of Japan entering the war Australia's oil supply lines could be drastically reduced, if not cut altogether.

On 29 June 1940 the Johannsens relinquished the mail contract and it was taken over by Mr L. M. Owen who carried mail and passengers on the Alice Springs–Tennant Creek sector and freight as well on the Birdum extension. Owen used an International D-15 truck. About a year later the army took over the conveyance of all mails north of Tennant Creek, and in November 1942 the Alice Springs–Tennant Creek contract was cancelled (with compensation to Mr Owen) and the army became responsible for handling all mail between Alice Springs and Darwin.

After the war Mr Owen submitted a tender when the army pulled out but he wasn't successful; the contract was won by Mr Len Tuit who used an International 15-hundredweight utility and a Lease-Lend Ford V8 5-tonner.

Soon after the war in the Pacific broke out Kurt fitted the prototype wood burner to the Studebaker sedan which he and his father had used on the mail-and-passenger service and drove to Brisbane to show that his invention really worked.

It was more efficient than the charcoal burner which so many vehicles were fitted with during the war. It was only about one third the weight and produced more power than a charcoal burner. It consumed about one and a half pounds of wood per mile [about 0.7 kg per kilometre] and it could operate on just about any kind of timber.

Going across to Brisbane I was travelling through some open plains which were devoid of wood. I found a railway sleeper which I chopped up and it fuelled the Stude for about 120 miles, by which time I was back in timbered country with unlimited supplies!

Soon after arriving in Brisbane Kurt was 'man-powered' into a machine tool company where he worked for 15 months. He was unable to get support for his invention in Brisbane but,

I eventually got the Melbourne firm of Malcolm Moore interested in my invention, which I patented in 1943. But by the time we got it off the ground, after perfecting the prototype, the war had turned the corner and nobody was interested in it. I drove the Studebaker with the wood burner on it until 1945 and in that time it covered 42,000 miles.

After his stint in Brisbane he returned to the Territory where he was 'manpowered' once more, this time into the Allied Works Council's Civil Construction Corps:

I was with the CCC for about six or eight months working in the Harts Range area but eventually I was able to convince the powers-that-be that I would be of more use to the war effort if I could get out to a mining lease I had at Winnecke where I'd done a bit of goldmining from about 1932. Out at Winnecke I'd found phlogopite some time about 1937 or 1938; it's a special type of mica used in aircraft spark plugs.

The only other place where phlogopite was being produced for the Allies during the war was Madagascar, but when Madagascar fell into enemy hands another source of supply had to be found and, fortunately, I was able to provide it.

All the good things come to an end, I suppose. With the end of the war the demand for phlogopite dropped off; my father stayed on at the mine for some time and I began to turn my attention to transport once more—but big transport this time.

If the logistics of a war failed to lead to the construction of a railway through the Northern Territory, it was obvious to a thinker like Kurt Johannsen that road vehicles of train proportions could become a viable proposition.

By the end of World War II he had established a general engineering and motor repair business in Alice Springs. A friend named Ted Dickson, owner of Waite River Station 100 miles to the north, started more than

a flicker of interest when he said to Kurt: 'Why don't you build a road train that would take about 100 head of cattle? There's plenty of ex-army gear around, so why don't you get some of their trailers and build up something big?'

Kurt mumbled something about not having the money to buy such equipment, to which Ted Dickson replied that he had a few quid which he could lend if Kurt saw what he wanted. Shortly afterward the government held a series of wartime equipment disposal sales at Alice Springs and Kurt's eyes fastened on some Bren Gun carrier trailers with stub-type axles and 'big single' tyres (1200 × 20):

I thought: if I can get hold of these—there were 23 of them—I've got a start . . . they'll make the running gear for my trailers. The government bloke asked me to make an offer, which I did, and I got them for a ridiculously cheap price; can't remember how much. Anyway, I had to dash up to the Barrow Creek races where Ted Dickson was that day and he wrote out a cheque for £2,000 to help me get my first three 36-ft trailers built. These units formed my original road train. I removed the stub axles from the Bren Gun trailers; they'd simply been welded to the frames of the trailers, so I had to then make up straight-through axles for the trailers and weld the stubs to them. Then, of course, I had to get a prime mover which was sufficiently powerful to haul three loaded trailers. I had ideas of building my own; I'd also bought ten heavy-duty International rear axles and I thought I'd make an eight-wheeler (four axles), something like the old AEC road train but much longer and much more powerful. I planned to power it with twin-six GM diesels; in fact I tried to get a twin marine power pack but wasn't successful. So I made inquiries in the U.S.A. but General Motors weren't very happy with the idea, nor was I when I found that the landed price was going to be in the vicinity of £25,000.

Around about this time the big military surplus disposals sales began in Darwin, and there were tank transporters listed in the catalogues. They appeared to be ideal; plenty of power and plenty of gearing. But again the question of money cropped up. At this stage I had an old mobile crane working around Alice Springs; it was my bread and butter, and it was in use day and night shifting stuff from the disposals sales to railway trucks.

I went up to Darwin; I had my return air ticket and £80 in my pocket. I saw a Diamond T tank transporter and decided that that was what I wanted. Well, the bidding went to £2,500 and the auctioneer said that it hadn't reached the reserve price. I said I was still interested and would deal privately. When the time came to 'talk turkey' they asked me what was my financial position. Now, that was a bloody silly question, wasn't it?

Fortunately, I had met up with a chap named Doug Wheelhouse who was at the sales buying a lot of equipment which he intended selling in Melbourne. He said that he hadn't bought as much as he'd hoped to, and therefore had a couple of thousand quid that he could lend me, provided I could repay him by the time the next disposals sales came on. So I borrowed his £2,000 and got the Diamond T plus a four-wheel trailer; I loaded both of them with stuff that other buyers at the sale had bought and wanted taken down to rail at Alice Springs. This loading helped pay back some of my debt to Doug Wheelhouse.

At the next sale about eight weeks later there was a Diamond T with a low loader which I wanted. I'd told Doug Wheelhouse about it, but I couldn't get to the sale in time. However, he bid £3,600 for the outfit and got it, and kept it for me till I got to Darwin. The problem was how to pay Doug back because he was there to buy a lot more stuff for his Melbourne business.

Well, I was lucky. There was a bloke who wanted 170 tons of reinforcing steel carted; I quoted him £20 but he only wanted to pay £10 a ton. We finally settled for £12 provided he could pay me in a couple of days. Well, the job turned out to be 230 tons and by the time I carted all that and some other consignments I'd earned enough money to pay back what I owed.

I now had two Diamond Ts, but if I was to set up my road train business properly I needed more prime movers. So I went across to Albury where there were more disposal sales out at the Bandiana army camp and got three more Diamond Ts! I 'cannibalised' one for spares. They all had Hercules engines— the DFXE model Herc—which did quite a good job. I later re-engined them with GMs.

Another real piece of luck that I had was to put in a successful tender for 63,000 40-gallon drums and three and a half tons of bungs for them. Mind you, at this stage I was up to my ears in debt because I'd ordered some big cattle trailers from McGrath's in Melbourne and they cost plenty. I put in a bid for fourpence per drum. Some had been used to carry fuel, others bitumen, they had to be sorted, cleaned and picked up at various old army and air force depots from Darwin down.

I began carting them 1,150 at a time on three trailers and a body truck. I sold them to a petrol company for £1 each first grade, and 15 shillings each second grade, landed at Alice Springs. I set up cleaning plants using chains and kerosene which did the job very well. Each drum cost me about five or six shillings to clean, but I was able to sell them all—even the third-grade ones which leaked; drums were in such short supply in those days that petrol companies and others would take anything as long as it was repairable.

Looking back, I took some horrible financial risks at the time but I got away with it!

The drum recovery operation proceeded steadily while Kurt developed the cattle transport side of his business. He extended the wheelbase of each Diamond T prime mover to increase its carrying capacity and his trailer fleet grew to ten units, most of which were four-axle cattle crates shod with big single tyres. The wheel bearings ran in oil instead of the conventional hub grease, and this method of lubrication proved highly successful. In fact, Kurt Johannsen said that when his trailers reached the end of their commercial life the wheel bearings were 'as good as the day they were first fitted'.

The cattle trailers were convertible to flat tops for general freight carriage. The majority of the trailers were 36 feet long and weighed seven tonnes; some of these were subsequently lengthened to 43 feet, adding another tonne to their tare, and one was extended to 51 feet (15 m), bringing its weight, including the crate structure, to nine tonnes.

Having seen the self-tracking trailers on the old Government Road Train in action, Kurt decided to make his trailers steerable. The steering mechanism on the government trailers was spring-loaded and this, he said, caused considerable 'snaking'. He did not incorporate springs in his system which proved quite successful when handling trailers at relatively slow speeds. On narrow, winding bush tracks that served station properties Kurt Johannsen's drivers found that self-tracking trailers were essential. Non-steering trailers cut in on corners and as they bashed down scrub and saplings they sustained damage and tyres were staked by the sharp stumps that remained after the upper growth had been snapped off. But as roads improved and the prime movers had their speeds increased by the

A Johannsen cattle train pulled by a Diamond T body truck. The trailers, mounted on single wheels instead of the more usual duals, were self-tracking and were fitted with steering mechanism designed by Kurt. *(Kurt Johannsen)*

CATTLE TRANSPORT

Rear view of a later-design cattle trailer with dual wheels, built in Melbourne by McGrath Trailers. The self-tracking feature was an advantage on narrow, winding bush tracks and station roads. *(Kurt Johannsen)*

fitting of higher ratio diffs, the self-tracking principle gave trouble because the movement through corners tended to become exaggerated; the lead trailer would move out a little on the corner, the next one would go out a little further, and the third unit went wider still. Finally he settled for putting one self-tracking trailer behind the prime mover and coupling two non-steerable units behind that.

The first basis of the trailer size—in fact, the total capacity of Kurt Johannsen's cattle trains—was related to the carrying capacity of railway cattle vans. Each trailer was the equivalent of two railway vans, which meant that a road train of three trailers and a body truck was the equivalent of seven vans; if the 15-metre trailer was in the combination the road train's capacity became eight vans.

The first consignment of cattle handled by Kurt Johannsen's road trains was from Murray Downs to Alice Springs, a distance of 233 miles. The second came from friend Ted Dickson's Waite River station to the railhead at The Alice 123 miles away. Most of the movements were within a 300 mile radius of Alice Springs, although occasionally there were longer hauls. There was one move from Wave Hill to Alice Springs, 754 miles; a couple from Wave Hill to Mt Isa, 835 miles;

as well as a 'test run' early in the piece from Anthony Lagoon to Alice Springs, 620 miles, for the edification of visiting transport and livestock experts from Canberra and several States, to assess the future viability of this form of transport and to see what effect road train operations were likely to have on Territory road surfaces. Ted Pettit was the first driver of Kurt Johannsen's road trains.

Ted helped me build the first train, and then he drove our first cattle lift from Murray Downs—about six or eight loads, I think. Then there was Carl Corner; he was a driver-cum-welder-cum-foreman. Others who were with us early on were Tom Denny, Roger Wait, Peter Ritchie, Jim Hodgman, Ivan Wiese, Bert Noske and a lot of others, of course, who worked with us and later went into their own businesses or got into other avenues of employment.

Back in 1947–48 road transport of cattle was in its infancy; the transition from the traditional droving method to the faster but costlier mechanised movement was slow because station owners had yet to be convinced that their cattle would arrive at the saleyards in better condition after travelling by road and would bring higher prices, thus offsetting the cost.

The beef roads scheme wasn't even thought of; the roads which the Johannsen vehicles had to use—other than the Stuart and Barkly Highways—were in fact only bush tracks and deteriorated rapidly after a few trips over them by these heavy multi-wheeled units. Boggings were frequent after rain; on more than one occasion trailers went down in mud holes so deep that the vehicles were laid over at an angle of 45 degrees and the beasts walked out of them. A favoured method of testing the hardness of a track after rain was to walk ahead of the vehicle plunging a crowbar into any suspect surface which might be a 'crust' covering a soft spot; when these were revealed a detour track around the danger spot

In a town procession at show time one year, Kurt Johannsen decided to impress the locals by attaching a fourth trailer to one of his cattle trains. *(State Reference Library of the Northern Territory)*

would have to be bush-bashed by the prime mover until the original route could be resumed.

On some of the tracks, *said Kurt*, it would take us hours, with two or three blokes, to clear the way because we were pushing through scrub where nothing wide had ever passed before. Overhanging branches of trees would be broken off and would finish up in the trailers and we'd have to clear them out before loading. Of course, after two or three trips along those same tracks there'd be less and less scrub.

Fortunately for Kurt Johannsen the fluctuations in demand for his cattle train caused by station owners' reluctance to accept the new medium and by seasonal limits on movements (confined to the April–October portion of the year) did not affect him greatly. He was able to utilise his vehicles on general freight transport and carting copper ore from Jervois mines to the smelter at Mt Isa. In addition to developing his road trains he also kept an active interest in mining:

I worked it out that if I could get into mining, with the big vehicles carting the ore, even if I didn't make anything out of it, at least I could keep my crews together and keep my expenses down. This paid off, particularly in the off-season for cattle cartage. I had leases at Jervois which produced copper and scheelite but as there was no money in scheelite after the war I concentrated on copper.

We hauled a lot of copper to Mt Isa; in fact the first year we moved about 2,000 tons. Each vehicle averaged about 60 tons a trip. We used to go through Tobermory and Urandangie, and the distance was about 310 miles each way.

Although the cattle train operation proved to be quite viable, there were problems as operating costs began to rise and several stations decided to buy vehicles to transport their own cattle as well as livestock from neighbouring stations at times. Around 1955 Kurt Johannsen decided to reduce his activities in the cattle transport business. Following hefty wage increases and a big rise in Commonwealth Railways freight rates, he put up his prices by 10 per cent; this was resisted by station owners who were members of the Cattlemen's Association.

They were going around saying they wouldn't pay the new rates. Johannsen's so far in that he can't back out, with all his road trains and all the money he's ploughed into them. Well, that was where they made their big mistake. I had bookings to bring in about 30 train loads and I just cancelled the lot. That's when I got stuck into other work such as ore cartage and moving a whole lot of rolling stock for the North Australia Railway from Larrimah to Alice Springs where it was railed south for overhaul. I moved four locomotives, each weighed 26 tons, and their tenders, plus 143 trucks, vans and fuel tankers.

I stayed out of cattle transport for some years. Then the drought of the '60s began to hit hard and I came back in with my gear. The station owners who'd bought rigs had bowed out; they found they were cattlemen, not transporters. I stayed with the cattle business for a time but it was becoming a bit of a rat-race; hauliers from down south were going through bad times so they came up here and began carting for ridiculous prices just to pay off their hire purchase instalments so they wouldn't lose their trucks.

Eventually I got right out of the game. I sold most of my equipment and I disposed of my Jervois mine to Petrocarb. I'd begun to develop another mine at Molly Hill and I eventually sold that to Petrocarb too.

I guess I've been part of the history of the Territory. I can justifiably claim to have been the operator of the first road trains after the war in the Territory; Dave Baldock was hot on my heels and of course others followed as they saw the viability of this type of operation in an area of no railways and big distances.

In the cattle off-season Johannsen's vehicles were converted to flat-tops and carried freight of all description, as can be seen in this photo depicting railway tank wagons heading north to the NAR at Larrimah.

CATTLE TRANSPORT

Even small locomotives were 'piggy backed' by Johannsen road trains over the rail-less stretch between Alice Springs and Larrimah.

End of the road for one of Kurt Johannsen's GM-powered Diamond Ts. It was photographed in a yard at Alice Springs.

In the midst of all his transport, engineering and mining activities Kurt Johannsen at one stage even found time to learn to fly. He acquired a Tiger Moth shortly after World War II and when he gained his pilot's licence he flew it to all corners of the Northern Territory.

One trip nearly ended in disaster.

The *Centralian Advocate* of 23 February 1951 reported that he had had to carry out a forced landing in his plane in a remote area near Lake Hopkins, 350 air miles west of Alice Springs, just over the Western Australian border. The plane's propeller was damaged in the landing and rather than wait to be rescued he cut off the damaged ends of the prop and flew back to Alice Springs. He had a passenger with him at the time who he had to leave behind with food and water because of the plane's inability to get back into the air with two aboard due to the reduced 'bite' of the airscrew. In 1970 he re-enacted the task of cutting the propellor tips for a BBC–ABC film crew which was making a documentary series on human survival.

In 1988 Kurt Johannsen was living in retirement at Alice Springs.

Big and Beautiful

For Roger Wait, who worked for Kurt Johannsen for three years, there were few dull moments and little time off, but it was a very enjoyable life.

He'd spent the war years in an Army transport unit and when he was demobbed he listened with great interest to other army drivers who'd been trundling up and down The Bitumen in convoys during the war, telling their stories of what a great place the Northern Territory was.

He was discharged in Sydney and the thought of settling down to a mundane life in suburbia had no appeal so he decided to see for himself what the Territory had to offer. He was 21 and looking for something different when he reached Alice Springs and the 'something different' that caught his attention was one of Kurt Johannsen's road trains. 'I saw this huge vehicle coming along the road—it was really big for those days—and I was flabbergasted. I thought: "I'll have to have a go at one of those" And I did!'

He started work on £7 a week. He asked Kurt if it was a permanent job, and the reply was that he didn't put on anyone permanently until they'd proved themselves.

'How will I know if I've proved myself?'

Kurt answered: 'If you're still here in three weeks you'll get £7 10s. a week and you'll know you're permanent.'

In addition to their wages drivers were provided with tinned food while they were on the road:

Some time later our wages went to £11 10s. a week and that was good money in those days. If necessary we had to work seven days a week and 24 hours a day. But we were happy with our work.

If we got back on Friday we'd have the weekend off, providing there was no cattle to be carted or a truck to be prepared. Sometimes we'd work all day Sunday getting ready and then we might have to drive 200 miles all night to our pick-up point because station owners preferred to have their cattle loaded at daybreak.

But we enjoyed it; there was always action. We got no overtime or anything like that. Now and then union stirrers would turn up but we used to buzz them off.

There was always work to be done. In quiet times the road train crews would be employed in Johannsen's Alice Springs depot:

When we came back from a job we'd have to hop in and give a hand at the depot, either helping build trailers or repairing them. Carl Corner did most of the work on the trailers and we used to assist him.

Roger Wait.

Bearing in mind that these were the early days of cattle transport and we had a lot to learn, our trailers weren't as sophisticated or well finished as they are today and consequently there were problems with bruising and other injuries. The condition of the roads and tracks contributed to that too.

Roger Wait said that the usual method of transporting cattle by road was in trainload lots; three road trains, each consisting of a body truck and three trailers would go together to a cattle station and pick up about 240 head and bring them in to Alice Springs, filling about 14 or 15 rail vans, depending on the size of the beasts.

Each road train carried a crew of two and sometimes three who took it in turns to drive. Having this number of people on hand meant that in the event of mechanical troubles or difficulties caused by the terrain they could overcome the problem without having to call for assistance. Sandy creek beds or big stretches of soft going caused little worry because two prime movers could be coupled up to haul loaded trailers through the trouble spot or pull them by cable one at a time.

We've even been known to connect three trains together by means of drawbars when we've come to a known trouble spot so that we could charge through, full bore. Those old Diamond Ts were very powerful, particularly in the lower gears.

Even on the main road there could be problems. For example, at Newcastle Waters there was a long causeway and after heavy rain there would be a lot of fast-moving water running across the road. We knew the bottom was solid but if the water was fairly deep we'd sometimes have trouble with the last trailer. You see, the idea was to load the body truck [prime mover] with the heaviest beasts to put weight on the drive axles for better traction. The load would get lighter down the train and sometimes the last trailer wouldn't have much on, relatively speaking. Thus it would tend to 'wag' like a dog's tail and if we weren't careful it could get caught by the water

Roger Wait at the wheel of a left-hand-drive Johannsen Diamond T. *(Roger Wait)*

and drag the rest of the trailers down off the causeway. We'd usually connect two trains together and put the last prime mover on the back of the second train; it would leave its trailers behind and then go back for them with another prime mover to steady the last unit.

If you were on your own, you'd haul two trailers across and then go back for the light one.

They could go through 3 feet of water but when you think of it there was a tremendous sideways pressure on a combination which was about 150 ft (45 metres) long.

Cattle haulage was only one part of the Johannsen operation. Roger Wait at times found himself picking up a load of empty fuel and bitumen drums anywhere between Darwin and Alice Springs, or bringing surplus railway rolling stock from the North Australian Railway to Alice Springs where it was put on rail to go to Adelaide. Sometimes there would be some loading to go northward prior to picking up the south-bound drums or rolling stock, but most times the vehicles would go up empty with some of the trailers piggy-backed to save tyre wear.

It used to take us a week to go up to Darwin and back, *said Roger.* After working most of the day preparing the trucks, we'd leave on Monday night about 10 o'clock after the pubs shut and would arrive in Darwin on Wednesday afternoon.

About a day or a day and a half would be spent loading, and then we'd head back, aiming to do the whole trip in six days but mostly taking seven.

We drove all day and all night, stopping only for meals. With a crew of three we'd have three hours at the wheel, during which we'd cover about 60 miles and then we'd have six hours off. In the box on top of each cab there was a stretcher on which one of the blokes could sleep as we went along.

A lot of the time we'd only average about 18 miles an hour, because some of the long slow gradients would send us back a cog and there were fairly wide gaps between the gears.

If there was a headwind or a three-quarter wind, that could send you back yet another cog. If the wind changed to one side, the temperature gauge would begin to climb and oil viscosity would get thin and you'd hope like mad that something would happen to change the wind direction and bring temperatures down and get the oil pressure up again. Suddenly you might find you've got a tail wind, and that was just like dropping a trailer off; you'd go up a cog or two and get her up to her top speed of 22 miles an hour.

The Diamond Ts had two gearboxes—a 4-speed up front and a 3-speed behind it—and of course two gear levers. Yes, we could two-stick them on the move; it was a bit fiddly but it could be done. It was something similar to the action on the Mack quad boxes when they came into vogue some years later.

They were pretty good vehicles really, but very slow. If you got behind schedule there was no way you'd pick up time because you were flat-chat at 22 mph. You could get them from standstill to their top speed fairly quickly—in a few hundred yards, actually—but that was it; there was no way of getting up any more speed! They had a very low diff ratio. In a more modern truck you'd have to go about five miles before you got into top gear.

We only had brakes on the prime mover, Westinghouse air brakes, and they're hard to beat. We didn't get into any strife with the unbraked trailers; I suppose if there'd been cause for an emergency stop we might have had the trailers around our neck but nothing like that ever happened because we made sure we kept out of trouble and used a bit of anticipation in our driving.

At times it was hard to stay awake, just plodding along at 22 miles an hour, but I guess if we'd dozed off we couldn't have got into much strife at that speed!

Three Johannsen drivers (left to right) Bert Noske, Henry Kunoth, and Roger Wait, in the days when ex-wartime Diamond Ts and Federals were the 'big iron' of the highway. *(Roger Wait)*

A mixed load of empty drums and underground fuel tanks on the move southbound to Alice Springs behind a Diamond T. Note the sleeping accommodation on top of the cabin! Open windscreens provided the 'air conditioning'. *(Roger Wait)*

Sometimes if we had to stop at night for a rest—if we were on our own for some reason or other—we'd roll out our swag and we'd sleep on the bonnet because it was warm and those winter nights in the Centre can be very cold. Inside the cab you'd have to be rugged-up because there were plenty of places where the cold air could get in.

We could cook a meal as we went along. We used to put tins of soup, baked beans, meat and vegetables, etc., on the hot manifold and in about half an hour the contents would be ready to eat!

They were good days; we were young and keen, and hard work didn't worry us. It was a great experience.

Those road trains were formidable vehicles and we were proud to drive them. They were the forerunners of today's more sophisticated operations which provide a network of services throughout the Territory which no railway line or lines could possibly cover.

Moving the Mobs

There is a distinct line between the operations of cattle transporters and freight operators in the Northern Territory and each has kept, in the main, to his own mode.

Within the cattle transport business, however, there has always been a varying proportion of for-hire operators and individual stations or pastoral groups with their own equipment, and it can be fairly said that the use by pastoral companies of their own vehicles in the infant days of cattle transport drew the attention of other station owners to the economics and efficacy of moving cattle by road and added impetus to the transition from droving to road haulage.

Although pioneers like Kurt Johannsen started to transport cattle in the mid-'40s and early '50s it was only in the 1960s that this side of the road transport industry began to grow, as the beef roads scheme got under way and a disastrous drought gripped the centre and the north of the continent. Almost overnight road transport of cattle began to expand; livestock too weak to attempt the long walk to the railheads, and with no hope of survival in the long months of drought still to come, were saved and their owners were enabled to hold on to their properties until the rains came.

Like any radical change of method or technology, the evolution of a new mode can be slow. Inertia and resistance to innovative ideas have to be overcome and in the case of moving cattle the seemingly disparate cost of road transport vis-à-vis traditional droving was a further detraction that had to be controverted.

Mr C. L. A. Abbott, Administrator of the Northern Territory from 1937 to 1946, was not really enthusiastic about the future of cattle transport in the Territory. In *Australia's Frontier Province*, published in 1950, he wrote:

Since the war there has been a pronounced tendency to think that motor transport will go a long way towards solving the Territory's transport problems, and that railways are out of date. The mechanisation of the Army and the extensive use of motor vehicles of all kinds have influenced many station owners to believe that they can market their stock by road transport alone. In certain favoured localities this may be possible but the Territory is a land of vast distances where many mobs of cattle move over hundreds of miles of stock routes. The use of motor transport is increasing in the Alice Springs district but . . . pastoral lands there extend in a radius of little more than 200 miles from the railhead at Alice Springs and haulage is comparatively short. A road cattle train, consisting of a power unit with trailers, operates from Alice Springs and can move seventy-five head of cattle on the trailers at an average

speed of twenty-five miles an hour. The yearly average of cattle moving out of the Territory by road and rail from Alice Springs is about 80,000 head, travelling an average distance of 650 miles. If these were moving by road trains of the type described, over 1,000 trips would have to be made.

Another point is that the bitumen roads of the Territory do not have heavy gravelled formations. The bitumen was poured over light screened gravel tamped down by heavy rollers and the surface is not likely to stand up to the heavy axle load of road trains moving at speed.

However the main argument is that the transport of stock by road is making little headway in the more closely settled Australian States, and none in the United States of America, which is the home of roads and speed.

But as history records, others saw the future differently.

One big company which was a proponent of cattle movement by road was the Northern Australian Pastoral Company. In 1952 its managing director, Mr D. M. Fraser, was proclaiming the economies and advantages of road trains for cattle transport.

(Truck & Bus Magazine)

(Haulmark Trailers)

For four years previously he had been using six Leyland six-wheelers and trailers to move fat bullocks from Marion Downs to Dajarra. Capital outlay had been £50,000 and he expected to write this off over eight years. Even with a heavy depreciation allowance he said that the actual cost of transporting the cattle, including all operating and running costs, was averaging £3 5s. per head. The cost of droving the cattle would have cost an average of £1 per head. His returns for the previous three years showed that cattle transported by road reached the abattoirs from 80 to 100 lb (36 to 45 kg) heavier than beasts which would have spent three to four weeks walking off that amount of beef. At rates of at least £5 per 100 lb the added weight more than compensated for the £2 5s. additional transport costs, showing a profit of £3.

But Fraser's voice, like that of the apostle John, was a voice crying in the wilderness at that time. The pastoral industry was proving to be reluctant to change from its conventional methods of moving cattle.

It was around that time—the early '50s—that Mr J. H. Kelly, an officer of the Commonwealth Bureau of Agricultural Economics, in the report of a survey wrote:

Road transport of cattle in Northern Australia is still in its infancy; to date efforts to establish this method of moving cattle offer little to justify the original optimism of pioneer operators. This method has been confined to two principal operators—Tancred Bros, of Bourke meatworks, and Kurt Johannsen in the Alice Springs district.

The question of motor transport of cattle was discussed with these operators at different stages of the survey, and with a number of graziers interested in the comparative economic results of the various methods of moving cattle.

From the experience of those who have engaged in large-scale road transport of cattle over long distances in Northern Australia, it is apparent that this method of moving cattle will not provide a solution of the major problem of cattle movement.

Mr Kelly said that Tancred Bros operated two large inland meatworks, at Bourke and Tenterfield, N.S.W. Many of the fat cattle treated at Bourke were walked in over long distances from the Queensland south-west Channel Country; some from the vicinity of Windorah and Innamincka, approximately 600 miles.

Over the previous 15 years Tancred's had transported cattle over formed and unformed earth roads. They regarded this method of moving cattle as a matter more of necessity than of choice; some cattle which had walked long distances got sore footed and it became necessary to send trucks out to pick up the 'tail' of a mob. In other circumstances, when stock routes leading in to Bourke were denuded of food, trucks were sent out to bring cattle over the last stages of the journey. Also, when the demand for carcase beef exceeded anticipation, a heavy draw was made on cattle immediately available for slaughter and these had to be replaced by trucking cattle in from mobs en route to Bourke. Kelly reported that

With fifteen years' experience of transporting cattle over earth roads, in Mr H. E. Tancred's opinion, nothing less than a sealed surface road is satisfactory to carry the heavy transporters, and

CATTLE TRANSPORT

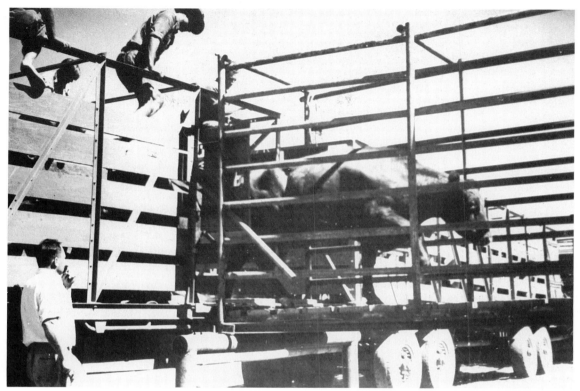

(Kurt Johannsen)

even then, these vehicles are suitable only for journeys of up to 160 miles.

Referring to Kurt Johannsen, Mr Kelly said that he was the pioneer of large scale road transport of cattle in the Northern Territory. His first unit was assembled and tested in 1946, with a capacity of approximately 60 head (more or less, according to age and size). The cost of this unit was not high, as the prime mover and most of the material used in the construction of the trailers were purchased cheaply from 'war disposal' sales.

The first practical test was the movement of a railway train load of about 280 head from Murray Downs station, 246 miles to the north-west of Alice Springs. The objects of this test were to find out the speed at which fat cattle could be moved and the cost of moving them. Of the distance travelled, 206 miles were over bitumen surface and 40 miles over unformed earth road. The charge for this trial was 3¾d. per ton mile, which worked out at approximately 17s. ($1.70) per head per 100 miles as against the then fat cattle droving rate of 7s. per head per 100 miles. In 1946, 600 head were transported, the longest haul being from Murray Downs. In 1947 the organisation was stepped up to two units, the second also being assembled at low cost, and 1,400 head of cattle were moved, within much the same range of mileages as in 1946.

Mr Kelly's report went on to say that another unit was added in 1946, but at greater cost than the first two, the two new trailers costing £2,200 each, landed at Alice Springs. In 1948, 2,200 head of fat cattle were moved to Alice Springs, including the longest road haul of cattle ever made in Australia—239 head in three drafts, from Anthony Lagoon to Alice Springs, over 402 miles of bitumen and 126 miles of unformed earth track.

In 1949, with three units in operation, 8,000 head of cattle were moved. The rate was raised to 5¾d. per ton mile, working out at about 26s. per head per 100 miles.

Six hundred and seven head of mixed cattle were moved 476 miles on bitumen all the way, from Helen Springs Station, on the western edge of the Barkly Tableland, to Mt Isa railhead. Three road trains were used and each train made three journeys. The cost of the Anthony Lagoon and Helen Springs trials worked out at 15s. and 15s. 9d. per head per 100 miles, respectively. In the summer of 1949–50 most of the Alice Springs district was affected by drought and the demand for the road transport of fat cattle eased. 6,800 were moved.

Continuing, Mr Kelly's report stated that by 1950 Johannsen was faced with steeply rising costs, heavy depreciation of vehicles, and the need for replacements. Early in 1951 he was forced to announce a substantial

MOVING THE MOBS

increase in transport rates, the new rate for fat cattle amounting to about £2 10s. per head per 100 miles, as against 17s 6d. for droving.

[The rates advertised by Kurt Johannsen in the *Centralian Advocate* of 5 January 1951 were £95 per 100 miles on bitumen roads and £105 on bush roads.]

The report then stated that the demand for road transport of fat cattle to Alice Springs railhead almost ceased. Johannsen took the view that the graziers would ultimately recognise the advantages of road transport over droving. The fact remains, however, that the grazier 200 or 300 miles from Alice Springs would have to be satisfied that a real advantage was to be gained from paying £5 or £7 10s. per head for road transport, compared with 35 s. ($3.50) or 52s. 6d. per head for droving.

Mr Kelly added that in general the attitude of graziers was governed by the cost of road transport compared with droving. Naturally, there was greater interest shown by cattlemen in the Alice Springs district than elsewhere, for the reason that they had had more practical experience of the road transport method. Channel Country graziers were interested in road transport development, but graziers generally did not appear to have studied the economics of the method closely.

Furthermore, Mr Kelly commented that to bring road transport of cattle within economic reach of cattle raisers, heavy governmental subsidy would be necessary, whether to attract contractors into this field of transport, or to cover losses on government-operated transporters, apart from the high cost of suitable road construction, which in itself would amount to indirect subsidy.

Despite this dispassionate assessment of the road train's future, the picture began to change just after the mid-'50s. In December 1957 the *Centralian Advocate* carried a news item saying that drovers were beginning to feel the effects of road trains; some had not been able to get work lately. By 1959 a new scene was unfolding. In a further survey of the beef cattle industry the Bureau of Agricultural Economics reported that the use of road trains had grown considerably and that the success of this type of operation was attributable to improved roads and the introduction of suitable vehicles with larger payloads and a better understanding of this form of transport.

The higher cost of road transport in comparison with droving was largely balanced by the minimising of weight loss by the cattle. On the other hand, its use was limited by the impact of distance on costs and the effect of travel on the condition of the stock, which travel quite well up to 400 miles, but suffered fatigue over greater distances.

The report stated the hauliers' charges were around 30s. per beast per 100 miles and the average cost of operating a road train was 24s. per beast per 100 miles. Droving charges were approximately 10s. per head per 100 miles for mobs of about 400, but there were advantages in transporting by road which offset the lower cost of droving.

Road trains varied in size from 125 bhp pulling a single trailer carrying 25 bullocks, to 150 bhp pulling two trailers carrying 50 bullocks. The cost per bullock carried varied according to road train capacity; unit costs for larger trains were 30 per cent less than for smaller, and it was reckoned that if the trains were running on bitumen roads the costs might be reduced by approximately 1 penny.

On 21 July 1959 the *Centralian Advocate* announced the formation of the Cattle Transport Association. Kurt Johannsen was president and the members of the association were said to have 15 units capable of lifting between 400 and 500 beasts. The aim of the association was to get uniformity into prices and service.

The success of the Co-Ord operation in getting individual carriers together in a cohesive group obviously had its influence on the thinking of the cattle hauliers because three months later the newspaper carried news of big lifts by members of the Cattle Transport Association which had won a contract to move large numbers of cattle from Mataranka to Mt Isa and from Mataranka to Alice Springs. The cattle were lifted from Elsey Station (made famous by Mrs Aeneas Gunn's *We of the Never Never*) for Smorgen & Sons who had bought Elsey and required the beasts at their meatworks in Brisbane and Melbourne.

The news item said that ten road units had moved 286 cattle to Mt Isa and had covered the distance of 748 miles in 32 hours with a stop at Camooweal to rest the stock. The same ten vehicles then took 331 head of Elsey cattle to Alice Springs covering the 682 miles in 27 hours.

The new transport organisation, said the newspaper, was the first of its kind in the Territory. Difficulties over prices and conditions had led to the formation of the association earlier in the year and since then it had been able to stabilise rates and coordinate operations. Nine operators had 13 units available ranging from road trains to trucks and trailers.

When referring to loads the association talked in terms of railway van capacity and the 13 units operated by the members converted to 34 vans, each of which could carry 11 fats or 15 stores. Rates quoted were 9s. per mile on bitumen and 10s. on bush roads for the first 100 miles; then the price dropped to 7s. 6d. per mile for 350 miles and over.

An indication of conditions in the pre-Beef Road era was provided in a description of a lift of 500 cattle carried out by association members. It took seven hours to cover 108 miles, with one stretch of 28 miles taking more than half that time.

Association secretary Paul Davies said that the following week five vehicles would leave Alice Springs for the drought-affected Oodnadatta area to move 450 cattle in a three-day lift to the railhead for consignment to New South Wales.

In another item the *Advocate* mentioned that Vestey's road trains had been busy. By the end of December it was expected that they would have moved 15,000 cattle, and like other pastoralists they were trucking cattle out to prevent them from perishing in the drought which at that time was affecting a large portion of the Territory.

The growth in the numbers of cattle moved by road transport from the mid-'50s to 1961 was illustrated in figures issued by the Acting Assistant Administrator (Mr Hugh Barclay).

In 1956–57, 4,480 cattle were carried by road transport, or 3.3 per cent of the total movement. In 1957–58 the volume grew to 22,815 (17.6%); 1958–59 it nearly doubled to 42,742 (25.9%); the figure for 1959–60 was 52,777 (38.5%); and by 1961 road transport was lifting just over 55 per cent of total movement, or in excess of 93,000 beasts.

Mr Barclay attributed this spectacular development to the government's program of beef and pastoral road construction during this period, which had improved access to the higher-carrying country and thus boosted beef exports. Over the next eight years the conversion to road transport became almost total. Northern Territory Department of Primary Production statistics show that by 1965 road trains were carrying 75 per cent of the Territory's turn-off, 85 per cent by 1967, and 95 per cent by 1969 (226,447 beasts).

Four years later road transport completely dominated the scene, carting 99.3 per cent of cattle moved off Territory stations, or a total of 222,855 beasts. Of these 40 per cent were transported to Queensland, 21 per cent to southern states, 4.2 per cent to Western Australia, 6.75 and 15.6 per cent to Darwin and Katherine respectively (for export), and 10.9 per cent for Territory consumption. The total turn-off of cattle in 1983–84 was 370,390 from 283 properties, plus 32,224 buffalo. The 1984–85 figures were down to 303,965 cattle and 28,892 buffalo, but in 1985–86 they were 364,018 and 26,414 respectively.

Although just about all cattle movements were by road train, not all were by livestock haulage companies, as many stations these days operate their own road trains.

The first program of beef road construction was commenced in Queensland in 1961 and soon after in Western Australia, South Australia and the Northern Territory. In the following 14 years 6,400 km of beef roads were built and over $109 million was spent on them in the three states and the Northern Territory.

It is estimated that the beef cattle industry earns more than $100 million a year for the Northern Territory. The predominant movement of cattle from the Territory is to neighbouring South Australia, Queensland and Western Australia. Live cattle are also exported to Brunei, Sabah, Sarawak, Indonesia and West Malaysia. In addition cattle are also transported to export abattoirs at Alice Springs, Mudginberri, Point Stuart and Tennant Creek, and to domestic abattoirs at Amoonguna, Corkwood Bore, Curtin Springs, Darwin, Marshalls, Meneling, Mudginberri, Nelson Springs, Urapunga and Victoria Valley.

The Cattle Transport Association was formed in Alice Springs in 1959 to get uniformity into prices and standards of service. The Leyland unit, photographed in a local procession, was one of 15 road trains controlled by the association.

The Vestey Road Trains

The Vestey operation was in its day the most progressive and best organised road train enterprise in the Territory. In 1957 this big British pastoral and meat processing group imported two Rotinoff Viscount prime movers from England to move its cattle from fattening areas to the rail head at Mt Isa for transport to the company's meatworks at Townsville and Rockhampton. At that time there were few for-hire operators in the cattle transport business, although their numbers were growing. There were Kurt Johannsen at Alice Springs; Len Wright of Mt Isa who had started in 1952 and was gradually expanding; Eric and Sid Ballard of Longreach; and companies such as Marion Downs (North Australian Pastoral Co.) and King Ranch (Qld) as well as other pastoralists such as Bill Braitling (Mt Doreen, N.T.), Webb Bros (Mt Riddock, N.T.), and Butcher Bros in Western Australia who had acquired their own road train equipment because they were convinced that this was the way to go. Vestey's decided likewise, having tested this new method by buying a complete road train—prime mover and two 45-foot trailers from Kurt Johannsen in 1954 to move drought-affected stock off Wave Hill.

At that time Vestey's pastoral interests spread throughout the Top End of the Territory and into parts of Western Australia and Queensland. The company had acquired its holdings over a period dating from the early 1900s and in 1917 has established a meatworks in Darwin, but this only operated for about four years due to persistent industrial action by intransigent unions.

By the 1950s Vestey's had holdings totalling in excess of 18,000 square miles, (more than 4.6 million hectares) including the famous Wave Hill Station. Among others were Nutwood Downs, Cattle Creek, Limbunya, Wateroo, Kirkimbie, Mistake Creek, Willaroo, Dela-mere, Manbulloo, Wallamunga, Birrinduda, as well as Ord River and Spring Creek in the days before the Ord River irrigation scheme came into being, plus Nicholson, Flora Valley, Gordon Downs, Sturt Creek and Turner just across the border in Western Australia.

Most of the properties were for breeding and raising cattle, but one of them, Helen Springs, on the western edge of the rich Barkly Tableland, was for fattening. Beasts were moved from the breeding stations to Helen Springs where they were fattened for a couple of years and then moved to the rail head. It was for transferring the prime cattle from Helen Springs to rail or to other fattening stations near Camooweal owned by Vestey's that the two road trains were introduced; droving on foot from the breeding stations was continued.

Vestey's formed the Northern Cattle Transport Company in 1957 to operate the Rotinoffs and a modern road train base which the group had built at Maryville on Helen Springs Station alongside the Stuart Highway about 117 kilometres north of Tennant Creek.

The *Centralian Advocate* of 15 November stated that Vestey's had just spent about £100,000 on a new maintenance depot at Helen Springs on the Stuart Highway. It included modern amenities for drivers and mechanics, plus inoculation and dipping areas for animals. Vestey's expected to lift 20,000 cattle with two new road trains from Helen Springs in the 1958 season. An accompanying photo of the Rotinoffs carried a caption which said that the units cost £40,000 and were capable of carrying 100 cattle.

In addition to running the 470 miles to Mt Isa, the Rotinoffs did occasional trips to the Larrimah terminus of the North Australia Railway (216 miles) with cattle destined for shipment out of Darwin. On occasions they also operated to and from Vestey's Nutwood Downs

One of the two Vestey Rotinoff road trains loading at the Maryville road train base at Helen Springs prior to departure for Camooweal in Queensland. The Rotinoffs were powered by 250 bhp Rolls Royce supercharged engines. *(Eric Prisgrove)*

What motorists saw when deciding to overtake a Vestey road train. Each trailer was 12 metres long, as was the Rotinoff prime mover. This photo shows three trailers behind the prime mover. Top speed was 75 km/h. *(Eric Prisgrove)*

One of Vestey's Rotinoffs pulling three trailers between Helen Springs, north of Three Ways, to Camooweal, across the Barkly Tableland. *(Eric Prisgrove)*

Station north of Helen Springs on the Hodgson River.

The Rotinoffs were spectacular vehicles in their day; they were bigger and more powerful than anything else available in Australia. The Leylands, AECs, Fodens, etc., of those times were in the 125 and 150 bhp class, and Thornycroft's Mighty Antar—with either 250 bhp Rover or eight-cylinder 315 bhp Rolls-Royce engine—hadn't arrived in Australia although it was available in England.

The two Rotinoffs were built by George Rotinoff Ltd, of Slough, England, a small custom-builder of heavy-duty vehicles. Each was powered by a Rolls-Royce 6SFL supercharged six-cylinder diesel engine producing 186 kW (250 bhp) at 2100 rpm and 950Nm (710 lb/ft) torque at 1300 rpm. This power was transmitted by means of a 6-speed synchromesh overdrive box with 3-speed synchromesh auxiliary and thence via a bogie drive rear end with hub reduction gears and a ratio of 10.18 to 1, calculated to produce a top speed of 75 km/h in double overdrive (overdrive in the main box and in the auxiliary).

Overall length of each unit was 12 metres and width was 2.4 metres. Chassis weight was a hefty 9525 kg and the gross combination rating was 61,234 kg. They were fitted with air brakes, power steering and twin 450-litre (100 gallon) fuel tanks. The double-skin insulated cab had sliding doors, leather upholstered driver's and co-driver's seats with arm rests, external adjustable sun visor and a sleeper berth.

Each Rotinoff pulled two 13.7 m freighter double-bogie steerable trailers and overall length of each train was 42.6 metres. The design for the trailer steering was basically that devised by Kurt Johannsen for his trailers.

As was frequently the case in those times, vehicles designed in the Northern Hemisphere weren't entirely suitable for Australian operating conditions.

Neil Pearson, who was an automotive engineer with Rolls-Royce of Australia at the time, checked over the engines when the Rotinoffs were landed in Sydney. A few months later he was called to the Northern Territory to advise on a problem with cracked exhaust manifolds. He said:

The engine was a supercharged six and our absolute peak rating was a one-hour automotive rating, as is usual, but what was happening was that the vehicles were leaving Maryville fully loaded with the throttle wide open and there it sat for hours. Instead of working for one hour at the peak they were going for up to 12 hours at the absolute maximum. The manifolds were a glowing mass at night, just below white heat. Shrewsbury (R-R works in U.K.) soon fixed this by supplying Meehanite iron manifolds which were all that was needed.

But there were other troubles.

The transmission tended to overheat and cause bearing failure. Neil Pearson said that it was a big gearbox and it sat relatively close to the ground. With the bitumen temperature around 75°C plus the friction generated in the five shafts and three gears it wasn't surprising that when the box was stripped down the shafts were blue and had 'grown' to such an extent that it was impossible to remove the bearings. Eventually they were replaced with Fuller boxes.

The fitting of Fuller transmissions also eliminated troubles that were being experienced with tailshafts. These were fitted at such acute angles that failures were frequent. Spare shafts were strapped on the top of each trailer and as the Rotinoffs travelled mainly at night it was possible to change a shaft without having to unload the cattle for watering as would have been the case in the heat of the day. The shorter, smaller Fuller box provided straighter angles for the shafts and overcame two problems simultaneously.

Fuel pump failures also caused upsets in the operation. Fuel under pressure from the spill ports bored holes in the aluminium casing of the pump. By inserting a steel sleeve in the gallery this defect was beaten.

The high engine temperatures induced by mechanical supercharging eventually led to the introduction of sodium-cooled valves and modifications to the cooling system.

However, Eric Prisgrove, who now lives in retirement in Alice Springs and who was in charge of maintenance on the Rotinoffs from late 1959 till late 1961, said that when he was appointed manager of the road train base he found the two Rotinoffs in a poor state of repair:

To put it bluntly they had been badly maintained and poorly driven. One of them was out of action with a damaged main gearbox. This had happened a week before my arrival and I'd been told that these vehicles had a bad history of gearbox and tailshaft trouble.

When I questioned the five drivers at the base all of them said that the vehicles were unreliable and frequently broke down. On probing deeper I found that these drivers were changing down from top to bottom gear without using any intermediate ratios. The reason they gave for this was that the brakes were in such poor condition that they had to use the gears in this manner so that they could slow the vehicles sufficiently to stop with the assistance of what brakes were available.

Obviously in doing this there was a very severe strain on the transmission. On examination of the braking systems on both road trains it was found that the brake shoes on the tandem rear axles were soaked with oil coming through leaking sales and their effectiveness was practically non-existent. Also the Westinghouse air system was out of adjustment and the brakes on all the trailers needed attention and repair.

With a lot of hard work during the off-season between November 1959 and February 1960 we overcame these troubles and we put both road trains on a schedule of three trips a week from the base to Camooweal and return, 700 miles, using five drivers who drove in pairs with the fifth man off duty resting and acting as relief to each crew so that they had approximately three days off each week. The drivers were quite content with this arrangement.

We completed the 1960 and 1961 seasons without any mechanical breakdowns. The only trouble we had was caused by a batch of defective prime mover tyres. With some training and with their own know-how these drivers proved to be very efficient.

Those two Rotinoffs, which were named Jackie and Julie, were the best vehicles I ever worked on during a lifetime in the automotive business, *said Mr Prisgrove.*

After 10 years Vestey's quit road train operations and closed the base at Maryville. Wright's Cattle Transport of Mt Isa, which by this time had built up a fleet of 23 road trains (mostly with Mack prime movers), leased the Maryville premises and looked set to expand in the Northern Territory. Unfortunately the founder, Len Wright, was fatally gored by a bull at Larrimah in 1968 and the company which had grown solidly since 1952 and had been one of the pioneers in establishing cattle transport by road in Queensland went into decline and other operators, including Buntine Roadways, secured much of the former Wright business.

George Rotinoff died in 1959. His company was taken over by Lomount Ltd, but no further vehicles were produced. In 1965 another vehicle manufacturer, Atkinson, bought up the Rotinoff spares, stock and designs and appeared to be planning production of Rotinoff-type prime movers but none was built. Of Vestey's two Rotinoffs, one was sold and the other was retained for a time to move bulldozers and other plant around the various Vestey stations for roadworks, dam sinking, and other property improvements. Eventually one ended up in Western Australia and was used by earthmoving contractor George Appelbee and the other was acquired by Kurt Johannsen's son Lindsay and was put to work hauling ore from a mine east of Alice Springs.

By 1982 the Vestey Group had considerably reduced its holdings in the Northern Territory but had increased its Queensland interests, with the result that Wave Hill and Helen Springs were its top remaining properties in the Territory, and in place of its own vehicles road trains operated by commercial carriers carried out all inter-station and turn-off movements for the group.

One of the Rotinoffs in its early days, pulling two trailers designed by Kurt Johannsen. Vestey's operated their two road trains for ten years, moving cattle to fattening areas or to rail for transport to abattoirs. *(Ron Knight)*

The Buntine Saga

Undoubtedly the best-known name in cattle transport in the Northern Territory was that of Buntine. For over 20 years the big green and white rigs with 'BUNTINE ROADWAYS' signwritten on them in red letters were to be seen right across the Top End of the Territory and far into Queensland, South Australia and Western Australia as they moved thousands of beasts each year to markets, abattoirs, ports and agistment areas as well as between stations for fattening and other purposes.

The sheer size of Buntine road trains, when compared with conventional transport in other States, has been a compelling attraction for tourists. The sight of a stationary tourist coach with its passenger complement strung out along the roadside in various standing, kneeling and even prone positions clicking away with their cameras was a familiar sight to Buntine Roadways drivers, and the results of such photographic activity must have given Northern Territory tourism an incalculable boost.

Noel Buntine, founder of Buntine Roadways, was born in Stonehenge, south-west of Longreach in 1927. Like a number of others who made good in transport he left Queensland for the Territory looking for work. After numerous unsuccessful attempts to find employment in Sydney, Adelaide and Port Augusta he landed a job in August 1950 with the Mines Branch at Alice Springs where a young man named John Ryan was also working at the time.

After a couple of years in the Mines Branch Buntine and Ryan decided to launch themselves into the world of private enterprise by setting up as mining commission agents, selling and servicing mining equipment as well as taking on agencies for various southern-based firms.

The break which put the young partners on the road to bigger things came in 1951 when the Territory Transport Association approached Ryan to take on its secretarial tasks as Percy Colson, the foundation secretary, was in poor health and wished to resign.

The business acumen of the two partners soon told them that there was a promising future for those taking part in the coordinated road–rail service which the Commonwealth Railways were pushing, so they decided to acquire a slice of the action; they purchased the Martin brothers' Overland Transport which held one of the ten shares in the TTA road-rail contract. This proved successful; Ryan assumed the secretarial responsibilities and Buntine contributed his efforts and expertise in running Overland Transport.

But in late 1959 Buntine decided to leave the Territory. The partnership was terminated and he took a Commer 'knocker' prime mover and semi-trailer as part of the settlement. Commers in those days were very

The sight of Buntine Roadways' cattle trains was a familiar one throughout the north of Australia for more than 20 years. At its peak the company operated 42 Mack and Kenworth prime movers and over 100 trailers. *(Truck & Bus Magazine)*

Noel Buntine.

popular with interstate operators on the east coast and he soon found work with Price's Interstate Transport on a sub-contract basis. Bill Price was operating out of the Valley in Brisbane and Noel hauled between Brisbane and Sydney with an occasional trip to Melbourne.

But after a few months in the cut and thrust of interstate transport, which at that stage was undergoing almost daily change as big companies absorbed small ones, he came to the conclusion that this wasn't his scene and he decided to go back to the Territory.

He'd dabbled briefly in cattle carting before he'd left Alice Springs but his equipment was unsuitable. This time, with better gear, he began moving cattle in the Alice Springs and Oodnadatta areas but soon found that those regions were well supplied with operators so he looked further afield and after talks with Peel River Land and Minerals and the L.J. Hooker organisation, he moved up to the Top End and began carting cattle into the Wyndham meatworks with a Mack B61 which he named 'High and Mighty', complemented by an elderly Foden. The operation expanded rapidly and he borrowed one of Kurt Johannsen's ageing Diamond T outfits. When it broke down it usually proved difficult to rehabilitate, but if a call went out to Kurt he would respond and fix the trouble in a matter of minutes, according to Noel, who regarded Johannsen as a 'mechanical genius'.

The first season's tally was 3,600 beasts; the bulk of these were lifted from Auvergne Station to Wyndham, a 240-kilometre haul. At the end of the first season the Foden was disposed of and a second Mack was purchased to assist the single-axle B61 which had served in Overland Transport before being used on cattle haulage. Noel Buntine was on his way to establishing a business which over the next two decades was to become one of Australia's biggest cattle road train operations. But it was to be a long, hard grind to the top:

In the early days we used to camp at Wyndham for the season. We had a tent fly strung between the trees and my 'office' was a briefcase under the seat of the Mack. After a couple of years we bought a Holden ute and a caravan; the ute was used for maintenance duties such as going out to breakdowns, and the caravan gave us something by way of sleeping and cooking accommodation. We used to move the caravan from station to station as our work required.

The Hooker group acquired Victoria River Downs about the time Noel Buntine began his cattle carting operation in the Top End but his first job for Hooker wasn't to move cattle; it was to transport 2,000 tonnes of fencing wire and pickets for property improvement on the huge 5 million acre (2 million ha) station in readiness for beef cattle production. In the initial stages the rolls of wire and the bundles of stakes were carried on open-top trucks, but as Hooker's began to turn off cattle and Noel's trucks were converted to stock crates, the wire and pickets had to be loaded into the crates and unloaded from them, which just about doubled the effort required to handle them.

We used to load and unload 60 tons a trip. The weather was hot and the tar with which the pickets were painted came off and our hands and faces were red raw. Sometimes we'd try to reach our unloading point about 5 p.m. or in the evening when it was cooler. We'd spray the surrounding trees with diesel oil and set fire to them so that we had some light to work by. We just couldn't toss the stuff off the vehicles; it all had to be properly stacked on the ground so that it could be tallied.

Sometimes we'd arrive at the station headquarters with a load and we'd be told they didn't want the stuff there, it had to go to some spot way out on the property. They'd give us a 'mud map' and off we'd go, perhaps following a wrong track or two on the way but eventually getting to the required spot. Occasionally they'd accompany us part of the way and they'd say, for example, 'This is No. 5 Bore, and No. 7 is six miles away

Early in his cattle transport career Noel Buntine used a Commer 'knocker' but it was soon found to be unsuitable. It is shown here bogged in a sandy creek crossing near Kulgera, on the South Australian–Northern Territory border. *(Bob Dodd)*

A B61 Mack which Buntine & Ryan operated on the Co-Ord freight service convinced Noel Buntine that this was the marque for cattle transport. This vehicle, named High & Mighty, was driven for a time by Bob Dodd, pictured here. *(Bob Dodd)*

CATTLE TRANSPORT

in that direction [pointing] and No. 12 is over the other way about 15 miles distant'. After we'd done a few trips we got to know where things were.

Some of the tracks were pretty rough and narrow and occasionally they'd send a grader ahead of us to knock down scrub and clear a road for us.

But the station tracks weren't as rough as some of the so-called main roads at the time. I remember when the Department of Works gravelled sections of the road through from VRD to Top Springs. However, they didn't do much about maintaining it; they'd probably only grade it once a year and the corrugations would get so deep that kangaroos could hide in them! The pickets and wire would vibrate so much that we'd have to stop every 30 or 40 miles to push them back under the chains that we had to hold them in place.

There were also big sections of bulldust. Some of them would be two to three miles long and at least a quarter-mile wide. We'd try to dodge going through this stuff by making a detour around the deepest section but these new tracks in turn became bulldust tracks. Bulldust is as fine as talcum powder and we had a lot of trouble with it getting into the engines of our vehicles. We also had problems with wheel bearings because the seals couldn't keep the dust out. We'd 'do' a set of wheel bearings every second trip, but nowadays with so many bitumen roads this problem doesn't exist. We used to carry tin boxes of packed wheel bearings on every vehicle. Sometimes getting the bearings off was quite a task because they'd weld themselves to the axles. We'd be stuck for hours belting away with a hammer and cold chisel trying to remove and replace wheel bearings.

Dust caused other problems, particularly at night when there was no breeze and it just 'hung' in the air. If more than one train was involved in a move, they would have to depart at half-hour intervals in order to give the dust sufficient time to settle. If, for instance, one of the leading vehicles had to stop because of tyre or mechanical troubles the time delay process would have to be repeated, leading to longer trip times and considerable frustration.

Although from time to time there has been controversy about cattle in the rearmost trailer suffering—and at times dying—from dust inhalation, Noel Buntine said that such claims were fallacious. Admittedly No. 3 trailer was often in a cloud of dust but the effect on bullocks was no different from that of being at the rear of a mob when they're walking; they inhaled some dust but it was not fatal.

When it began, the operation was seasonal. Buntine Roadways vehicles would work into Wyndham for up to 16 weeks between April/May and August. Then they'd be switched to work between the Victoria River area and Mt Isa until the summer heat and the onset of the Wet began to make their presence felt. Vehicles would then be laid up and after reconditioning the trailers, all operations would cease until the next round commenced in the following April or May. Prime movers were overhauled and those which were not

considered fit for the next year's activities would be taken to Brisbane and traded in on new (and more) vehicles as the business grew.

At the finish of the second year of operations we had two Macks. Next year it was three and so on. I started with the Mack that John Ryan and I bought from Champions in Adelaide; it was a B61 single-drive with a 170 hp engine. I think I must have traded that thing four or five times. I'd work it into the ground and then I'd take it to Brisbane and trade it in on a new one but I'd tell Mack not to get rid of it because they'd reconditioned it because I'd probably be back for it when I had enough money.

In those days I'd try to buy a new truck every year plus a couple of trailers. I received a lot of assistance from the late Cyril Anderson [managing director of Westco, Queensland distributor for Mack, and later of Mack Trucks Australia] and from the trailer people such as McGrath initially and later Haulmark in which I was a shareholder.

When I switched to Haulmark trailers I stuck to a standard design for quite a few years because I was scared of going broke and having to sell my equipment. I reasoned that it would be easier to sell standard trailers than specially designed ones. But in the '70s I got away from that notion and I think that through the efforts of Doug Foster, Spencer Grammer [Haulmark] and myself we got trailer design very close to the ultimate for conditions in the Territory—elsewhere for that matter. We goosenecked them for years, using a drop-deck design for double-deck cattle haulage.

Cattle trailers used on road train work up here are different from those used by operators down south. Being confined to semi-trailers, southern operators end-load which means that cattle simply walk through to the front. Up here, with multiple trailers, we have to side-load and we have to avoid the problems of beasts walking up to a 'blank wall' and refusing to move.

As the Buntine livestock fleet grew, so did the diversity of trailer sizes. The 'body' trucks (prime movers) were standardised on 8 metres but trailer lengths varied from 10 through 12 and 13 metres to over 16 metres.

To avoid complications in cartage rates Noel Buntine settled on the 'K' to indicate vehicle capacity. It derived from the capacity of the Queensland Railways K-class cattle waggons; depending on size and age, the average figure for a K-waggon was between 18 and 22 beasts.

Thus a modern triples combination—three double-deck semi-trailers, each about 12 metres long, within a maximum overall train length of 50 metres—can carry 7½ 'K' or approximately 135 to 165 beasts, depending on size and weight. By comparison, in earlier times a body truck and three single-deck trailers could carry 4 or 4½ 'K' or between 80 and 100 animals.

In the Alice Springs region cattle hauliers calculated their truck space as 'vans'. This unit of capacity related to the number of animals which could be accommodated on a 17 × 8 foot (5.1 × 2.4 m) Central Australia Railway cattle van, and varied from 11 fats to 18 thinner stores.

1963 was the year of opportunity for Noel Buntine. The Kimberley region which covers approximately 360,000 square kilometres of the north of Western Australia and spills over into the Northern Territory, was hit by drought. This plateau country with rugged mountains normally surrounded by grasslands had become a virtual wasteland through lack of rain and station owners began to realise that although road transport was relatively expensive when compared with droving, they could at least get their cattle moved out.

'We brought in trucks from everywhere, even from as far south as Alice Springs, to move cattle,' said Noel. 'We didn't make much money but at least we supplied a service and established road transport as a viable medium.'

Also in 1963 the Katherine meatworks was opened by Northern Meat Exporters Pty Ltd, a company in which the Hooker interests had a majority shareholding. But the seasonal nature of cattle cartage and the fluctuations in demand caused Noel Buntine to cast around for some means of cushioning the inconsistencies and with this in mind he fell back on his experience in the general freight field as a partner in Overland Transport. In 1964 he bought John Ryan's interest in Overland and this gave him two full shares in Co-Ord. In later moves he acquired to Co-Ord shares Des Jury (Rumble & Jury, Shell agents and transport operators) and Tom Corry, as well as the share of Jucor, which was a joint company owned by Jury and Corry. This put him on a level footing with Fleet Owners, for by this time Buntine Freightways, which he had named his freight operation, also had a 50 per cent shareholding in Co-Ord. He appointed Doug Foster, who had been a road train driver with Fleet Owners from 1956 to 1959 and then maintenance manager in that company's workshop, as manager of the operation at Alice Springs in 1966.

Co-Ord was travelling very well at the time, *said Noel*, and we were able to work our plant very efficiently. We were able to bolster the Alice Springs requirements with plant from the cattle operations when livestock movements were down and likewise we could get some help from Alice Springs prime movers if we were short up our way. Similarly when vehicles required overhaul we could swap around so that there were no interruptions to either operation.

During the '60s Co-Ord was a really big, strong operation. The tonnage it moved was almost unreal. We seemed to be loading and unloading trucks day and night and, of course, Buntine Freightways shared this volume 50–50 with Fleet Owners. We had nine road trains on Co-Ord work.

Noel's son Denis joined the business in 1968, virtually straight from school in Brisbane. He was assigned to the Wyndham depot as a road train driver until 1971 when he was moved to the Katherine office to act as operations manager. Then when Doug Foster

was moved from Alice Springs to Katherine in 1974 to become general manager, Denis took over Doug's job at The Alice as manager of Buntine Freightways.

In the world of commerce change is constant and transport, being a service industry which has to move with every trend and whim of the economy, usually 'sniffs the wind' early. Opportunity and chance also come into the scheme of things.

As the '60s merged into the '70s several factors had a marked influence on the future direction of the Buntine operations.

In November 1968 Len Wright, the Mt Isa cattle haulier who had built up a fleet of 23 road trains, was fatally gored by a bull during loading operations at Larrimah.

At the beginning of the 1969 slaughtering season a disastrous fire closed down the Katherine meatworks for most of the year and this in turn meant the diversion of cattle movements to other centres, stretching the vehicle resources to their limits but at the same time increasing the scope for new business as station owners sought other destinations for their turn-off.

Also in the late '60s, noises off-stage indicated that Vestey's were looking at disbanding their cattle transport operation. And there were distinct signs that the Co-Ord business was slowing down. In fact figures were showing that where Buntine Freightways had been literally propping up Buntine Roadways, the reverse situation was becoming manifest; furthermore, the gradual lengthening of the cattle carting season was strengthening the viability of Buntine Roadways. Additionally, a swing in freight movement into the Territory from traditional South Australian sources to Queensland traders was exacerbating Co-Ord's problems.

We stayed with this deteriorating situation for quite a while, *said Noel*. At one stage we decided that if we couldn't lick the Queenslanders we'd join 'em so we began a doubles operation from Brisbane via Mt Isa, Dunmarra and the Murranji Track to Victoria River Downs and other Hooker interests in the Territory, but other people in Co-Ord screamed a bit and the Queensland Railways did likewise because it was said we were interfering with their road–rail service to the Territory so we had to pull out. Which was just as well, perhaps. Every Joe seemed to be getting into the act so we decided to concentrate on cattle cartage.

In 1976 the decision was made to quit the freight business. By that time the combined fleets of Buntine Roadways and Buntine Freightways had grown to 28 Mack and 5 Kenworth prime movers, plus over 100 trailers. The Buntine Freightways operation (but not the vehicles) was sold to the O'Neil interests, giving them the total Co-Ord operation. From ten shareholders in the original Co-Ord when it was founded by the TTA in the early 1950s, this unique operation 25 years later came under single ownership—a prospect which was apprehended and guarded against in the early days but to which the operation eventually, and ironically, succumbed.

Prior to quitting the general freight side of the business Noel Buntine had acquired a sizeable portion of the late Len Wright's business. Wright's Cattle Transport had a number of clients in the rich Barkly Tableland region which consists of 76,000 square kilometres of open plains well covered with Mitchell and Flinders grasses extending from Newcastle Waters eastwards to the Queensland border.

Buntine Roadways had also become involved in taking over some of the Vestey transport operations. According to Noel, Vestey's had wanted 'out' for some time and had approached him—and no doubt others— to take over the total transport operation, including the road train base at Helen Springs. One of the conditions was that the two Rotinoff prime movers would have to be taken over:

We'd done some transporting for Vestey's at various times and we knew that the Rotinoffs had been designed for bitumen roads in the main. We had carted for Vestey's over all sorts of tracks and rough-formed roads and there was no way that we could envisage those Rotinoffs in our kind of operation.

Another aspect was that I couldn't see that the Maryville road train base at Helen Springs would do much for us except add enormously to our overheads. Furthermore, I was pretty financially extended at that time because the business was growing strongly. And yet I still wanted the Vestey work if I could get it.

So I went to them with the proposition that I'd take over their six trailers but not the Rotinoffs if they would guarantee our purchase of two V8 Mack prime movers to pull their equipment. We said we'd also bolster the two Macks with prime movers from Buntine Roadways as required and this would give them all the necessary plant to meet their requirements.

We pointed out that we could handle their western requirements satisfactorily through Katherine and Wyndham, and we offered to establish a base at Mt Isa that would cater for their Queensland movements.

They accepted our propositions and the Vestey operation became a 'branch' of the Buntine Roadways, operating under contract. We used the road train base at Helen Springs for a while but eventually handed it back to them because it didn't fit in with our type of operation.

In the mid-70s Buntine Roadways purchased East Kimberly Transport which operated nine road trains out of Wyndham. This brought the total Buntine fleet to 42 prime movers and over 100 trailers.

As the business grew so did the ability of Buntine Roadways to handle the fluctuations in market destinations which are a feature of cattle cartage. Katherine was the home base and depots had been established at Wyndham, Mt Isa, Tennant Creek and Alice Springs, and occasionally a part-time operation at Broome was 'activated' for moving store cattle as required.

Quoting examples of fluctuations in demand, Noel said that vehicles can be pounding up and down the Tanami Track for a season and then the whole movement will swing in a different direction and they won't be near the Tanami for the next couple of years. Likewise much of a season's operations can be concentrated on hauling from the Kimberleys to Meekatharra (in Western Australia) or from the Victoria River area to Katherine or across to Mt Isa. Then suddenly somebody's perception of the market will change in favour of Adelaide or to any of the ten certified abattoirs or the four export abattoirs in the Territory.

In addition there are exports of live cattle through the ports of Darwin and Wyndham and these require almost instant attention when the pick-up vessels arrive.

Another complicating factor in livestock is drought.

Buntine Freightways, a contemporary of the cattle operations, Buntine Roadways, had this Foden in its fleet which grew to a total of nine in the Co-Ord service. The load pictured here grossed 40 tonnes. *(Bob Dodd)*

If there's a drought, for instance, on the Barkly Tableland there's usually good pasture in Queensland or South Australia, and this means a heavy demand for transport to agistment areas. When the drought breaks the task of re-stocking is tackled but in this event the numbers to be moved aren't as high, and there's usually a lull in turn-off for a couple of years while herds are built up.

By 1980 fleet numbers had grown to 50 road trains plus ancillary vehicles and there were approximately 120 employees on the payroll. The company's turnover had risen to over $6 million a year. It was the largest road train livestock haulage operation in Australia, and was capable of lifting no less than 3,000 head of fat cattle at any one time. In addition to livestock transport the company had a valuable contract to haul bulk lime from South Australia to the Ranger uranium mine east of Darwin. Six road trains were engaged on this operation.

Buntine Roadways was pre-eminent in Territory transport and its star appeared to still be in the ascendant. Then suddenly, and to the surprise of most people in the industry, new ownership came on the scene. In May 1981 Buntine Roadways became a subsidiary of Transport and Property Holdings.

To outside observers the reasons for selling appeared to be twofold. Retirement or semi-retirement would have been in the Buntine rationale so that he could engage in other pursuits, high among which would be the development of horse racing and bloodstock interests which he had cultivated in recent years; and there was a need for more capital to expand Buntine Roadways which was riding high on the wave of development following self-government in the Territory in 1978.

The view from the purchaser's side of the desk would have been that of a highly successful business with solid potential and good cash flow. The new owners opened an office in Darwin and transferred general manager Doug Foster up there from Katherine and put Denis Buntine in charge at Katherine. But in a matter of

months both Doug and Denis resigned due to conflicts with the new management over policies which were quite different from those of the founder. Doug decided to set up a transport consultancy practice in Darwin and Denis mortgaged himself to the hilt to establish a livestock haulage operation which he named Victoria River Transport, based in Katherine.

But in less than two years from the time he sold out, Noel Buntine found himself in the position of having to buy back the farm. Transport and Property Holdings had 'gone down the tube' as they say in the finance world. Then, certain liabilities suddenly found their way to Noel's doorstep. He was thus faced with the choice of walking away from it all, or going to the finance companies involved and getting their okay to return to cattle transport and work off the indebtedness in which he'd unwittingly become involved. He chose the latter course.

At public auction 20 prime movers and 100-odd trailers came under the hammer. Noel bid for most of the prime movers and for 50 trailers. Between December 1983 and April 1984 he traded-in 17 prime movers on 14 new Mack Superliner V8s; he sent some trailers to Haulmark in Brisbane for rehabilitation and employed welders and spray painters at Katherine refurbishing the remainder so that he had sufficient rolling stock to hitch behind the new Macks and two 1979 Kenworth body trucks which he had also acquired at the auction for use on special applications and 'hack work' where this type of vehicle is more efficient, such as in rough country or on sub-standard tracks. The Macks with three double-deck trailers provided a capacity of 7.5 K whereas the Kenworths with two double-deckers could lift a total of 6 K.

Drivers were selected and trained on the new 298kW (400 bhp) Macks and, capitalising on the Buntine name and expertise he approached some of his former customers and got the show on the road once more, but under a different name—Road Trains of Australia— as Buntine Roadways technically was in receivership.

Compared with the days of Buntine Roadways,

Kenworth body truck and trailers were retained by Buntine's long after the company had changed over to using triples because of the versatility of configuration in the tough going on some station roads. *(State Reference Library of the Northern Territory)*

CATTLE TRANSPORT

Road Trains of Australia was a smaller and trimmer operation. Total inventory was reduced to 16 road trains operating out of Katherine and Wyndham where there were repair and maintenance workshops with smaller staffs and lighter overheads and less industrial disputation. Total office staff at Katherine and Wyndham was five, including a girl traffic manager, Lorraine Burbidge, who directed and monitored movements by two-way HF (high frequency) radio. Most of the work at that stage was concentrated on the Kimberley and Victoria River areas and RTA vehicles could be seen in Western Australia, South Australia and Queensland as well as throughout the Territory. Although they were individual companies, Noel's RTA and son Denis' Victoria River Transport cross-fed work to each other when there was too much for one to handle at any given time.

The contraction of Noel Buntine's operations could be compared with similar changes that have taken place in recent years in the cattle industry itself. Companies which over a long period had owned strings of stations divested themselves of many of their properties, and some of these were acquired by people or firms which preferred to run their own road trains to move cattle between their stations or to abattoirs.

Noel Buntine called it a day in transport on 30 November 1985. He sold Road Trains of Australia to Dick David, a former Buntine Roadways employee who had built up a string of BP fuel depots. In association

with Ken Warriner of Newcastle Waters station, Dick set about expanding RTA in different directions across the continent. In 1986 he took over Klopper Transport in Perth (13 road trains) as well as two Toowoomba cattle transporters, Baskett's and Bain's, whose combined inventory comprised 20 road trains. Towards the end of 1986 he acquired Alice Springs-based Tanami Transport and its eight road trains. Thus in 1987 Dick David's and Ken Warriner's cattle transport interests covered approximately 60 road trains.

Two years after he sold Buntine Roadways, Noel Buntine returned to cattle cartage and named the new company Road Trains of Australia. This Mack-hauled triple was photographed after delivering cattle for export through the port of Darwin.

From Cars to Cattle Crates

Bob Dodd worked for Noel Buntine and became his foreman driver. Later, with Noel's assistance he went into business on his own account; he now has three Macks on road train work and is the Ampol fuel agent at Katherine.

Bob got into the transport industry in 1958 when, at the age of 18, he began driving a car carrier for Don Tottey; in fact he was Don's first driver, and his 'mount' was a Leyland Comet.

The driving conditions were good; I was young and I drove hard. I'd do one and a half trips a week from Alice Springs to Larrimah with the Leyland hauling a single-axle semi-trailer with five cars on it plus another car on a small dog trailer towed behind the semi.

Later I worked for other operators and graduated to Fodens. They were great machines in those days. They pulled a 70-ton payload: 20 on the body truck and 25 on each of the two trailers. The Fodens I drove had either a Gardner 6LX or an 8LW. They were wonderful engines, although I must say I preferred the 6LX. Despite the fact that the 8LW had two more pots and was an 11-litre engine as against 10.4 litres and six cylinders in the 6LX, both were rated at 150 horsepower but the smaller engine had more torque over a wider rev range. The 6LX had a 4¾ inch bore, compared with 4¼ inches for the 8LW. Both had the same stroke—6 inches.

When I was driving on the Co-Ord service I used to do a run from Alice Springs to Mt Isa with steel and I'd bring back lime for the mines at Tennant Creek. The 8LW took eight hours to go from Alice Springs to Tennant Creek (500 km/312 miles); it was governed to 38 miles an hour but I used to 'fly' in the 6LX—45 miles an hour!

One of the Gardners I drove had a crack in the block. To stop the crack widening there was a steel strap with a turnbuckle and my daily routine was to check the oil and water and tighten the turnbuckle!

But the Foden cabs were very hot; heat from the exhaust manifold came up through the opening for the pre-select lever for the range-change. I used to stuff towelling and anything else I could find down the hole to keep out the heat.

Bob Dodd.

Bob also worked for Noel Buntine and John Ryan (Overland Transport). He drove a Foden 8-wheeler with 8LW Gardner engine. When Buntine entered the cattle transport business Bob went with him.

'I drove "The High and the Mighty" for a time when I was with Noel,' said Bob. 'It was a B61 Mack and it was real class in those days.'

Dodd Transport's three Mack prime movers all have V8-400 power.

'Macks have always impressed me,' he said. 'I had an F88 Volvo for a while; it was the first in the Territory. I had a good run out of it for two seasons but I decided to trade it on a Mack.'

His Macks haul road trains of Ampol fuel to such distant stations as Inverway (700 km from Katherine) near the Western Australian border, and Wollogorang (920 km) on the Northern Territory/Queensland border south-east of Borroloola. They're also used on cattle train work 'from anywhere to anywhere' on a sub-contract basis hauling crates owned by other livestock haulage companies.

Speaking of the changes that have taken place in the past 30 years, Bob says:

Haulage work in the Territory, particularly in the Top End, is seasonal, but it's not as seasonal as it used to be. In times gone by, once the Wet came we simply packed up until it was over. But these days, you're looking at $170,000 for a prime mover when not so many years ago the price tag was about $27,000 so you've simply got to get more work for them. Thus, when the cattle season finishes we look for other work, and we've found that there are plenty of opportunities around. Even so, everything comes to a halt in February and March; the Wet is just too much for us—and everyone else—in those months.

The old days are gone forever. Trucks are faster, and travel times are tighter. There's less time to dally along the way like we used to and get into bother at the roadside pubs! The investment is big and the result is that vehicles have to be kept moving.

Tanami Transport

Tanami Transport, the biggest stock hauler in the Alice Springs region, was originally RPM Transport, which was built up in the early '60s by Dick Rogers.

Dick came to the Territory in 1939 and for a period he was engaged in yard building and general contracting. Looking for something different he joined a stock transport business which was 'limping along' and he became its managing partner. Calling it RPM Transport (the initials represented the three partners, Rogers, Petrick and Menzel) Dick's 'foundation fleet' was two Ford F600s each pulling a two-van 34-foot semi-trailer which averaged around 30 beasts.

Eventually Dick bought out the other partners and one of his early moves was to buy a second-hand AEC Mandator which, he said, provided the basis for a very successful operation. He built the fleet to 12 vehicles, which included five AECs (three Mandators, a Mammoth Major and a Matador) plus Leylands, Bedfords and diesel-powered Fords.

As well as cattle haulage Dick Rogers established regular scheduled services to Ayers Rock and to stations north-east of Alice Springs carrying general freight, station stores, machinery, etc.

As the fleet expanded so did its carrying capacity, and the AECs were replaced by International and Mercedes-Benz prime movers. The two-van trailers moved over for combinations that could lift four and six rail van loads at a time.

In 1978 Dick Rogers acquired Arapunya Station, a 2434 square kilometre (1520 square mile) property 320 kilometres north-east of Alice Springs, and around the same time he handed over the management of the transport business to his sons Alan and David.

With the typically enthusiastic and confident outlook of the younger generation of business management, Alan and David as managing director and partner respectively, set about reshaping RPM Transport. Recounting the happenings of '78 Alan said:

We traded-in all the old stuff. There were no double-deckers in the old fleet, just a couple with shallow top decks, not really suitable for fully grown cattle. So we changed all that around and instead of hauling four and six vans per road train we upgraded our capacity to 15 vans in each road train of three 40-foot double-deckers.

We've got eight road trains now, of which five are hauled by Macks and three by Kenworths. All the trailers are Haulmark. We can lift 120 vans of cattle. We like the biggest prime movers we can lay our hands on. We specify double

RPM Transport (Rogers, Petrick and Mengel) was the predecessor of Tanami Transport. One of Dick Rogers' AEC road trains is shown in this 1961 photo.

This rig can carry between 165 and 200 head of cattle, depending on size and weight. Dick Rogers' AECs had a capacity of between 70 and 90 beasts.

Alan Rogers.

chassis rails and we look for 400-plus horsepower (300 kW) and around 1500 16/ft torque (2090 Nm) because that's the minimum 'poke' that in our experience will handle our type of work. Our trains operate off the highways for much of their time and each is fitted with two-way HF radio to improve the safety and efficiency of the operation.

We go anywhere, wherever cattle has to be shipped. We go to Birdsville, we go up and down the Strzelecki Track, we bring stud bulls back from Toowoomba, Cloncurry and other places in Queensland, and we cross into Western Australia.

We're always busy. The brucellosis campaign may have caused problems for station owners but when they de-stock they have to re-stock eventually. It's a two-way operation for us, moving cattle out and bringing cattle in. Agistment is also a two-way thing. Consequently our road trains are always on the move.

The name of the company was changed to Tanami Transport in 1978 because at that time a lot of the company's business was being done in the Tanami area.

Alan began driving for his father at the age of 17 and after seven years on the road he took over the reins of management.

In 1986 Tanami Transport came under the operating flag of Dick David's and Ken Warriner's Road Trains of Australia.

CATTLE TRANSPORT

Buntine Mk II

Although the Buntine name no longer appears on road trains in the Northern Territory, it is still very much a force in livestock transport. Denis Buntine is carrying on the family tradition in transport as owner of Victoria River Transport, based at Katherine, as was the famous Buntine Roadways founded by Denis' father, Noel.

After his schooling in Brisbane Denis began as a driver with Buntine Roadways working out of the Wyndham depot. He spent three years on the road and then was moved into the company's head office at Katherine as 2ic to the operations manager.

In 1974 when Doug Foster was moved from Alice Springs to take over management at Katherine Denis went to The Alice as manager of Buntine Freightways, the general freight operation. At that stage Buntine Freightways operated six road trains on the Co-Ord Service alongside those of Fleet Owners. This number was increased to nine when in 1975 Buntine bought out Tom Corry's T.C. Transport share in Co-Ord, thus putting Buntine Freightways on the same footing as Fleet Owners. Then, in 1976, Noel sold Freightways to Fleet Owners and for the next two years operated on a sub-contract basis for Fleet Owners which by now owned the Co-Ord service completely.

In 1981 when the big cattle transport operation Buntine Roadways was sold to Transport and Property Holdings, Denis stayed with the new owners for some months but as he didn't see eye-to-eye with their business philosophy he decided to quit.

With little money but plenty of confidence in the future of livestock transport in the Territory, Denis returned to Katherine in July 1981. He sounded out some former Buntine Roadways' clients to ascertain the likelihood of their becoming customers of his if he was able to 'set up shop' in the cattle haulage business and encouraged by their response he mortgaged everything

Denis Buntine.

to put an outfit on the road. In August that year he bought a new Mack prime mover and four trailers and began hauling for Vestey's in September. In the following year he bought another Mack and two more cattle crates and also leased a block of land on the western outskirts of the town where he built an office, maintenance shed, etc., whilst living in a demountable on the site. Two former Buntine Roadways drivers— Jack Taylor and Kevin Renahan—joined him and Victoria River Transport was born. As business built up he utilised a Mack prime mover owned by Bob Dodd of Katherine on a sub-contracting basis.

At the end of 1986 VRT had six road trains with a total capacity of 40 K (about 800 beasts). They're kept busy throughout the April–November cattle cartage season hauling for Western Grazing and other big stations in the Top End.

Although Noel Buntine is out of cattle transport his son Denis is in the thick of it, thus ensuring that the name of Buntine continues to be known in the road transport industry throughout the Territory and adjacent States.

Victoria River Transport is the cattle hauling business which Denis, son of Noel, established from scratch in 1981. His Mack-hauled outfits operate throughout the Top End and into Western Australia and Queensland.

PART THREE

Towards the Twenty-first Century

Lifeline of the North (1)

Up till 1940 the Territory's road system could best be described as rudimentary. Then things began to happen. The exigencies of war led to rapid upgrading of the rough tracks which connected Alice Springs with Darwin, and Mt Isa across to Tennant Creek. In the following three or four decades 'beef roads', mining development roads and general highway improvement programs gave the Territory a network of routes which have been—and always will be—essential to the development and economy of Australia's seventh 'state'.

Prior to 1940 the Overland Telegraph Line served as a communication medium and at the same time provided a south–north route firstly for the camel teams and then the motor transport pioneers and occasional intrepid travellers in motor cars. Each side of the line a 20-metre strip was kept clear of timber and scrub, and became the overland road.

The iron poles ran in straight lines for distances of between 30 and 50 km before turning slightly to avoid some natural obstacle; they resumed their straight course until some other obstruction necessitated a small alteration in direction. The vehicle track twisted between the poles as users sought out the most favorable path to avoid hazards such as bogs, tree stumps, rocks etc.

The track was anything but a highway. There were ups and downs in and out of dry creek beds and over small ridges and jump-ups. It crossed sandy terrain, stony plains, alluvial flats and hard-baked claypans, and dodged around termite nests which seemed to be rebuilt as fast as they were knocked down by the axles of travelling vehicles.

Likewise the track across the sparsely settled country between Mt Isa and Tennant Creek was only just able to cater for freight and passenger requirements, and the widely contrasting weather pattern of the Territory, ranging from floods in the wet season to thick dust and scorching temperatures in the longer dry season added to the difficulties of Territory transport. The Mt Isa–Tennant Creek route was in reality a series of tracks between bores, deviating and wandering as station owners cleared or fire ploughed them for their own use. In turn they formed a meandering link across the Barkly Tableland.

In 1928 a young engineer named Smith came to the Territory. There's a memorial in a park on the corner of Parsons and Hartley Streets in Alice Springs and the plaque attached to it reads:

D. D. SMITH PARK

This park is dedicated to David Douglas Smith J.P. first Resident Engineer, Department of Works of Central Australia, 1928–1957. He played a leading role in planning and supervising the construction of the Stuart Highway between Darwin and Alice Springs. He assisted in opening the Outback to travellers and settlers by developing roads, stock routes and bores. He made the needs and wishes of the people of this area become his major concern. His name appears in the records of almost every facet of the development of Central Australia.

D. D. Smith.

D. D. Smith came to this place when it was a small outback settlement and on this site set up his home and office in tents. The tents have long since disappeared but the mark of the man who erected them shall remain.

Before he became first resident engineer for Central Australia, Smith was an engineer with the Commonwealth Railways and carried out surveys for proposed railway lines between Daly Waters and Dajarra (Qld) and from Daly Waters to Wyndham (W.A.). These projects, like the north-south connection between Larrimah and Alice Springs, came to nothing. Thus Australia lost a railway line across the top of the continent and through the centre.

D. D. Smith resigned from the Commonwealth Railways in 1928 to take on, as he put it, 'the whole of the inland development of the Northern Territory. I was responsible for all works south of the 2½ mile bridge in Darwin.'

To his credit, in view of the fact that he was firmly convinced of the importance and value of rail routes in remote areas, D. D. Smith pushed ahead as best he could within government financial restraints with a program of road building. He would have preferred to construct the two rail lines he'd surveyed as well as another he had in mind from Anthony Lagoon north to Borroloola and the Pellew Islands area in the Gulf of Carpentaria where, in his opinion, the main port for the Northern Territory should have been located rather than where it is, in Darwin:

All that would have been needed was a causeway between some of the islands from the mainland and you'd have had a marvellous port. You could put the whole of the American and Australian fleets up there!

A rail line from there to connect at Anthony Lagoon with my suggested Dajarra–Daly Waters line would have completely opened up the Barkly Tableland and all of The Centre. All the lines from the Queensland coast could have been linked to it at Dajarra, and thus the whole of south-east Australia would

have been served. It would also have had value from the defence aspect, too.

I tried several times to persuade the Federal government to complete the north-south rail line but I was politely told that Alice Springs would only ever be an up-country town. Actually, when the Northern Territory was taken over by the Commonwealth government from South Australia in 1910 one of the clauses of the agreement was that the Commonwealth would build a rail line between Oodnadatta and Darwin. But all they've done is tear up the Larrimah-Darwin section!

When war broke out a bunch of American railway engineers came up; we escorted them to Larrimah and back. They decided they could build a railway from Alice Springs to Larrimah faster than they could build a road. They offered to build it free of cost to the Commonwealth Government and hand it over when war was finished. They went to Canberra and were told by the prime minister at the time that he would not allow the railway to be built by American Negroes; they would have to use Australian workers. So the Yanks packed up and went away.

In the late 1930s D. D. Smith put aside his long-range plans for strategic rail lines and began concentrating on straightening and relocating the road from Alice Springs to Darwin; he was becoming convinced of the inevitability of war and of the vulnerability of the northern coastline to attack and even invasion. He pushed on with his highway work with such dedication that he frequently ran foul of higher authority and when he overspent his budget by £67,000 the Administrator of the Northern Territory and the Commonwealth government made known their disapproval in no uncertain manner but Smith dismissed the official please-explain with the retort, 'Too bloody bad'. Years later he told the author:

I opened up the road and graded it from Alice Springs to Adelaide River before war broke out. In the main I kept to the OTL alignment because with the exception of two or three spots they made a very good job of selecting the higher areas.

I would have liked to straighten the road alignment between

World War II military vehicles pounded up and down the newly constructed all-weather road north from Alice Springs. The movement of troops and supplies was a top priority operation as the Japanese advanced southwards. *(Australian War Memorial)*

Alice Springs and Taylor's Well, just north of Barrow Creek. Going from Burt Well to Taylor's Well the road runs in an arc to the west, whereas if we could have constructed it so that it ran more or less due north we could have cut off 35 miles. But the then owner of Ryan's Well went to Canberra and put a spoke in my wheel and so I had to go around his property.

Everybody suddenly discovered the Northern Territory when the war broke out. Up till that time they had no idea it even existed.

Local communities are rarely isolated from national and global events and in this instance the Territory's remoteness proved to be no exception. The lumbering government road train and the trucks and semi-trailers with which a handful of pioneer operators were establishing transport services on the north-south route were suddenly shouldered aside by convoys of military vehicles carrying thousands of troops and their back-up supplies, fighting equipment and all the other paraphernalia of war.

In August 1940 the Commonwealth government decided that an all-weather road had to be built between Tennant Creek and Birdum by December; there was already a formed road from Alice Springs to Tennant Creek. The movement of troops was given top priority.

A popular myth is that this road was built by American military personnel. In fact the Americans had very little to do with its construction. The work on the Tennant Creek–Larrimah sector was carried out with extraordinary speed and efficiency by the road authorities of New South Wales, Queensland and South Australia.

In broad terms the specification for the road was a gravel surface capable of carrying vehicles of six tons (exclusive of loading) at 30 miles at hour 'without undue wear and tear on the vehicles'. This surface was to be sealed after the road had been in operation for two wet seasons. A further requirement was that the road should be capable of carrying 200 tons per day in each direction. Causeways, river and creek crossings were to be constructed to restrict delays to three days or less through flooding and such crossings to remain in good trafficable condition when water subsided.

And. . .work was to be completed before the 1940/41 wet season set in.

The New South Wales Department of Main Roads (DMR) was allocated the 86-mile length from Larrimah to Dunmarra; Queensland's Main Roads Board was responsible for the 90 miles from Dunmarra to Ferguson's Springs; and the Highways Department of South Australia was to construct the 129-mile strip from Ferguson's Springs to Tennant Creek. At the same time the Department of the Interior was to upgrade the standard of the Alice Springs–Tennant Creek track.

By 6 December 1940 the DMR had finished its sector, using two and three shifts of construction workers each day, seven days a week. The job was completed in 66 working days and it was claimed as a record at the time; it probably still stands.

The next task for the DMR was the construction of a 70-mile all-weather road from Darwin to Adelaide River. This was completed between August 1941 and the beginning of the 1941/42 wet season. Then this authority was handed the job of building the Adelaide River–Katherine sector (145 miles), while South Australia's Highways Department took over the Katherine–Larrimah sector (111 miles) and the Royal Australian Engineers worked on the Katherine–Maranboy length (30 miles).

Although the north–south road was pushed through in record time there were problems caused by weather and traffic. Due to very heavy rains in late 1941 large sections of the unconsolidated road became quagmires and upwards of 100 vehicles were bogged at times. In summer these bogs turned to bulldust as the projected movement of 200 tons a day rose to 2,400 tons and U.S. troop movements added to the volume of traffic.

In February 1942 the Japanese offensive came directly to Australia's shores and Darwin was bombed. In the following months there were 65 air raids by Japanese aircraft over the Darwin region, reaching as

Before the Mt Isa–Tennant Creek highway was bitumen-sealed it was carrying upwards of 1,000 military vehicles a day. It was a dustbowl in dry weather and a series of bogs after rain fell. It was sealed in by May 1944. *(Australian War Memorial)*

far south as Katherine. Over 300 lives were lost and 50 per cent of Darwin's buildings were destroyed.

The road between Tennant Creek and Alice Springs was sealed with bitumen between June 1942 and December 1943. During 1943 the DMR sealed from Darwin to Adelaide River and from Larrimah to Mataranka. In 1944 Victoria's Country Roads Board sealed the Mataranka–Adelaide River length, thus completing the tar-sealing of the north-south road.

In the meantime the gravel-surfaced Mt Isa–Tennant Creek road was carrying more than 1,000 defence vehicles daily and under these conditions it began to fail in many places, so it was sealed between January 1943 and May 1944.

The cost of constructing the north–south road was estimated at £15,000,000 and for the Mt Isa road it was said to be in the vicinity of £3,233,000.

For some years after the war the two highways were maintained at the wartime standard and sealing was maintained at a width of 16 feet. There was a dramatic drop in traffic volume after the war, and C. L. A. Abbott, Administrator of the Northern Territory from 1937 to 1946, wrote in 1950 in *Australia's Frontier Province* that 'Since the war traffic over these roads has dwindled, and it is doubtful whether the road from Tennant Creek to Mt Isa carries more than one car a day'.

He was pessimistic about the future of road transport:

The maintenance of these roads is a big problem. From Daly Waters north to Darwin the road runs through the monsoonal belt and though it is well sited and graded the heavy tropical downpours are the cause of much damage. . .

The lesser roads running to the stations and particularly to those towards the Western Australia border will be a less formidable problem with the more general use of modern road-making machinery but it is exceedingly doubtful whether permanent all-weather roads can be laid down east and west of the Stuart Highway for very many years, and this is an additional reason for railways.

The Allied Works Council and various state road authorities were responsible for the wartime reconstruction of the north-south road. This Federal, operated by the AWC, moved roadmaking equipment to various construction sites. *(George Maff)*

Among the vehicles used by the Allied Works Council and later the Department of the Northern Territory was this left-hand-drive White prime mover. *(George Maff)*

In 1949 a 'pilot' beef road program was introduced in the Kimberley area of Western Australia, involving the construction of a route from Wyndham down the Ord River Valley. Two years later a scheme to improve rural pastoral roads in the Territory was begun and then in 1961 the 'real' beef roads program got under way and when it ended in 1974 over £32 million had been committed to constructing or sealing roads serving the pastoral industry, and it included the upgrading of sections of the Victoria Highway east of Katherine.

During 1961–62 five roads were constructed: Dunmarra–Top Springs–Timber Creek–Western Australian border (gravel), Barkly Highway–Anthony Lagoon (sealed), Stuart Highway–Yuendumu (gravel), Stuart Highway–Plenty River (gravel), and Top Springs–Wave Hill (sealed).

By 1969 roads between Katherine and Top Springs via Willeroo, Daly Waters to Cape Crawford on the McArthur River, Mataranka to Roper Bar, Willeroo to Timber Creek, and Anthony Lagoon to Borroloola were sealed or were in the process of being sealed.

In 1975 the Federal government embarked on a policy of developmental roads in place of beef roads and decided to upgrade the Petermann Road from Erldunda to Ayers Rock, the Tanami Track from the Stuart Highway to Yuendumu, the roads from Jay Creek to Hermannsburg and Glen Helen, and the Daly River road.

Although considerable construction and maintenance work was carried out in the 1950s and 1960s on the Stuart Highway, it was not until 1971 that major reconstruction began to take place. The Federal government approved an upgrading program worth $15 million. Official statistics show that 29 contractors were employed on 12 new bridges, 221 kilometres of realignment, 269 kilometres of strengthening and widening, and 311 kilometres of resealing. A standard roadway width of 7.4 metres was adopted.

Between 1976 and 1980 another $26 million was spent on providing 26 more bridges and 1,168 kilometres of highway reconstruction including elimination of the notorious twisting climb up out of Alice Springs and the equally treacherous stretch between Adelaide River and Pine Creek. These two improvements alone cut travel time considerably as well as improving the road safety factor.

Since self-government in 1978 the Department of Transport and Works has continued heavy expenditure on major projects along the Stuart Highway including the construction of a five-kilometre causeway and three bridges at Newcastle Waters, known as George Redmond Crossing, to eliminate a trouble spot which plagued the transport industry, private road users and road construction authorities every year during the wet season. George Redmond was the director of Works in the Territory from 1962 to 1967.

Very little trace is left of the old wartime road. But had it not been for World War II it's a matter of conjecture when the Stuart Highway would have been constructed.

Until 30 June 1978 the control of roads in the Northern Territory was vested in the Administrator of the Northern Territory under the Control of Roads Ordinance. The responsibility for advising the Administrator rested with the Department of the Northern Territory, usually acting in accordance with technical advice from the Department of Construction.

On 1 July 1978 the Department of Transport and Works was formed, with responsibility to the newly-formed Northern Territory government. It took over the road function from the Department of Construction and the Department of the Northern Territory.

There were no road ordinances prior to World War II. The administration came under the following Commonwealth departments:

Interior	April 1932 to May 1951
Territories	May 1951 to June 1968
Interior	June 1968 to February 1973
Department of Northern Territory	February 1973 to June 1978

Today the Roads Division of the Territory's Department of Transport and Works maintains 20,000 kilometres of roads, of which over 5,000 are sealed and all-weather.

One can only speculate about the benefits or otherwise for the Northern Territory that the scheme put forward in the early 1960s by the Federal Inland Development Organisation (FIDO) would have had if it had gone ahead.

FIDO proposed a highway from north-western New South Wales through western Queensland to Camooweal and thence via the Barkly and Stuart Highways to Darwin. The projected route was via Bourke, Thargomindah, Eromanga, Windorah, Boulia and Mt

Isa, and the proponents of the scheme envisaged a 900-mile bitumen road which would link sealed highways in the Northern Territory with those in New South Wales. This Pioneer Highway, as it was to be named, would not only facilitate the movement of cattle and freight by providing direct access to northern areas from the heavily populated south, but would also develop tourist potential and, be useful for Defence purposes.

The estimated cost was £15 million which the scheme's promoters suggested could come from the Defence allocation. In any case, they said, there would be vast economies for the nation by way of reduced transport costs, the saving of at least 100,000 head of cattle per annum that would otherwise be lost by drought, increased population density in northern Australia, improved access to mineral wealth, and a number of other related factors.

In its manifesto the organisation stated that it was making a concerted effort to 'awaken the Commonwealth Government to the vital necessity for developing and populating Inland and Northern Australia'. It continued:

Through lack of proper road access, through lack of development of available water resources, over half our continent is neglected and empty.

Beef cattle produced in the north waste on stock routes and die in waterless desolation through national neglect.

£40 million worth of beef cattle perished in this way from 1958 to 1961.

Across the water the millions of Asia starve while our fertile north lies unoccupied.

Although it was an apolitical organisation, FIDO failed to get support from government and in fact met with opposition from various interests, including Queenslanders in eastern regions who could see adverse effects on their railways and their State's economy generally due to, for example, stock being moved from north to south instead of from west to east.

South Australian interests also withheld support as they could see Channel Country beef being diverted to New South Wales and Victoria.

Typical of the attitude of some grazing interests was that of Mr W. S. Kidman, chairman of directors of S. Kidman & Co. Ltd, who said that he thought the FIDO plan was impracticable. The proposed highway would have to cross the flood plains of the Diamantina and Georgina Rivers and Cooper Creek which became 15 or more miles wide when in flood. Priority should be given to extending the rail line from Quilpie to Windorah in Queensland, and from Dajarra or Mt Isa to the Barkly Tableland.

After some years of valiant fighting for its cause, FIDO finally subsided into oblivion.

Lifeline of the North (2)

The Stuart Highway runs from Port Augusta in South Australia to Darwin at the top of the Territory. Its total length is 2,670 kilometres, of which 1,745 traverse the Northern Territory and 925 are in South Australia. It was named after John McDouall Stuart who led the first successful expedition across the continent from south to north in 1862. The highway traverses the same harsh regions of the continent that Stuart crossed on horseback on a journey which occupied nine months and terminated at Chambers Bay, north-east of the present city of Darwin.

The highway took shape over many years from a series of tracks connecting various pastoral properties between Port Augusta and Kulgera on the border. Very few sections of it had been properly constructed and for most of its original 1,075-kilometre length in South Australia it was unformed and despite regular grading it was rough and dusty in dry weather and usually impassable after even moderate rainfall.

A massive reconstruction and realignment program on the South Australian side was completed in February 1987 and this not only reduced the length of the highway by 150 km but it also gave the nation its first bitumen-sealed north–south transcontinental highway. (The east–west transcontinental route, known as the Eyre Highway, was sealed in 1976.)

Although road train operations have always been concentrated on the Alice Springs–Darwin sector for the obvious reason that these unique combinations took up where the rail train left off, many a transport operator has looked at the possibility of competing with the railway for the haulage of freight from Adelaide to Alice Springs, but the general condition of the highway on the South Australian side has invariably been a deterrent. Furthermore South Australia did not allow road train combinations such as those in the Territory to operate on its highways; it permitted doubles only, and these were restricted to the area between Port Augusta and the border—in other words, no further south than Port Augusta.

Before the commencement of the upgrading project in 1979 there were murmurs by many that the South

In the 1950s and 1960s scenes such as this, with road trains hopelessly bogged when the bitumen road surface collapsed, were common during the Wet and resulted in delays of a week or more while roads dried out and vehicles were retrieved. *(Ken Moody)*

Australian sector of the highway would never be improved; it would be always sub-standard to discourage competition from road hauliers with the railway service.

Some idea of the nature of the old highway may be gained from the following description of conditions around 1956, as experienced by Doug Foster:

The south road from Alice Springs to Port Augusta was dirt for the whole 800 miles. There was no bitumen whatsoever.

The South Australian section, from the border to Port Augusta, was about 650 miles and it was formed and maintained to some extent. It was rough but there were usually a couple of graders working here and there on it. But the Territory end of it, from the border to Alice Springs, was just a series of tracks; it wasn't a formed road at all. Some of these tracks had been graded at one time or other but there was no proper road formation.

At Erldunda Station, for instance, there were tracks leading off all over the place. There were a few sandhills in that area and when you got there you simply picked the best-looking track, or if you met someone beforehand you'd ask which was the best track and they'd tell you. If you were a bit concerned about the soundness of a particular track you could walk through the doubtful area looking for solid ground and then make a new one.

That was the highway from Alice Springs to the border! One particular spot on the South Australian side down near Lake Hart was a bitch. After you left Pimba the road descended from the plateau down to the edge of the lake and ran alongside the railway line. It was sort of wavy sand, and I got bogged every trip. Coming north I'd try to leave Port Augusta after dark so that I got to Lake Hart about 2 or 3 in the morning when the sand was cold and firmer than by day. That way I'd probably only bog twice in that region.

I carried Marsden matting on the truck. Also there were plenty of railway sleepers laying around; the unwritten law was that you left them where they were after you'd used them so that other drivers could get some help from them. But invariably they'd have to put more sleepers down to get themselves out of trouble. I reckon in some places those sleepers must have been at least six deep; they seemed to just settle down in the sand and others would have to be put on top of them to get traction.

We used to get a lot of tyre trouble on that road. I remember one particular trip that I had seven flat tyres between Alice Springs and Port Augusta. I always carried two spares. The worst part was that there was a mixture of Budd wheels on the Ford prime mover and spider wheels on the trailer. I carried two spares, one of each type of wheel, but if I got more than one flat for a particular wheel, I had to not only patch tyres but also had to demount them and swap them around.

Pumping-up was the worst feature. I had one of those old Dead Easy pumps with a wooden handle on the top. The truck didn't have a compressor; its brakes and change-speed mechanism were vacuum-operated. So it was a matter of pumping for hours. I think it took about 100 strokes for ten

Bogged on a bitumen road seems an unlikely happening but as this photo shows it could and did happen on the Stuart and Barkly Highways after prolonged rainfall. After vehicles were extricated road authorities were faced with a tremendous repair task. *(Ken Moody)*

TOWARDS THE TWENTY-FIRST CENTURY

psi. The pump I had was a double-acting one; it had two barrels and it used to pump air on both the down stroke and the up stroke. It was a good pump but it still took a couple of hours to inflate a tyre to correct pressure.

It was all part of the job; it didn't faze me. I guess I was young and stupid and didn't think about the hardships and hard work!

The Alice Springs–Kulgera section of the highway was reconstructed and sealed by 1976.

Road train drivers in the Top End during the 1950s were reminded of the Territory's—and Australia's—involvement in World War II as they passed abandoned airstrips along the Stuart Highway between Katherine and Darwin. There were Tindal, Fenton, Manbulloo, MacDonald, Pell, Coomalie, Batchelor, Hughes, Sattler, Strauss and Livingstone. Having served their purpose, most were in various stages of deterioration due to the ravages of the sun and monsoon rains as well as the encroachment of sub-tropical vegetation. Although the aircraft and the men who crewed them, both in the air and on the ground, had long since gone—with the exception of those buried in the Adelaide River War Cemetery—little imagination was needed to picture the activity and the action that took place as squadrons of Spitfires and Kittyhawks (P40s) flew off to defend the northern coastline against Japanese attacks, and as bombers such as Hudsons, Beauforts, Mitchells, Liberators and Flying Fortresses roared down the runways with their bellies full of bombs to 'smarten up' the enemy in Timor and other places as the tide of war began to turn.

The memorabilia of war were still very noticeable in Darwin itself. There was the wreckage of ships in the harbour, derelict anti-aircraft and artillery posts around the foreshores, deserted groups of huts and campsites, and further afield over a wide area of sparsely settled bushland were the remains of crashed enemy and allied aircraft.

Despite the superior condition of the highway, thanks to its wartime upgrading, there were times when its function as a supply link was severely dislocated. Dozens of small rivers and creeks which lie dormant or are bone dry for nine or ten months of the year turn into raging torrents when the Wet arrives and cuts the highway, interrupting freight and passenger services and stranding motorists. Road train drivers with any length of service at all can recount stories about delays and episodes at Newcastle Waters, Warlock Ponds, Attack Creek, Morphett Creek, Adelaide River, Chambers River and other notorious spots along the Track. Since self-government in 1978 most of these problems have been eliminated but before then it was a different story.

A 60-ton road train would come to an instant stop when the road surface collapsed. At times axles would be ripped out but fortunately it was rare for the load to shift forward, otherwise there would have been fatalities. *(Ken Moody)*

On 15 March 1957 the *Centralian Advocate* carried a story headed 'DAMAGED ROADS HOLD UP DARWIN PERISHABLES', and went on to quote Stan Cawood, then managing director of the TTA, as saying that everything possible was being done by the Co-Ord service to ensure that three iceboxes of perishables which had been held up due to the state of the highway between Daly Waters and Larrimah were kept in proper condition. The iceboxes had left Adelaide nine days before and were re-iced at Alice Springs. Then two and a half tons of ice had been rushed to Daly Waters to keep the boxes at the correct temperature, and he expected them to reach Darwin in the next two days with their contents in good condition.

To prevent further damage to the highway a load limit of 6,000 lb (2,720 kg) per wheel or 12,000 lb (5,440 kg) per axle was imposed between Elliott and Adelaide River.

Then followed four years without rain in the southern region of the Northern Territory, but when the drought broke the *Centralian Advocate* reported: 'April 21 1961: Rain at last! But it brought problems for transport. A road train loaded with copper concentrate capsized when a sudden surge of water caught it as it crossed a swollen creek. The driver escaped but lost his belongings.'

In the following year the monsoon rains extended well to the south, and the *Centralian Advocate* of 16 February 1962 reported:

Dozens of semi-trailers and several smaller private vehicles have been hopelessly bogged over the past week at Gilbert Creek, just south of Wauchope. Semi-trailers went down like ninepins on Wednesday night following more than three inches of rain at Wauchope. One semi-trailer pulled the dolly axle completely off its second trailer. Some of the semi-trailers have broken completely through the bitumen where it has been undermined by water. Trucks have been bogged side by side as drivers tried to get around others already in trouble.

When dawn broke over the highway last Saturday morning it revealed a scene of complete havoc. Vehicles lay at acute angles in slush and mud.

One of Outback Transport's units loaded with fuel tried to fight through the bog but failed. Drums of fuel cascaded from the trailer and piled up as another hazard. The danger was increased when some of the drums began leaking and petrol oozed across the bog. Light traffic was still getting through as it was just possible to bypass the stranded trucks in a light vehicle along the sodden shoulders of the road.

The bogged transports were pulled out on Saturday by Works Department equipment. This allowed a refrigerated van to get through to Alice to load Darwin perishables—more than 24 hours late. However, on the return trip the truck bogged down again at the Gilbert late on Sunday night.

The Fleet Owners truck which had torn off its axle was still in the bog. The true spirit of Australian comradeship came to the fore as drivers of trucks, both bogged and not bogged, jumped in and helped Don Tuck, the driver of the Fleet Owners

vehicle, to transfer his load of copper concentrate from the bogged trailer.

Early on Monday morning two north-bound trucks were bogged at Gilbert Creek and another two just south of Wauchope. A Department of Works Euclid was swung in to pull them out but the bog won and the Euclid was itself bogged. The road was now impassable to all traffic.

The road was later cleared and opened to all traffic again on Tuesday morning. But it was not long before two more trucks were bogged at Wauchope. On Tuesday night there were six vehicles waiting to go north. With this new impasse the District Engineer immediately advised that once the bogged vehicles were cleared he would set up radio control posts at each end of the bog and allow only one-way traffic from each side of the bad area until repairs could be effected.

Nine years later the *Centralian Advocate* of 1 April 1971 was again reporting troubles on the Stuart Highway:

Following heavy rain overweight permits on the Katherine–Darwin section of the Stuart Highway have been suspended.

The manager of Baldock's and Fleet Owners, Peter Gunner, said: 'We're not bucking about this because we don't want the roads damaged. The Administration has our full support.'

Manager of Buntine Freightways, Doug Foster, said: 'If loadings had been restricted straight away after rain in previous years we would have been much better off.'

The maximum bogie axle loading has been reduced from 16 to 13 tons.

Perhaps the most damaging period in the Territory's history was that of the first three months of 1974. Newspapers began carrying stories of floods in western

Newcastle Waters was a notorious trouble spot for many years when the rains came. There were times when floodwaters cut the highway for up to two weeks. Numerous other crossings could cause long delays until water subsided. *(Bob Dodd)*

TOWARDS THE TWENTY-FIRST CENTURY

New South Wales and western Queensland mid-January 1974. Then the Territory 'copped it' as this summary, taken from the *Northern Territory News*, indicates:

January 22: RAAF alerted to airlift food supplies to the Northern Territory because of floods in Central Australia and Queensland. Talk of restrictions on weight of loads on vehicles using the Stuart Highway. Rail line closed. Road to Western Australia closed on both sides of the border.

January 23: Most major roads out. Load limit of 10 tons on the Daly River road.

January 25: Coles, Co-Ord Transport and Linfox arranging a massive airlift to Darwin from Melbourne totalling 47 tons.

January 28: 'Truckers ask for ban on S.A. Link.' Police and trucking companies have asked the Government to close the Stuart Highway from Alice Springs to near the South Australian border to prevent further damage.

January 29: All traffic banned on the Stuart Highway from Alice Springs to the border. Stuart Highway is cut at Barrow Creek, McLaren Creek and Wycliffe Creek. All traffic banned indefinitely between Alice Springs and Tennant Creek, but highway is open between Darwin and Tennant Creek. Drivers asked to use extreme care.

January 30: Darwin had 736 mm (28 inches) rain for the month. Previous record was 708 mm in 1896. Alice Springs had 303 mm.

January 31: Minister for Northern Development, Dr Rex Patterson, said that parts of the Northern Territory are in the throes of the worst catastrophe recorded in the region.

February 1: Daily airlifts of food into Darwin, Alice Springs, Tennant Creek and Katherine. Highway reopened between Barrow Creek and Tennant Creek.

February 4: Safeways, Woolies, Coins, Tully, flying in supplies.

Water across the highway was frequently only shallow, but there was always the risk of a deep hole or washaway which could 'drown' an engine and cause serious damage if the vehicle dropped into it. *(Bob Dodd)*

February 7: Schools still closed in Katherine and Tennant Creek. Teachers stranded.

February 8: Flood effects easing; road from Alice Springs to South Australian border open to four-wheel-drives but weight restrictions on the Barkly Highway have been extended until 14 February.

February 12: Stuart Highway again cut 65 kilometres north of Tennant Creek; Victoria Highway cut 65 kilometres south of Katherine. Load restrictions still applying on major roads. Katherine running short of food.

February 14: Most highways still closed; detours available in some places.

February 15: Darwin's fresh food worries are almost over, as supplies come in by sea and air.

February 16: Rail head set up at Finke; containers to come up by Co-Ord, Gulf Transport and other companies. Cement and flour being carried in containers.

February 18: All highways open.

February 20: Widespread rain has again closed most Northern Territory highways.

February 21: Building problems caused by Alice floods which have cut the rail link. Many building workers laid off.

February 22: No petrol in Mt Isa. Some freight getting to Alice Springs and as far as Tennant Creek. Airlifts of food continuing.

February 27: Road trains stranded. Stuart Highway cut south of Tennant Creek and several road transports are stranded. Stuart Highway cut north of Tennant Creek and Newcastle Waters. Barkly Highway closed at Sandon Station. Victoria Highway cut at King River.

February 28: Darwin hit by beer shortage.

March 4: Stuart Highway closed 166 kilometres south of Tennant Creek by two bogged oil rigs and a tanker road train. Katherine-Darwin section open; Barkly Highway closed at Rankin River.

March 5: Stuart Highway blocked south near Ti Tree by a capsized petrol tanker. First supplies of milk from Malanda for two months reaches Darwin.

March 8: Floods close all Northern Territory highways. Newcastle Waters causeway covered by more than one metre of water.

March 12: (front page) New Flooding Causes Chaos in Territory. New airlifts being organised. All roads out.

March 13: Fuel shortages cut power at Tennant Creek and Alice Springs.

March 14: Stuart Highway still out but Barkly Highway open to Mt Isa.

March 15: Stuart Highway between Tennant Creek and Alice Springs should be open in five days.

March 16: More rain cuts all roads out of Darwin.

The 17 March issue of the *Northern Territory News*

carried on its front page an interview with Jim Cooper, owner of Gulf Transport which at that time was operating five road trains on car carrying and general freight haulage.

'The Stuart Highway is a disaster area,' said Cooper. 'Vehicles and heavy machinery worth more than $2 million are at a standstill.' The story then continued:

Gulf Transport is under contract to Civil Defence to bring in vehicles left by their owners on flooded Queensland and Territory roads.

Mr Cooper estimates it will take three months.

He said most people in Darwin had no idea how bad conditions were along the highway.

In normal wet seasons he budgeted for the loss of eight road train loads but already this wet he had lost 30.

'We rely on the rail to Alice Springs to feed us but there has been no rail delivery to Alice Springs since January 12,' Mr Cooper said.

'In turn this has given us delivery to Darwin of only 49 vehicles in January, five in February and none in March.

'This represents an average loss to the motor industry and general public of 450 cars.

'The last road train arrived in Darwin on February 24 and the last to leave Darwin was March 5.

'This vehicle is still waiting 450 miles south of Darwin loaded with 55 tons of cement.'

Mr Cooper said about 50 cars were stranded at Mount Isa by the floods.

Another 100 were at Alice Springs and 150 were on rail between Finke and Port Augusta.

About 400 vehicles were stockpiled at factories in the south, waiting to be brought to the Territory.

The litany of disruption continued to be reported by the *Northern Territory News*:

March 19: Fuel coming in by road from Queensland.

March 21: Record rains have again cut Northern Territory roads, but the Barkly and Victoria Highways are open.

March 25: Food still being airlifted by RAAF into Darwin. Stuart Highway still cut south of Katherine.

March 28: Stuart Highway officially open all way from Alice Springs to Darwin for first time in several weeks. Load bans lifted between Dunmarra and the Three Ways. Barkly Highway also open but some load restrictions are in force.

April 1: Gulf Transport road train left Mt Isa on Saturday with a full load of 12 vehicles. Gulf is under contract to bring in all vehicles which had to be abandoned along roads which became impassable more than two months ago. Jim Cooper said that 12 vehicles would be moved from Tennant Creek, 50 or 60 from Mt Isa, and between 120 and 150 from Alice Springs.

April 3: Road trains roll as weight curb ends. The last limits to be lifted were those applying between Katherine and Tennant Creek. Since early January road

trains have operated for only two periods of a fortnight. Twenty-five staff men and 30 drivers were laid off by Co-Ord.

The myriad stories told by road train drivers describing delays, boggings, strandings, etc., caused by rain and floods would easily fill a book the size of this one, so we'll just focus on some of the experiences of a veteran driver and later an anecdote of more modern times.

Peter Ritchie drove road trains for 24 years, and in that time he'd been marooned and bogged on countless occasions on the Stuart and Barkly Highways:

It was nothing to be held up for three or four days at a time, waiting for creeks to go down or for softened road surfaces to dry out. The longest period I was stranded was nearly two weeks. We were held up at Newcastle Waters, which was no novelty, and after we'd been there a few days some other drivers and I decided to go back to Dunmarra and wait it out. I was working for Shell at the time.

Next thing we were instructed to bring our road trains back to Katherine because there had been a lot of rain higher up in the creeks feeding into Newcastle Waters. But we only got back as far as Warlock Ponds just south of Mataranka and the water was at least two metres over the bridge so we had to turn again and go back to Larrimah where we waited it out for about a week and a half. Bob Holt, who was the Shell dealer at Katherine, later came down with a boat and took the other three drivers and myself across the creek, which was about 2 kilometres wide by this time. Anyway, we got back to Katherine and Bob lent us his car and we returned to Darwin. We retrieved the tankers some time later.

On another occasion we were again stopped at Newcastle Waters by monsoon rains filling the creeks and covering the road. The water wasn't very deep except in one spot. There were three of us with road trains so we coupled the whole lot together. It must have surely been the longest road train in the world! It would have been nearly 500 ft long!

We pushed the first train in, with its engine turned off. Then, as the water got deeper, I switched off my engine (I was number two) and the third train did the pushing. By this time the first prime mover was just about out of the water so he started up and pulled us through.

Sometimes we'd be able to push through water which wasn't too deep after taking the usual precautions of taking off fan belts and so on, but occasionally a motorist, seeing you were going through, would try to sit in behind and take advantage of the wave we created but nearly always he'd come unstuck because we could get through much deeper water than he could and he'd end up 'drowning' his engine.

But I think the worst experiences I had were in the Foden days when we'd sometimes get bogged in the bitumen. Yes, in the bitumen!

It would happen after very heavy rain. You'd be driving along, keeping your eyes open for possible soft spots caused by water seepage under the tar. Then, when you'd least expect it, down you'd go, through the bitumen surface. The whole train—60 or 70 tons all-up—would stop instantly and you'd be very lucky if the steering axles weren't ripped out or the axles under the trailers weren't shoved back several feet. Luckily the load on the prime mover didn't move; otherwise if it had slid forward under the sudden impact I'd have been history.

Of course that was the end of operations for days and days. We'd have to wait for the place to dry out because there was no way that any other vehicles could get in to unload the stuff on the trailers or to pull the trailers and prime movers out of the bog. It also meant that very little other traffic could move—except for motor cars—until we'd been removed.

We used to have some really scarey times up in the Top End in the Wet, especially when the rivers were in flood because we had to use the railway bridges at some places and we prayed that we wouldn't meet someone coming in the opposite direction because it means reversing all the way back to the road. You can imagine the problems of reversing with a couple of trailers along a narrow railway bridge!

I remember a bloke who was driving a Federal Styleliner over the Adelaide River railway bridge. He was moving very cautiously because the timber sleepers weren't always secure. Well, one of the sleepers gave way and the front wheel dropped down. Fortunately he stopped immediately, but I'll bet his heart stopped too!

In another incident the driver of a 180 Inter owned by McCarthy's Transport was crossing the old Ferguson railway bridge, which was about 300 yards long or more, with no sides and the sleepers were not much wider than the truck's wheels. It was a black night, raining in torrents, and the only noise he could hear other than that of his engine was the roaring of the river some 50 ft or 80 ft below. After creeping almost right across the bridge he came to a dead stop; a railway gang had ripped out a number of sleepers to replace them with new ones, but hadn't done so. You can imagine his feelings when he had to reverse all the way off the bridge, which was no mean feat.

In those days, if someone was in trouble up ahead, or a creek was in flood, or the road was boggy or for some reason it was not safe to proceed, we used to put a branch of a tree across the road. This was a universally recognised code or signal and I'm sure it prevented a lot of accidents.

There's a wry twist to another road train driver's story of a bogging on the Stuart Highway just before the new Pine Creek section was opened. John Frazer-Allen tells it this way:

We're not real keen on people knocking our Territory roads about. Sure we know some overloading goes on but gross overloading—that's a different matter.

One time I was travelling in convoy with a mate, as we'd done for a couple of years, when we came across a Queensland bloke about 3 a.m. just out of Pine Creek. He was driving a Scania pulling a double and he'd got bogged. As he tried to get out he'd done his axles in—in the middle of the highway, mind you. It was the old section of highway. We asked him how heavy he was and he said about 72 or 73 tons.

Well, the way he was situated we couldn't get a semi and dog around him so we had to unhook the dog from one of our vehicles and then take the prime mover and semi up front to

The George Redmond Crossing has overcome the problems experienced at Newcastle Waters. It is shown at left. Inset: Mr and Mrs Redmond at the official opening in 1979.

LIFELINE OF THE NORTH

pull, while my mate intended to do some pushing. Well, we pulled and heaved and pushed and swore but we couldn't move him. Then along came a milk tanker with a rigid bar so he got into the act too. But we still couldn't shift him.

That fellow's got to be heavier than 70-odd tons, we thought. Anyway we were just about to give up when the thing started moving and we got him out.

We said: 'Hey, are you sure you're only 73 tons?'

'Oh yes, I'm sure. That's payload, of course!'

The bugger must have been around 120 tons all-up. If we'd known that we'd have broken him up and got him out a bit at a time, like semi first, trailer later.

We said: 'Why didn't you tell us instead of letting us knock our trucks about?'

He answered by saying that he thought if he told us how heavy he was we'd have knocked him back.

Well, we got ourselves sorted out and hooked up our trailers again and towed him and his load into Adelaide River. My mate went to the front and hooked on to me, as I'd given my vehicle a helluva hiding trying to get this bloke out. Between us we got him down over the low-level bridge and up to the Adelaide River police station where we pulled up and left him parked there, right in front of the cop shop.

We thought: 'Bugger you, knocking hell out of the road and letting us belt our vehicles around. We've got to use these roads to earn a living!'

His rig was brand new, so I guess he was hocked to the hilt and was trying to pay it off quick by overloading. But it doesn't work that way.

Anyway the police must have got the message somehow because he was parked there for several days. I think they might have had a word in his ear before they let him move after his truck was fixed.

When the Track was sealed from Alice Springs to Darwin in 1944 it was constructed to the standard of the time. It was 4.8 metres wide and capable of withstanding loads of around 16 tonnes. Since then it has undergone a metamorphosis and the design standard embodies a sealed width of 7.4 metres, ability to resist a 1-in-50-year flood cycle, and vehicle speeds of up to 130 km/h.

As part of the rejuvenation two difficult sections which caused so much trouble to road train drivers— up through the hills north of Alice Springs and the twisting section between Adelaide River and Pine Creek—have been eliminated and another problem stretch of the highway has been rebuilt through Newcastle Waters with a causeway and bridges to lift the road above the troublesome currents that flow during the Wet.

Although there is still spasmodic talk of the possibility of a railway being built between Alice Springs and Darwin, the Track will continue to serve the Territory as it has done since the days of the camel teams and road trains will utilise it to provide the most efficient form of transport for Territorians' freight and livestock.

After Cyclone Tracy

Jim Cooper arrived in the Territory from New Zealand in 1971 after coming to the conclusion that road transport in his home country had no future for him. Anyone with any knowledge of the industry in New Zealand in the 1970s would have to agree with his contention that it was over-regulated and had little to offer anyone with progressive ideas. It was precisely for these reasons that he sold up his business in Tapanui and headed for the climatically opposite Darwin where soon after he arrived he purchased Gulf Transport which at that time was operating two road trains between Alice Springs and Darwin hauling general freight and motor cars in competition with Co-Ord and the North Australia Railway.

The prime movers for the road trains were a pair of AEC Mammoth Majors similar to those which Jim had operated on log haulage in New Zealand but which, he said, 'like most Pommie trucks of that era weren't designed for a hot climate'.

In the following year the sales manager for White Trucks in Brisbane paid a visit to Darwin. He was a fellow Kiwi from Jim's home town. One thing led to another and not only did Jim buy two White 4000s to replace the AECs but he also acquired the White franchise for the Northern Territory. With it came the Autocar agency which proved to be particularly worthwhile as the big and powerful Autocars were well suited to road train operations.

Gulf Transport expanded under Jim Cooper's ownership to the point where it was operating nine road trains hauled by White, Autocar and Volvo prime movers. Much of the business was in transporting motor cars, both new and privately owned, with containerised general and refrigerated freight also playing a significant part.

I guess at one stage Gulf handled every motor vehicle—every marque and model—coming into the N.T. from all parts of Australia. We brought them through the rail head at Alice Springs and distributed them throughout the Territory to dealers and we also handled cars coming over the wharf at Darwin. The contract for cars coming in by ship involved not only transporting them but also checking them through quarantine and preliminary servicing.

In addition we handled just about every private car whose owners wanted them moved into or out of the Territory, including the armed forces, private companies, etc. It was quite a busy period in the life of Gulf Transport.

Our perishables traffic also grew. We were hauling for Coles, Tullys, Crowhurst and other clients. We were running about two and a half road trains a week on perishables and

Jim Cooper.

about four or five on cars. We also carted beer and general freight and some fuel consignments in cross-tanks as well as cars back down the Track, dropping off at all points south of Adelaide River, including stations such as Newcastle Waters, Banka Banka, Kalala, and other properties which ordered their stores, general supplies, fencing, machinery, etc. through Darwin.

Gulf's road trains were all flat-tops with portable frames for carrying cars. This meant that the operation was very flexible; freight was loaded on the floor of the trailers and cars were carried on frames above.

Immediately following Cyclone Tracy in December 1974, Gulf Transport's fleet was stretched to the limit for months, even though Darwin was in effect a 'ghost town'; its population was scattered throughout Australia and for the relatively small number of people who stayed on there was very little required by way of transport of goods and equipment until the big reconstruction program began in 1975. Consequently most transport was virtually at a standstill—at least for the first few weeks of 1975. But Gulf was on the move from day one:

We were scarcely game to open our eyes on Christmas Day, 1974, *said Jim*. We just couldn't imagine anything surviving the night. Eventually we screwed up our courage and went around to our depot at Winnellie—just getting there from home in Fanny Bay was an experience in itself. There was debris of all description and fallen power poles everywhere. We wanted to see if there was anything left—whether we had any premises or trucks or anything that might be salvaged.

It seemed almost incredible that anything could survive, yet that's what happened. When we got there we found that everything was reasonably intact. There was a lot of damage to our property but we could see that our vehicles were okay and if we could get them out and onto the highway we could get into the action that was to follow. So on Boxing Day, with the aid of a front-end loader we cleared a track from our depot which was then in Coonawarra Road, to the Stuart Highway and we got our first road train out. It had been loaded on Christmas Eve to go south after the Christmas holiday break, and we knew there were containers of perishables at Alice Springs awaiting pick-up. There were no communications of any sort; all phone contact was out, all radio frequencies were taken over by the emergency services. So we sent the first road train off anyway; the two drivers were told to get down to The Alice as fast as possible, load up and get back as quickly as they could. Ironically it took them five days to get permission to pick up the perishables which were so urgently needed up at the Top End! Everything at that stage was under the control of the emergency services and nothing could be moved without sanction by the authorities.

But once we got that sorted out we then got stuck into the job. A day or so after Tracy struck there was an urgent call for caravans to house people whose homes had been destroyed. We knew we had 20 or 30 caravans down in the rail yard at Alice Springs so we began moving them immediately. We thus started a big shuttle operation in reverse to our normal movements; we carried caravans northward and motor cars south out of Darwin. Caravans became top priority loading and we hauled for probably every caravan maker in Australia during the following weeks, as literally hundreds of their products were hastily assembled and railed to Alice Springs to house Darwin folk who chose to remain there. The cars which we were back-loading south belonged to people who'd been evacuated under the emergency regulations.

We simply couldn't cope with the volume of traffic and we had to get assistance from other operators. We even had the 'punishment truck' on the job! It was a Ford F8000 with a 160 Cummins engine. Hot as the hobs of hell to drive—a terrible vehicle! It pulled two trailers. We were also involved in local work, carrying loads of building materials flown in to Darwin airport for the commencement of the reconstruction program.

In Cyclone Tracy 95 per cent of Darwin's housing was destroyed by winds which reached 217 km/hr before the recording apparatus was wrecked. The death toll reached 49 plus another 16 drowned at sea. During the following week 35,000 people were evacuated to other parts of Australia, but 11,000 chose to stay on.

The pace was hectic for many months. But Jim sensed that not only had the cyclone changed the face of Darwin but there were fundamental changes coming over the entire Northern Territory transport pattern. When he bought Gulf Transport in the early '70s the industry was relatively insulated from interstate competition due to the atrocious condition of roads to and from the Territory borders and few interstate operators were prepared to risk the possibility of damaging their equipment and loads. Most freight at that time came from or through South Australia to Alice Springs, which was, and still is, the natural freight corridor.

Whatever changes may have been in store for transport in the Northern Territory as a result of advances in techniques and technology as well as improved roads, the turning point came with the 1974 wet season in the Territory and record rains in other parts of the continent. (See chapter, Lifeline of the North.)

Floodwaters cut the rail line to Alice Springs for lengthy periods and the Stuart Highway was knocked out for the first three months of the year. Shops ran low on stocks of foodstuffs and other essentials, fruit and vegetables were virtually non-existent, and in general

Gulf Transport moved out of general line-haul work to specialise in hauling ore and other bulk materials for mining companies. The company's operations are mainly concentrated in the Top End and in the north of Western Australia.

TOWARDS THE TWENTY-FIRST CENTURY

life in the Territory was seriously disrupted. Suppliers and retailers began looking around for alternatives; shipping services from Perth and the eastern States were stepped up and road freight began to move in from Queensland via the Barkly Highway. Increased penetration later by southern operators as well as the entry of Western Australian hauliers into the Territory considerably sharpened the competition for available freight.

The growth and development of the Territory over the next few years was strong, particularly after self-government in 1978, but the increase in freight movements was more than matched by the number of operators jockeying for business. So Jim decided in 1979 to leave the line haul scene. He sold the car carrying and general freight side to Ascot Haulage which well-known South Australian transport figure, Alan Scott, had set up in the Territory to cart Mobil fuel and later expanded to cover other transport services. In 1981 Jim severed his connection with White Trucks just before that company 'went under' in Australia, to be replaced later by Western Star. His last sale of White vehicles in the Northern Territory was five Road Bosses to Peko Mines:

I could see the writing on the wall, *he said*. Fuel prices were rising and so were wages. I reckoned that only the big blokes would survive. I wasn't making much money. When I sold I had about 35 staff and a depot at Alice Springs which, incidentally, was on the site of Len Tuit's former bus depot on the northern outskirts of the town.

Jim Cooper re-shaped Gulf Transport from line haul to local work associated with major construction projects in the Top End. His five vehicles, all heavy-duty tippers, include one of his original White 4000s which has had the benefit of a couple of 'transplants' such as a new engine and a fresh transmission. Some of the early tasks for the revamped operation included the cartage of several hundred thousand tonnes of rock from Mt Bundey and other quarries to the new Darwin Naval Patrol Base and the Fort Hill roll-on, roll-off wharves. Gulf also supplied equipment for the construction and grading of 65 kilometres of road in the Borroloola area for Amoco Oil Co.

The latest move by Gulf has been into the field of hauling bulk commodities by road train for mining companies with a long contract to carry zinc and lead concentrate from the Woodcutters Mine (near Rum Jungle) to the Darwin wharf for export and another contract with Australian Development Inc. to haul gold ore to that company's processing plant at Nobles Nob (Tennant Creek).

Helped to Advance Technology

If nominations were called for the most widely experienced man in Northern Territory Transport the vote would have to go to Doug Foster. His curriculum vitae (if he ever had to prepare one) would read:

- Commenced employment in automotive repair and maintenance;
- Began driving trucks and semi-trailers in 1955 in the Northern Territory;
- Graduated to road trains (five years);
- Was promoted to workshop Supervisor for Fleet Owners (four years);
- Became Alice Springs manager for Buntine Freightways (8 years);
- Moved up to general manager's job with Buntine Roadways (ten years);
- Won a Winston Churchill Fellowship to study livestock haulage in the U.S.A. and Canada (1979);
- Was accepted as a member of the Society of Automotive Engineers (Australasia) for his contribution to the development of road train technology;
- Set up a transport consultancy in Darwin in 1983;
- Introduced the multi-trailer concept (an Australianised version of Canada's B-train combination) to the Territory;
- Is now general manager of a large diversified transport operation based in Darwin.

That sort of experience would be rather hard to top anywhere in Australia.

Doug's days at the wheel are described elsewhere in this book. They span a period when Fodens and Leylands were kings of the road. He also knows Macks and Kenworths quite intimately.

When he eventually got down from the cab and later left the workshop behind, Doug Foster's real talents began to show. He soon got into his stride on the management side of things and made his way up to one of the top transport jobs in the Territory. He had the 'feel' for transport and this was augmented by experience in the rough and tumble of highway operations.

Doug Foster.

When he moved into the position of general manager of Buntine Roadways in 1974 he faced a totally different set of conditions and challenges from those experienced in the freight operation over the previous eight years. Here was a strongly developing business in which no two days' problems were the same, and despite what must have been a natural inclination to match demand by expansion, Doug Foster had to keep a foot on the brake to stop the company over-revving but that foot had to be judiciously applied. The transport industry is littered with cases of boom and bust; rapid expansion to meet a perceived demand only to be faced later by strengthening competition as others move in for their cut.

Doug's policy was to get the best from what you've got and if that doesn't meet demand then go for more equipment. In other words, increase operating efficiency to avoid financial over-commitment and in doing so keep down the costs to the client.

An early target for change was the livestock trailer. The trailers in the Buntine fleet and, in fact, throughout Australia, hadn't changed in any significant way since the 1950s and at best were only flat-top trailers with stock crates built on them. Here was an area, in his view, where efficiency could be greatly increased by designing specialised equipment to take advantage of the economies of scale and at the same time transport livestock in conditions leading to less bruising and loss. Increased carrying capacity was essential to keep costs and rates down.

Although double-deck crates had been in operation for a few years, their design had a number of short-comings. Deck heights were too low, leading to back injury (rubbing) and bruising; and nobody had devised a satisfactory internal ramp which would allow fat cattle to be loaded into double-deckers without bruising. Mechanically-operated ramps in vogue at the time led

to bruising by causing cattle to stand facing fore and aft in the trailer instead of their preferred position at 90 degrees to the direction of travel.

Discussions with Haulmark Trailers, Brisbane, led to the manufacture in 1977 of the 'Volume' crate which was a 40-foot double-decker with a goosenecked underframe to provide more height per deck within the overall height regulations. By-products of this design were a lower centre of gravity and elimination of injury through back-rubbing, but a distinct limitation was in the carrying capacity, particularly in the area over the turntable. In effect, the Volume turned out to be two decks of 28 feet (8.3 m) and a single deck of 12 feet (3.6 m) within the 12-metre overall length, instead of two 12-metre decks. Thus there was an effective loss of 15 per cent utilisation.

The Mark 2 version of the Volume came on the scene in 1979. The Volume Plus, as it was named, was also designed and manufactured by Haulmark with an unusual frame design in which the major load-bearing chassis beams were moved to the outer periphery of the vehicle and a deep member ran down the outside to provide strength. Thus it was possible to build the bottom floor between the beams and provide two full decks of 12 metres each with 5 foot 6 inch (1.7 m) internal height. Whilst the Volume Plus overcame the internal deck clearance problem, its tare weight plus the weight of two decks of cattle brought it very close to, if not beyond, the legal weight limits. And there were difficulties in the internal loading ramp area.

The problems encountered in the quest for more capacious and more efficient trailers led to Doug's application for a Churchill Fellowship to study America's and Canada's technology, having in mind that livestock haulage in North America had begun in the mid-1930s. In general his study was focused on ascertaining American and Canadian experience, and in particular he was looking at the design and application of specific door widths, ramp angles, internal trailer construction and fixtures aimed at eliminating or at least reducing injury to animals.

His observations of Northern Hemisphere standards and practices were pertinent and candid.

'In the majority of cases,' he said, 'cattle were handled with some consideration for carcase damage but instances were observed where no consideration whatsoever appeared to be given to handling practices which at times were brutal.'

With regard to equipment he was of the opinion that the majority of trailer gates, ramps and fixtures were designed, manufactured and used with the economics of the trucking industry in mind rather than concern for the beast being transported. The fact that death and bruise ratios were generally low was a credit to the placid, well-handled beasts rather than to design considerations by trailer manufacturers. But, he added, in fairness to the manufacturers, they were merely responding to the demands of the livestock trucking industry for less tare weight and more payload and in turn this was a result of pressure by livestock producers for operators to more closely control their costs.

Doug listed a number of common faults on trailers he studied in North America:

- Absence of floor cleating thus allowing cattle to slip and fall. A common claim was that cleats or grids hampered cleaning and washout procedures.
- Internal ramps without side panels resulted in animals having their legs caught during loading/unloading operations.
- Recessed ramps allowed animals to step over the side of a one metre drop rather than use the ramp when entering the dropped 'pot belly' section.
- Hinged roof panels, which, in the case of one manufacturer, allowed the hinge to protrude 8 inches (20 cm) below the roof line, causing back injuries to animals.
- Excessively steep ramp angles in confined areas on some vehicles.
- Sharp, hip-high protruberances adjacent to the 'pot' section.

Doug added that whilst it would not be possible to operate U.S.A. standard trailers legally in Australia, the trailer building industry could well consider the advantages of monocoque construction which is a dominant feature of the North American scene and results in considerable reductions in tare weight and maintenance cost. But . . .whether the limited volume demand for a completely new style of trailer construction would justify the tooling-up by any livestock trailer manufacturer in Australia would be a debatable point. A further complication could be the cost of special high tensile steels and treated aluminium extrusions.

Whilst in Canada, Doug Foster also looked into what is known on the West Coast as the B-Train and which, in his opinion, should have a strong future on Australia's East Coast routes—if the regulatory authorities don't apply unreal restrictions which would hamper its innate efficiency as an economical load carrier.

In essence the B-Train—or MTC (multi-trailer combination), as he prefers to call his version which has been modified for Australian conditions—is different from the conventional double or triple combination inasmuch as the first trailer (A-trailer) is connected as usual to the prime mover by a turntable but the coupling point for the second unit (B-trailer) is by means of a turntable mounted on the rear end of the A-trailer's bogie frame which projects beyond the A-trailer body. Thus the dolly under the nose of the second trailer is eliminated, as is one pivot point (the drawbar pin), with consequent improvement in stability, tracking and manoeuvrability. In more densely populated areas such as the seaboard States where combinations are restricted to semi-trailer and truck-and-trailer configurations,

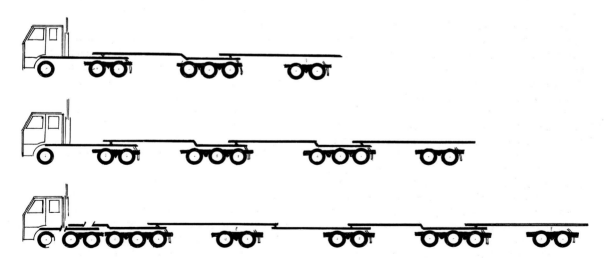

The MTC (multi-trailer combination) is different from conventional doubles or triples in the method of coupling between the first and second units. The rear bogie of the first trailer projects beyond the body and the second trailer is connected to it, eliminating the dolly under the forward end of the second unit and forming a 2 MTC or B-train as this configuration is also known. A third trailer can also be coupled by this method, as the middle drawing shows, forming a 3 MTC (or C-train, in southern and eastern States parlance). Where a fourth trailer is connected, the combination becomes a 2 + 2 MTC, as can be seen in the bottom illustration. The prime mover and first trailer have been foreshortened in the bottom drawing to save space. *(Drawing Lindsay Paish)*

HELPED TO ADVANCE TECHNOLOGY

Close-up of the bogie-sharing arrangement between numbers 1 and 2 units in a 2 MTC or B-train.

the B-train could be considered as a viable intermediate between conventional articulated vehicles and road trains, provided they meet safety standards and axle weight limits and are confined to set routes.

Increased load capacity and reduced running costs are, of course, advantages claimed for MTC combinations. In South Australia, for instance, a two-unit MTC tanker operating for Shell was permitted by road authorities to carry 55,600 litres, compared with 40,000 litres in a conventional semi-trailer.

The Review of Road Vehicle Limits (RORVL) initiated by the National Association of Australian State Road Authorities (NAASRA) and released in 1986 put forward the idea that B-Trains up to 23 metres in length should be permitted on selected routes on a terminal-to-terminal basis in the more populous states.

The MTC is not limited to two units in the Northern Territory; others can be coupled so long as they comply with the Territory's overall length limit of 50 metres as well as, of course, the axle load maxima.

Doug Foster is general manager of M. J. Hannon Pty Ltd, Darwin, and its subsidiary Ace Transport which has been operating MTCs since 1984. Hannon's specialise in industrial waste collection and the Ace operations cover a wide range of transport activities from road trains to town cartage and from taxi trucks to forklifts.

Under his guidance Hannon's introduced a two-trailer MTC combination. Then as experience was gained by the company and the regulatory authorities this was increased to a four-unit rig with an overall length of 41 metres. It is used for hauling quicklime (calcium oxide) in containers to the Ranger uranium mine at Jabiru, 250 kilometres south-east of Darwin, and back-loading with yellow cake (uranium ore).

In essence the combination is a two-plus-two; it could be described as two B-trains connected in the middle by a conventional drawbar and dolly.

One of the lesser-known episodes in Doug Foster's transport career was his successful appearance in a Section 92 case involving interstate transport.

The repercussions of the famous Hughes & Vale

appeal to the Privy Council under S.92 of the Constitution were slow to reach the Northern Territory. In November 1954 their Lordships of the Privy Council in London ruled that State laws prohibiting road transport from competing with State-owned railways were invalid in relation to interstate haulage. In other words, the Privy Council interpreted S.92 to mean what it said—that commerce and trade between the states should be absolutely free.

Doug Foster, who was driving for Donald's Transport (Don Bale) at the time, was 'picked up' by Alice Springs police for driving an unregistered Ford transport on Gregory Terrace on 11 April 1957.

He pleaded not guilty and in his defence said that he was engaged in carrying a load of uranium ore from the Pine Creek area to Adelaide which involved crossing the border of Northern Territory and South Australia. His legal representative pointed out that S.10 of the Northern Territory (Administration) Act was practically the same as S.92 of the Constitution which provided for freedom of trade and commerce between the States. Therefore he was not obliged to register his vehicle in the Territory or elsewhere.

His case was upheld by the magistrate in the Court of Summary Jurisdiction at Alice Springs and became the first constitutional case involving the movement of transport vehicles across Northern Territory borders to and from adjacent States. At the time there was a spate of cases heard by the courts in all States as governments continued to resist the consequences of the Privy Council's decision upsetting their so-called sovereign right to control transport.

In another episode involving the transport of uranium yellowcake, Doug was driving for Noel Buntine and John Ryan (Overland Transport). His vehicle was a wartime Federal with a five-cylinder Gardner engine pulling a trailer in the Co-Ord operation. At Larrimah railhead drums of yellowcake had been transferred from the NAR train to the trailer and he proceeded toward Alice Springs. South of Dunmarra he had an encounter with a stray bullock on the road and in the process of trying to miss the beast six of the heavy 44-gallon drums fell off.

The lid came off one of the drums and fearful of what the boss would do when he heard of the incident Doug scooped up the yellowcake by hand and put the lid back on and waited for someone to assist in lifting the drums back up on to the trailer. Peter Gunner, who was then driving for Len Kittle, came along and with the aid of a drum skid the two men loaded the heavy containers and got on their way. Doug reported the incident to Noel but nothing more was heard about it.

'I don't know what's supposed to happen to people who handle yellowcake,' he said, 'but so far in thirty years nothing's happened to me!'

Operator with a Difference

Mike Flynn's road train operations aren't involved in either general freight or cattle. They're in the field of bulk liquids. Something else that's different about Mike Flynn is that he can't reminisce about the days of driving Fodens or ex-wartime Diamond Ts or vehicles of that generation because he wasn't old enough to hold a driver's licence in those times.

But he can recall his experiences later driving B-model Macks, Leyland Beavers and the like hauling single-axle trailers in north Queensland between Cairns and Cooktown, Laura and Lakefield, and from 1968 pulling 11-metre cattle crates in doubles with a Beaver and triples with a two-stick Mack 240 kilometres from Elizabeth Downs to Darwin for a couple of years before moving down to Katherine and working for the local Shell agent there, Bob Holt, where he got his first experience in fuel cartage.

Mike's direction then changed; he left truck driving to take over the Shell retail outlet (service station) on the highway at Katherine but he still retained contact with transport. In addition to selling fuel to road train drivers—mostly owner-operators, as company-owned vehicles usually carry sufficient distillate to take them through to destination—he designed and built a couple of heavy duty truck retrieval units, one of which had a tilting deck for getting under the nose of a disabled semi and securing the kingpin to the plate by means of chains in each corner, then towing it into Katherine.

In 1981 his big opportunity came when the Shell dealership in Darwin became available. He bought it and immediately set about getting rid of a motley collection of vehicles that went with the business and put on a new Kenworth and a new Mack plus the last of the old Atkinson eight-wheelers which Shell put on road train work in 1970.

The Kenworth and the Mack haul triples of fuel throughout a large area extending as far as Pine Creek (223 km from Darwin) and along the Arnhem Highway to Oenpelli and Nabarlek. Bitumen haulage also comes into Flynn Petroleum's sphere of operations; triples of bitumen in tankers owned by Spraypave are hauled by the Mack or the Kenworth from either Darwin or Townsville to places along the Barkly Highway and along the Buchanan Highway to Top Springs and distant centres in Western Australia according to road program requirements.

The company's road trains can carry up to 100,000 litres of super-grade petroleum or 93,000 litres of diesel

Mike Flynn's Kenworth road train with a mixed load of petroleum products for various destinations in the Top End. His company's tankers can carry up to 100,000 litres of petrol or 93,000 litres of diesel fuel.

Mike Flynn.

fuel. All-up (gross) weight limit in the Territory for road trains is 115 tonnes.

The Atkinson is a relic of the days when 'body' prime movers pulled two or three trailers, depending on overall length and weight. But with the advent of a more-or-less standard 12.2 metre (40 ft) trailer length adopted by operators, a body-and-three would have gone beyond the allowable 50 metre (164 ft) overall length, because there is a minimum drawbar length of 3 metres and a maximum of 5 metres, and it is not possible to use a body truck of any reasonable length with three 12-metre trailers. A body-and-two is not regarded as being economically viable.

Other aspects of the body truck's dis-economies are: maintenance cost is high, particularly in the drive line area; capital cost is higher than for a conventional prime mover; it has to be a heavily constructed vehicle to pull 115 tonnes, including some payload on its own 'back'; and being heavy and specialised its resale potential, even for tipper work, is very limited.

The only body trucks working these days are in the cattle industry, mainly on intra-station roads where at times traction is a problem for conventional prime movers.

Mike Flynn has studied the MTC (B-train) concept to see what advantages there might be in it for his operations. The optimum, in his view, would be a five-unit MTC running on big single tyres and line-hauling fuel between, say, Darwin and Jabiru or Darwin and Alice Springs. But much would depend on what reduction could be achieved in tare weight, which is all-important in tanker operation—and, for that matter, most other types of operation. The removal of compart-

ment dividers to increase compartment sizes and thus eliminate some of the plumbing would lead to weight savings, but the structural strength of the tank might have to be increased and this in turn might bear a weight penalty. Tankers these days are chassis-less and have been for many years and the MTC concept must incorporate this principle if it is to be weight-effective.

Ideally the MTC would be purpose-built for a specific type of operation with regular loading. An advantageous situation would be the movement of containers, where one 20-tonne box per conventional trailer would be under-capacity and uneconomical (i.e., three containers per road train, making a 60-tonne payload) but five carried by a five-unit MTC would be a better financial proposition.

Mike Flynn said it would not be feasible to adapt the MTC to his own operations because with a conventional triple travelling to Jabiru, he can split the combination and drop off one unit at, say, Cooinda and another at a mine site further along the highway leaving one trailer to finish at Jabiru. This sort of arrangement is not possible with an MTC.

However, he and other operators are watching developments with the MTC. In his view the next logical step would be to remove the dolly set-up which is now required by law in the middle of an MTC train of three or four units and replace it with a fifth trailer so that there are five freight 'platforms' or five tanker units or five vans forming the train within the 50-metre length limit. It would be a very stable train; there would be only five pivot points—the same number as on a conventional three-trailer road train with two dollies. In theory an MTC train should be more stable under heavy braking than a triple is.

He doesn't see the MTC or B-train concept taking over but for specific applications it could be adopted more widely in future, depending of course on the attitude of the regulatory authorities.

In 1988 Mike Flynn was serving his third term as president of the Northern Territory Road Transport Association. His view of industry/government relations is:

We get on well with government in the Territory. Due to the work of fellows like Doug Foster and Jim Cooper who put in a tremendous effort setting up the framework of the system we've got, the Northern Territory Road Transport Association and the Government have worked together to produce a set of regulations that are fair and reasonable and right in line with the Territory's unique conditions. We have very good lines of communication with the N.T. Government and the liaison between us is beneficial to both sides. We don't envisage the introduction of regulations or conditions which, whilst they're suitable for the situation in other States, would jeopardise the transport lifestyle and efficiency of the Territory.

TOWARDS THE TWENTY-FIRST CENTURY

A Voice for the Industry

In 1978, with self-government for the Northern Territory getting closer, there came the realisation that new laws would have to be drafted for just about every aspect of commercial and social life in the Territory once Canberra's administrative hold was loosened.

Jim Cooper and Doug Foster and others involved in transport and in the supply of equipment to the industry could see that it was time to act to ensure that road transport would be treated more as a partner in the new phase than as a barely tolerated illegitimate offspring which the governments of the old-established States had historically regarded it as for half a century or more.

There was also the realisation that the industry did not at that stage have a voice. The Territory Transport Association which had been formed in Alice Springs and which had played such a significant and beneficial role for the industry for over 20 years was defunct. The question was: should the TTA be revived or should it be allowed to rest in peace? The situation was entirely different from that which led to the formation of the TTA. Back in the 1950s there'd been an urgent need for operators to band together to protect their businesses; subsequently this led to their forming a unique and profitable commercial operation—the Co-Ord—which was now in private hands.

Now, in 1978, the action had moved from the Centre to the Top End. Darwin was to be the seat of government and it was in Darwin that decisions affecting the transport and other industries would be made. Furthermore road transport was looking toward a change in its traditional stance of reaction, to one of initiative, contributing its knowledge and experience in the formulation of regulations which would set the parameters for its operational activities and safety standards.

Gulf Transport's phone bill increased noticeably as Jim Cooper contacted fellow operators throughout the Territory and sought the support of transport equipment suppliers. Then, with the assistance of Colin Quan Sing (Quan Sing Transport) and Bernie Brock (Fruehauf Trailers) he convened a meeting on 20 July 1978, at the Berrimah Hotel in the heart of Darwin's transport district. It attracted 35 persons who, in addition to deciding to form an organisation to be known as the Northern Territory Road Transport Association, also voted to make it representative of the various spheres of operation such as line-haul, livestock, gravel cartage, interstate transport, owner–operators and off-highway carriers, as well as equipment manufacturers and others associated with the transport industry:

Line Haul: Jim Cooper (Gulf Transport), Tom Byrne (Byrne Transport);

Livestock: Alan Rogers (Tanami Transport), Doug Foster (Buntine Roadways);

Gravel Carriers: Ron Docking (North Australian Haulage), Peter Harris (Arnhem Sands & Aggregates);

Interstate Transport: Ross McMahon (Ascot Cartage Contractors), Colin Quan Sing (Quan Sing Transport);

Owner-Operators: David Barnes (Barnes Haulage), John Ottley (Ottley's Live Lift, Ottley's Freight Lift);

Off-Highway Carriers: Ivan Wiese (Northern Transport), Ron Thomas (RH Thomas Transport);

Associate Members: Bernie Brock (Fruehauf Trailers), Peter Rau (TriStar Sales).

From this committee Jim Cooper was elected president, with Ivan Wiese as vice-president representing the region south of Elliott. Bernie Brock was elected honorary secretary–treasurer.

Although initially some thought was given to linking with the Australian Road Transport Federation the eventual decision was against this because with the new 'clean slate' approach of self government it would be more appropriate for the newly formed body to make its own way without being influenced by other organisations' policies on industrial matters, rates, and negotiations with authorities. It had also been decided by consensus even before the inaugural meeting that there should be no attempt to revive the old TTA.

Jim Cooper's initial term of office lasted two years. He was succeeded by Peter Rau who took over for 12 months. Then Doug Foster did a three-year stint as president, and Jim Cooper came back into the chair in 1984. In 1985 he was succeeded by Mike Flynn (Flynn Petroleum), who was re-elected in 1986 and again in 1987.

Relations between the industry and government in the Territory are unique in Australia and have developed into a mutually productive liaison. The new government consulted the association before rewriting the transport legislation and many of the suggestions and recommendations from transport operators represented by the association were accepted and written into the new regulations. This has resulted in improved operating conditions and a break with the 'Hume Highway syndrome' which appears to influence the thinking of legislators in the southern States.

Size and Safety

Undoubtedly the revolutionary principle of a trackless train for remote area operations, exemplified by the government road train in the 1930s, must have had at least a subliminal influence on the thinking of Territory transport operators of the day. It's quite possible they might have developed train-style operations earlier if suitable prime movers with the required power had been available at a price they could afford.

At the end of World War II ex-defence force vehicles of adequate power and acceptable price became available through disposals sales. This was the impetus that was needed to trigger enterprise and launch into the sphere of multi-unit operation.

And 'multi' was the operative adjective. Trains of up to seven unbraked trailers began to appear, hauled by powerful air-braked prime movers at a sedate speed. Dave Baldock's road trains were a sight to behold. Hours would be spent hauling the loaded trailers two at a time out of Alice Springs up through the hills to the start of the flat country about 20 kilometres north of the town where they'd be coupled to the waiting prime mover. They would then weave their way to Tennant Creek at a steady 22 mph as eight army pintle hooks—all with some play in them—and eight flat-plate turntables contributed their bit to directional instability. Overall length would have been well in excess of today's allowable limits and as for axle loads—well it was anyone's guess what they might be. Brakes weren't considered to be necessary; the aim was to go, not to stop. There was no great cause for concern at these shortcomings because traffic was very light in those days and car drivers seemed to have no wish to self-destruct.

Obviously such a laissez-faire situation couldn't be allowed to continue; in fact operators themselves had begun to straighten it out by phasing out their wartime equipment around the mid-'50s. They were given a nudge in the form of a threat to implement the Control of Roads Ordinance which the Northern Territory Legislative Council had passed in 1954 but had not enforced. It would have drastically reduced loads—and carriers' viability—by imposing limits which would have prohibited a body truck (rigid prime mover) pulling more than one trailer, restricting the length of trailers to 30 ft (9.1 metres) and trucks to 31 ft (9.4 m), semi-trailers to 45 ft (13.7 m) and banning trailers behind semis. The overall effect would have been crippling and costs to the industry's clients would have risen dramatically.

In defence of the ordinance the acting administrator of the Northern Territory Mr R. Leydin said at the time that the limits on dimensions and weights had been decided 'after close consideration of the carrying capacity of the highway', but he promised that before fixing the date for introducing the ordinance consideration would be given to representations by the Territory Transport Association and truck owners generally.

Apparently the TTA's case was convincing because the Ordinance limits were still not enforced, although they remained 'on the books', more or less for use as a big stick to keep the industry in line so that it kept to the unofficially agreed upon maxima of 145 feet (44 m) for road trains, 31 feet (9.4 m) per trailer, and 20 feet (6 m) for a dog trailer behind a semi.

But by 1958 officialdom had gained more experience and had become more specific in its requirements. In the public notice columns of the *Centralian Advocate* the following limits were spelt out:

As postwar road trains increased in length and weight, it was inevitable that regulations controlling size and safety would be introduced. Trains of up to seven unbraked trailers, such as the combination pictured here, could have caused problems for operators and other road users alike. *(Peter Ritchie)*

The Territory's road construction authorities must have looked askance at loads such as this in the early '50s. Note the bend in the semi-trailer. *(John Ryan)*

Prime mover	40 ft (12 m)
Articulated vehicle	45 ft (13.7 m)
Self-tracking trailer	55 ft (16.7 m)
Non-self tracking trailer	31 ft (9.4 m)
Trailer (in train of three)	45 ft (13.7 m)
Dog trailer (behind semi)	20 ft (6 m)
Body truck and one trailer	100 ft (30 m)
Body truck and two or three trailers	145 ft (44 m)
Vehicle width	8 ft (2.4 m)
height	14.5 ft (4.3 m)

The fine for exceeding any of the above restrictions was £50.

By 1960 it seemed as though the 'Hume Highway syndrome' was influencing the legislators. It was not beyond the bounds of possibility that they were being 'heavied' by the Australian Transport Advisory Council and its Australian Motor Vehicle Standards Committee which was at that time pushing for nation-wide uniformity—obviously for the sake of uniformity and not necessarily in the best interests of industry efficiency.

The upshot of this pressure was the drafting of a series of amendments to the Control of Roads Ordinance and the appointment of a select committee of the Northern Territory Legislative Council to study and report on the effect of the proposed changes. It must be borne in mind that at this time the Legislative Council was, in effect, controlled by Canberra. It was legislative in name only; strictly speaking it was merely an advisory body to Canberra, hence the eastern States type of thinking in transport matters.

The *Centralian Advocate* of 12 August 1960 ran a front-page story with the banner heading: 'FREIGHTS WOULD RISE BY 130 PER CENT'. It described evidence given by hauliers at hearings of the select committee in Alice Springs. The amendments were designed to restrict the all-up weight of goods vehicles to 30.5 tons, and to severely curtail their size.

Jim McConville (D. R. Baldock & Co.) representing hauliers operating out of Alice Springs told the committee that the proposed amendments would completely dislocate the road transport system and make its operation uneconomical. He pointed out that under the amendment a rigid prime mover (body truck) and two trailers could carry only 11.5 tons payload, and this would have a devastating effect on the transport of copper concentrates from Tennant Creek which was the principal back-loading for Alice Springs operations. He added that the lighter semi-trailer type combination was not economical. Overheads would be increased, and wages would rise about 200 per cent. Road trains were more efficient and more economical, he said.

Len Kittle explained the anomalies arising from the proposed 47-foot overall length limit, particularly with bonneted vehicles. He said that his company was carrying three rail tankers of fuel weekly from Larrimah to the Peko mines. A prime mover and two trailers were used, and if the proposed amendments came into force it would reduce the payload from 10,000 to 2000 gallons (45,460 to 9,092 litres).

John Ryan (Overland Transport) said that freight rates from Alice Springs to Darwin (£22 per ton) were lower than they were seven years ago. This was a big factor in the Territory's economy and had been brought about by heavy investment in vehicles and better management. When the previous ordinance came into force, he said, operators went out of semi-trailers and invested in road trains because they were far more economical. If the proposed amendments were adopted, freight rates would have to be increased by about 130 per cent. He added that a diesel unit with two trailers would cost £15,000 and would only be allowed to carry a payload of ten tons.

Fortunately for the transport industry, common-sense and the public interest prevailed and the restrictions were rejected. Other skirmishes followed from time to time as the transport myrmidons in Canberra, failing to appreciate the unique conditions that prevailed in the Territory, endeavoured to bring Northern Territory transport into line with that which served the more populous areas using roads which carried a much heavier volume of traffic.

As the pace of progress toward self-government in the Territory quickened it could be seen by some of the pragmatists in the industry that if the Territory wasn't to be saddled with regulations that were simply derivatives or clones of other governments' laws, there would have to be some positive moves to get alongside government and assist in a constructive way with the shaping of transport legislation.

Jim Cooper, who led the move to establish the Northern Territory Road Transport Association in 1978, put it this way:

I could see quite plainly that if we didn't get our act together by the time they brought in self government we'd probably find ourselves in much the same position as transport operators in other states. We formed the association a few months before self government came in and then we went to the new government; we informed them that we were representing the transport industry in the Territory and they were very receptive to the idea of sitting around the table with us and framing legislation and regulations that would be appropriate to the unique requirements of the Territory. We didn't want a carbon copy of outmoded state laws which had had the Band-Aid treatment over the past 40 or 50 years.

In July 1978 the Northern Territory threw off the hobbles of remote control and assumed responsibility for its own future. It gained the right to govern itself and with this historic metamorphosis came the opportunity to bring new thinking to bear on transport generally and on road trains in particular. A meddling and uninformed government could have wrecked road transport, on which the Territory depends so much. Fortunately hauliers and legislators in the Territory formed the Road Transport Committee to advise the new government on the framing of regulations which were in step with today's technology and public requirements. The industry gives credit to the common-sense approach of men like Noel McAdie, Brian Webb, Tom Sheppard and Mel Trainer who represented the government on the Road Transport Committee.

It was around this time that the use of triples (prime mover, semi-trailer and two full trailers) was sanctioned. They'd been officially frowned upon for many years; the traditional rigid or 'body' truck prime mover and three full trailers had been favoured. In fact, as late as 1979 triples could only be operated under permit in the Territory and were prohibited north of Katherine (principally because of the narrow, twisting nature of the Stuart Highway in the Pine Creek region) although body trucks and three trailers were allowed to traverse that section.

The new government's Department of Transport and Works eventually sanctioned the use of triples throughout the Territory.

Numerous other recommendations from the Road Transport Committee were accepted and implemented and the result has been one of the most efficient and productive liaisons between industry and government in Australia.

Whilst recognising the unique Territory transport requirements and tailoring regulations to meet them, the Department of Transport and Works has also adhered to the strict safety standards and axle load limitations which have been adopted by all states following the recommendations of such bodies as the National Association of Australian State Road Authorities (NAASRA) and the Office of Road Safety in the Commonwealth Department of Transport.

In broad outline the dimensional limits which are approved in the Northern Territory are:

Road Trains:

Prime mover and three trailers (triple):	50 metres (164 ft)
Rigid vehicle and two or three trailers:	50 metres
Prime mover and two trailers (double):	33 metres (108 ft)
Prime mover and semi-trailer:	17 metres (55.7 ft)
Truck and trailer combination:	17 metres (55.7 ft)

In the Territory, any vehicle longer than 17 metres is classified as a road train.

Other vehicles:

For individual vehicles such as tippers, tray tops, vans, buses, etc., the length limit is 12.2 metres (40 ft) and the maximum length of the semi-trailer portion of an articulated vehicle is restricted to 12.5 m (41 ft). Maximum height for all vehicles is 4.3 metres (14 ft) although a double-deck cattle crate may go to 4.6 metres (15.5 ft). Exhaust stack height is restricted to 4.5 metres (15 ft).

Maximum width for all vehicles is 2.5 metres (8 ft 2½ in.) plus an allowance of 150 mm (6 in.) each side for mirrors on small vehicles and 230 mm (10 in.) each side for vehicles grossing over 8.5 tonnes, provided in the latter case that the mirrors are collapsible.

For road trains there are numerous additional conditions that have to be met in relation to safety,

As the Territory's transport regulatory people and road train operators began to point in the same direction modern well-designed equipment such as this Gardner-powered Foden in the Co-Ord operation replaced the ad hoc combinations of the immediate postwar era. *(Ron Knight)*

TOWARDS THE TWENTY-FIRST CENTURY

Load regulation changes are reflected in the axle spacings on the trailers in this photo. As tighter restrictions were introduced, operators endeavoured to meet them by utilising spread tandems, as seen under two of the trailers. *(Geoff Bullen)*

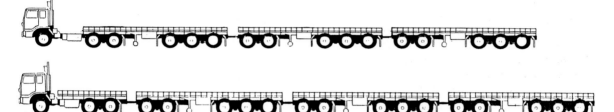

Drawings show (top) a triples combination, consisting of a semi-trailer coupled to two trailers, and (below) the superseded body truck and three trailers which was the original road train concept.

performance, vehicle standards, axle loads and so on. Well and truly gone are the days when it was simply a matter of hooking up as many trailers as the prime mover could haul, or putting on loads that nearly bent the springs double.

Here are some of the special requirements for road trains:

- If grossing more than 42 tonnes a road train prime mover must have bogie-driven axles which are fitted with a locking device for the inter-axle differential (limited slip diffs are not acceptable).

- Road trains must not exceed the gross combination mass or gross road train mass (all-up weight) rated for the prime mover by the manufacturer or calculated by a qualified engineer, and they must be capable of sustaining a speed of 80 km/h when fully laden. Moreover they must be capable of being started from rest, fully loaded, on a 5 per cent gradient. These requirements are aimed at preventing the use of under-capacity prime movers.

- Prime movers are compulsorily limited to a top speed of 85 km/h either by gearing or engine governing. At first this regulation stipulated speed control by gearing, which caused considerable debate about adverse fuel economy particularly when vehicles were running empty, but the problem was eventually resolved to the satisfaction of the Road Transport Committee by adopting the principle of engine governing as a means of controlling road speed.

- All wheels on the train must be braked, and there

are specific requirements for adequate air supply to every axle. Test adaptors are required so that inspectors can check the air brake system at any time. Brake equipment has to comply with Australian Design Rules and the requirements of NAASRA (National Association of Australian State Road Authorities).

- All multi-axle groups must be fitted with load sharing suspension.

- Fifth wheel and turntable assemblies must have manufacturers' ratings for the gross tonnage to be carried, up to a maximum of 120 tonnes. All dolly trailers have to be fitted with turntables carrying manufacturers' appropriate ratings.

- Tow couplings must be of European type such as Ringfeder, Rockinger, etc; they must have a clearly visible safety lock; and clearance between the eye bush and the pin must be no more than 4 mm (0.15 in.).

- In addition there is a rating system for trailers and dollies to ensure that compatible equipment of adequate capacity is used in road train combinations.

- A Class 3 trailer or dolly is 'top of the grades'. It can be used anywhere in a triple, double or single road train combination. It usually has a three-axle rear bogie arrangement and must be fitted with a rated kingpin and a 90 mm European-type tow coupling. Dollies in this class must have a turntable capable of accepting rated kingpins and, of course, must have brakes on all wheels.

- Class 2 trailers can only be used in the No. 2 or No.

SIZE AND SAFETY

3 position in a road train. They ordinarily have two rear axles and the kingpin and tow coupling requirements are 50 mm.

- A Class 1 trailer, which is defined as a semi-trailer or a dog trailer with fixed dolly, without a European-type tow coupling or with no tow coupling at all, or is built of fibreglass (as some fridge vans are), is restricted to the No. 3 (last) position in a road train.

In other words, trailers are rated for their suitability for use in a combination and in what position they may be used. A label attached to the number plate identifies each trailer's category and this facilitates policing of the system.

Vehicle safety standards, important as they are, have to be complemented by safe driving practices and on the recommendation of the Road Transport Committee higher grades of licences have been introduced as a means of inculcating in road train drivers the need for a professional approach to their job.

A C5 licence is the top category. Typical of the close working relationship between the industry and government is the fact that an applicant for a C5 licence is given a practical driving test by one of an authorised panel of driver examiners from the transport industry. For other licence categories Department of Transport and Works inspectors test all applicants. A C4 licence is issued to drivers who pass the departmental test on double bottoms, a C3 to semi-trailer and truck-and-trailer drivers, and a C2 to tyros and others capable of handling trucks, vans, etc. at the lighter end of the commercial vehicle scale. In the change-over to the new system current road train drivers were awarded a C5 upon production of a satisfactory report from their employers as to proficiency standards. But others have to achieve the 'top ticket' by moving up through the various licence stages after gaining experience in each classification.

In its Guide to Vehicle Limitations and Safety Requirements, the Department of Transport and Works says:

The heavy vehicle driver in the Northern Territory has advantages over his counterparts in other States. In order to preserve these advantages and prevent injuries and death on the road, it is in the interests of all transport drivers to recognise the important role they have to play.

The Northern Territory has a good record with respect to accidents involving heavy vehicles. The most common accident is caused by Mr Average attempting to pass a road train without ensuring he has sufficient room to do so, or the same Mr Average with his caravan in tow claiming his right to the bitumen. He does not know that the vehicle coming towards him can have an all-up weight of 115 tonnes. Given these situations the professionalism shown by heavy vehicle drivers

makes the difference between disaster and a 'near miss' situation.

A leaflet circulated through Territory information and travel centres and Department of Transport offices warns motorists to be alert to the difference between road trains and other vehicles they've been used to encountering:

When behind a road train remember. . . sections of the Stuart and Barkly Highways are 4 metres wide. Road trains are 2.4 metres wide. That doesn't leave much room for you!

On narrow sections, soft and loose gravel edges make overtaking road trains especially dangerous. From the time you start to overtake you will probably travel about three-quarters of a kilometre before you are completely past.

Be patient. The road train driver will make room for you when it is safe.

That leaflet is sponsored by one of the Territory's large operators, Northern Territory Freight Services, in conjunction with the Road Safety Council of the Northern Territory.

In addition to encouraging motorists to adopt a more responsible attitude to driving it also highlights the unique nature of transport operations in the Northern Territory.

Western Australia

In Western Australia five combinations of road trains are approved for operation on designated roads under permits issued by the Main Roads Department. They are:

Prime mover and three trailers (triple bottom)	50 metres (164 ft)
Rigid vehicle ('body truck') and three trailers	50 metres
Rigid vehicle and two trailers	44 metres (144.3 ft)
Articulated vehicle plus one trailer (double)	33 metres (108.2 ft)
Rigid vehicle plus two trailers	33 metres

Fifty metre triples and rigid-and-three combinations are confined to the area north of a line drawn from Carnarvon to Meekatharra and Leonora. South of Carnarvon and Meekatharra 33-metre doubles are permitted to operate to Upper Swan on the outskirts of Perth. In addition 33-metre doubles can use a limited network of specified roads in other parts of the State, particularly in the south-east where there are big movements of livestock, grain and fertiliser. As in the Territory, the maximum length of the semi-trailer and trailer portions of road trains is 12.5 metres.

Mechanical requirements for road trains in Western Australia include assessment of appropriate power and gearing for specific transport tasks; for example, livestock carriers are restricted to a maximum laden geared speed of 95 km/h. The prime mover must have a tandem-drive axle with provision for inter-axle locking regardless of whether limited slip devices are incorporated.

Western Australia's Main Roads Department specifies that turntables be either the ballrace or stabiliser plate type (or equivalent) and that turntable kingpins and trailer towbar eyes meet specified standards. All-up weight limits are more liberal than in the Territory. Gross combination mass for a rigid prime mover plus three trailers is 124.5 tonnes; this can be increased to 136 tonnes with the provision of load sharing steer axles and the inclusion of tri-axles. Similarly the GCM allowance for a triple, normally 104.4 tonnes, goes to 119.5 tonnes under the same conditions.

There is a requirement that road trains stop at least once every hour on the hour for a minimum of five minutes to allow following traffic to go past. Road trains must not overtake each other when in motion.

For livestock combinations there is a further requirement that on roads where the speed limit is in excess of 60 km/h a road train shall, when following another vehicle more than eight metres in length, be kept more than 200 metres behind the other vehicle.

South Australia

Although South Australian regulations make provision for 50 metre triples and rigid-and-three-trailer combinations, road trains in that State are effectively confined to doubles and rigid-and-two-trailers by means of a system of approved routes on which only 35-metre combinations may operate.

When this chapter was written the final section of the new Stuart Highway had been bitumen-sealed near Marla and the limited use of triples between the South Australian border and Port Augusta was being considered by the Highways Department. However, from Port Augusta southwards to Adelaide only semi-trailers are permitted to operate, thus in reality restricting multi-unit vehicles to the north of the State.

In common with other States and the Northern Territory, South Australia requires that a road train prime mover must not be capable of a speed greater than 85 km/h and where the gross combination mass (all-up weight) is in excess of 42 tonnes it must have tandem drive axles with inter-axle locking. Maximum gross weight for doubles in South Australia is 79 tonnes.

Road train trailers must not move more than 100 mm to either side of the line of the prime mover when travelling on a straight road.

As in Western Australia road trains in South Australia travelling on roads where the speed limit is in excess of 60 km/h must keep more than 200 metres

behind any vehicle which is more than eight metres long.

There are, of course, specific standards laid down for braking, kingpin strength and numerous other safety factors which correspond with standards observed by regulatory authorities throughout Australia.

Queensland

In general terms 49-metre triple bottoms or 44-metre rigid-and-two-trailer combinations may be operated east of the Northern Territory border throughout what is basically the western region of Queensland, as far as a line drawn from Mt Garnet through Charters Towers, Clermont, Charleville, Cunnamulla and Hungerford on the New South Wales border.

However, in that region there are several designated roads on which only 33-metre doubles or 28-metre rigid-and-one-trailer combinations are allowed. In various other parts of the State, the Main Roads Department approves the use of two-unit road trains but elsewhere, such as in the more populous areas, semi-trailers or truck-and-trailer combinations are the largest vehicles permitted.

There are specific requirements detailing the pulling power of road train prime movers and they must be governed to a maximum speed of 85 km/h. The MRD requires that all prime movers pulling road trains grossing more than 42 tonnes must have tandem drive rear axles. Trailers are given ratings according to their structural strength and kingpin size and there are strictures on the positions in a road train configuration in which variously rated trailers may be coupled. In other words, trailers must be coupled so that the lightest unit is at the rear of the train, and the strongest up front.

As in most States there's a proscription that 'ROAD TRAIN' warning signs 'must not be displayed on vehicles that are not coupled together as a road train'. This is obviously aimed at the 'cowboy' element who get rather carried away driving rigs which, whilst they're bigger than the majority of other road vehicles, are less than one-third the length of an outback road train.

New South Wales

In New South Wales the Department of Motor Transport approves the operation under permit of 35-metre doubles west of a line taken from the Queensland border at Mungindi through Walgett, Byrock, Cobar and Ivanhoe to the Victorian border at Wentworth. At Hungerford, north of Bourke, a third trailer can be added for the haul through the western Queensland region and into the Northern Territory.

There are, of course, regulations relating to the safety, mechanical, dimensional and weight aspects similar to those applying in other States and the Northern Territory.

In the United States of America and in Canada the use of triples is confined to specified four-lane highways in a small number of states and provinces. Doubles are permitted but these do not enjoy the same length allowances as in Australia. For instance, the most 'generous' U.S. state is Wyoming, which allows 88-foot (27 m) doubles, and in Alberta and British Columbia (Canada) there are 'Rocky Mountain Doubles' which consist of a 14-metre articulated unit with 12-metre dog trailer. In Australia the limits on doubles range between 33 and 35 metres.

Railway Metamorphosis

Over a period of 70-odd years at least 22 reports and studies of transport in the Northern Territory have been made—and pigeonholed—and the majority of these have found against the likelihood of any economic benefits stemming from the expansion of railways. Some, of course, did favour rail for social, defence and developmental reasons; in fact lines branching from the recommended north–south route to such places as Camooweal (Qld) and Bourke (N.S.W.), to the Pellews in the Gulf of Carpentaria and across to Wyndham and other places in Western Australia, to provide a network of interstate services, were suggested by various official bodies and individuals who had been given the task of studying and prescribing for the Territory's future economic benefit. But nothing came of them, and road transport continued to not only bridge the north–south gap but also develop subsidiary routes which cover the entire Northern Territory and provide interstate links which criss-cross the continent in all directions.

An announcement in 1980 that the Federal Liberal government had approved a survey and preliminary

In the early days of the coordinated rail–road service just about every ton of freight was manually transferred from train to truck and vice-versa. Copper concentrate from Tennant Creek is shown in this photo being manhandled from a Baldock road train to railway wagons alongside. *(K. Moody)*

planning for a rail line from Alice Springs to Darwin may have caused some apprehension among road train operators, particularly those whose activities hinged around road–rail interchange, but a later Labor government turned thumbs down on the project and a subsequent inquiry in 1984 into the prospects of such a line by the then chief executive of the State Rail Authority of New South Wales, Mr David Hill, reinforced this decision and found, inter alia, that for the projected traffic levels the total cost of transporting freight and passengers by rail would exceed the cost of accomplishing the same task by road by a large margin.

Among the principal findings of the Hill Inquiry it was stated that

economic analysis revealed that in present value terms the project would have a direct cost of $516 million and direct benefits of $142 million. This would mean that . . . it would cost an additional $374 million to transport the projected traffic by rail rather than by road.

The freight and passenger flows projected for the railway in the 1990s could be carried by 130 heavy trucks and 20 buses—a total of 150 vehicles. The total outlay on the railway construction, rolling stock and equipment and interest payments would represent an investment of $5 million for every truck and bus the railway would displace from the Stuart Highway. While there would be some subsequent savings in line-haul costs of the railway compared with trucks, these savings are quite small in relation to the investment required for each truck and bus removed by the railway.

A submission by the Queensland government contended that, relative to the construction of a rail link between Alice Springs and Darwin, 'the development of the Barkly Highway, together with a rail link between Tennant Creek and Mt Isa, would give benefits to many more Australians. And these benefits could be acquired more economically and efficiently.'

The overwhelming majority of views put to the Inquiry was in favour of a railway; in fact, 91 per cent of representations were 'for' the railway line.

The road transport industry as such did not present a case either way. As one operator told the writer, he saw the possibility of a through-rail link between Alice Springs and Darwin as being advantageous for the Northern Territory's economy in the long term, but in the short term it could have some harmful effects on the line haul operations, particularly those running up and down the Stuart Highway.

However, assuming that establishment of a railway service would result in lower freight rates, it could enhance the prospects of numerous potential mining and other projects which had been the subject of feasibility studies but had been shelved because of transport costs. Then, instead of the major road transport movement being north–south it would be east–west, serving new industries and feeding to and from points on the rail line.

The Northern Territory Government's enthusiasm for a transcontinental line to the north apparently was not shared by the Australian National Railways Commission whose name was missing from the list of organisations and individuals who submitted presentations to the Hill Inquiry. No doubt ANR's attitude was that it had had a long and costly experience in serving the Territory in the days when the service was operated by Commonwealth Railways, and it had trimmed and tightened its operations to reduce its annual deficit and would not be at all keen about taking on a project of doubtful financial expectation.

The origin of Comrails' Central Australia Railway troubles could be traced back 40 years when the early railway engineers apparently 'guesstimated' that the furnace-red land through which the line was constructed was drought country and consequently there was no need for ballast; they simply laid the sleepers and rails on the ground. They didn't realise that they'd located the line in one of the most flood-prone regions in Australia and this wrong guess was a formidable contributor to the misfortunes that befell the train service during its lifetime. Additional complications included the inconvenience of freight and passenger transfers at break-of-gauge points and the use of light rails which limited the weight and length and speed of trains. It was a railway which renowned British cartoonist Roland Emmett would have enjoyed.

Since 1929 it had served wayside settlements with such euphonious names as Oodnadatta, Rumbalara, Ooraminna, and Abminga, as well as those with anglicised appellations like Deep Well, where Kurt Johannsen was born; Finke, named after one of John McDouall Stuart's expedition patrons; Strangways Springs, commemorating the Hon. H. B. T. Strangways who was instrumental in inducing the South Australian Parliament to agree to the construction of the Overland Telegraph Line. Abminga, incidentally, was the unloading point for the supplies and equipment carried on Dr C. T. Madigan's crossing of the Simpson Desert from west to east in 1939.

In the late 1960s the Central Australia Railway, on which the co-ordinated road service depended, was beginning to show disturbing signs of strain as more and more pressure was placed on it by the increasing volume of freight moving to and from the Territory.

The reality of the situation was outlined in a report to the federal government in 1968 by the then commissioner for Commonwealth Railways, Mr Keith Smith, who said that the line between Oodnadatta and Alice Springs, which was completed in 1929, was constructed to 'extremely poor engineering standards'. It was laid with 60 lb (27 kg) rails on timber sleepers, was not ballasted, and crossed most rivers on its route by means of low stone embankments:

It is a pioneer railway in every sense of the term, but it has outlived its claim to be a useful asset in a modern world and can be fairly classed as an operating and economic embarrassment...and a hazard to the security and natural development of Alice Springs, its hinterland and the country north to Darwin.

He strongly recommended relocating the route 150 miles to the west on a flood-free alignment from Tarcoola, on the Transcontinental Line, to Alice Springs. At the time he was no doubt strongly influenced in his thinking by severe disruptions to services caused by floods and washaways in 1967 and 1968, which were in addition to other lesser troubles which plagued the system.

Up north the North Australia Railway was in similar difficulties. Although it had been significant in the development of the Top End from the time the first section from Darwin to Pine Creek was opened in 1889 and had carried phenomenal traffic (up to 147 trains a week) during World War II, its usefulness in the postwar years was declining, despite efforts by its parent, Commonwealth Railways, to bolster its productivity by means of the coordinated road and rail service. It too, like the CAR, was causing trouble for the operators of the connecting road services.

In 1950 the total of all rail freight moving through Alice Springs in both directions was just over 39,000 tonnes. By 1968, with six freight trains a week arriving and departing, the throughput was 149,512 tonnes. Of this, 58,272 southbound tonnes were handled, and this figure included 33,590 tonnes of copper ore from the Peko Mines.

It was a gloomy picture that the Comrails Annual Report painted in the year 1973–74:

It is depressing to record that traffic levels declined to a marked degree on the Central Australia Railway and the North

Australia Railway and that this was brought about solely by disastrous floods...which caused the railway between Stirling North and Alice Springs to be closed for a total period of nine weeks and brought about the cancellation of 126 scheduled freight trains. There were no through services between January 13 and March 16 1974.

The prolonged Wet season also knocked out the Stuart Highway for long periods (see chapter, Lifeline of the North) in the first half of 1974, and the second half of that year came to a disastrous climax with Cyclone Tracy ripping through and devastating Darwin. For the 12 months to 30 June 1974, the CAR moved 184,978 tonnes of freight. Piggyback traffic totalled 5,888 tonnes and the figure for coordinated road-rail freight was 40,017 tonnes.

It was around this time that freight movement through Queensland began to increase as Territory businesspeople sought ways of overcoming the problems created by the unreliability of the railway. This, of course, aggravated Comrails' difficulties and affected the traditional freight flow from the south via Alice Springs.

Troubles persisted. The first report by the new management of the CAR, Australian National Railways, covering the 1975–76 fiscal year, stated that floods and washaways along the line and flooding of the Stuart Highway at Newcastle Waters led to 'a decrease of almost 20 per cent in the tonnage of through goods traffic conveyed, compared with 1974–75. Road freight services from Mt Isa to Larrimah and from Alice Springs to Wyndham and Kununurra were discontinued.'

In 1976 two significant events marked a turning point in railway fortunes and activities in the Territory, with consequent influence on road transport operations: the North Australia Railway was closed down and work began on the construction of a standard gauge (1.4 metre) line from the south via Tarcoola to Alice Springs.

With the closure of the Larrimah–Darwin line Co-Ord services were able to operate direct by road from Alice Springs to Darwin—something that hauliers would have preferred all along. More or less stating the obvious, the ANR's Annual Report for 1977–78 recorded that 'transit times between Alice Springs and Darwin have shown a marked improvement', and added that the coordinated service had handled 26,000 tonnes of freight between these two centres during the year.

The ANR was an anachronism and its troubles were compounded by being distant from the seat of railway administration in Adelaide and from the funding source in Canberra. It was simply allowed to wither on the vine.

With the commencement of work on the new line from Tarcoola the ANR management must have been collectively praying for the day it would be completed so that it could stop the rot in its services caused by the deteriorating condition of the old line.

As soon as the new line reached Kulgera, in February 1980, Australian National put in a temporary terminal there with gantry cranes and vehicle ramps and began operating freight trains to and from that point whilst at the same time reducing the number of trains on the ageing narrow gauge Marree–Alice Springs line to four a week.

With the new line came indications of a changing trend. The ANR's Annual Report for 1979–80 had this to say: 'Traffic through the [new Kulgera] terminal is predominantly pick-a-back units, driven off rail flat cars. Large numbers of containers are also handled.' And again: 'A further 18,000 tonnes . . .was largely new traffic generated in response to a marketing drive'.

The new line from the south was opened to Alice Springs in December 1980 and simultaneously the interchange facilities between road and rail at the Alice Springs terminal were expanded and modernised.

It was no doubt with a great sense of relief that the new ANR Chairman, Mr L. E. Marks, announced in the Annual Report for 1980–81 that the Marree-Alice Springs line had been closed on 31 December 1980. He said that there had been a substantial increase in the volume of rail traffic on the new line. In the 1978–79 financial year, which was the last full year of operation on the old narrow-gauge line, north-bound freight into Alice Springs totalled 113,500 tonnes. In the 1980–81

A view of portion of the Alice Springs rail yard as seen by the operator of the overhead gantry which traverses several tracks. *(Australian National Railways)*

Most freight from the south comes into Alice Springs in semi-trailer pantechnicons 'piggybacked' on Australian National flatcars. *(Australian National Railways)*

Containers are still widely used for incoming and outgoing freight, and Australian National's travelling gantry transfers them to and from road vehicles. *(Australian National Railways)*

Pipes for oil and gas lines in the Territory are 'palleted' for easy transfer to waiting road train trailers at Alice Springs. *(Australian National Railways)*

financial year north-bound freight was 219,500 tonnes, an increase of 93.3 per cent over a two-year period.

'There are opportunities for even greater levels of traffic on this route,' said Mr Marks, 'and the direction of ANR's marketing thrust into the Northern Territory is an important part of our planning process.'

Lou Marks, who was also chairman of the Commonwealth Government's Transport Industry Advisory Council, came from a private enterprise road transport background. In the 1950s he was driving four-cylinder Albion prime movers with semi-trailers for Collier's Interstate Transport in the eastern States earning £15 a week. He was featured in a magazine in the Melbourne *Herald* written by the late John Hetherington, a well-known author.

Lou Marks' career in road transport was a success story in itself, and culminated in his being appointed a director of the national and international multi-modal transport group, Brambles Industries Ltd.

Around the time of Mr Marks' appointment ANR's business image began to change and phrases like 'commercial enterprise' and 'corporate objectives' began to appear in the commission's reports and that overworked word 'coordination' which should have really been 'coercion' in many instances back in the '50s and '60s was replaced by '80s language such as 'intermodal traffic' and similar.

Ten years down the track Australian National was reporting 251,600 tonnes of piggyback freight carried between South Australia and the Northern Territory, an increase of 27 per cent over the previous year. In the following 12 months (to June 1986) this traffic moved up another 19 per cent to over 300,000 tonnes. In addition, 42,500 tonnes of freight forwarder traffic were handled in 1984–85 and 36,400 tonnes in 1985–86. The 1986 report notes:

Based on American experience we expect the intermodal business to be the mainstay of ANR's business growth over the next five years. Progress during the year included express freight services to Alice Springs, new trailer handling terminals at Islington and Alice Springs and a 'piggypacker' for lifting trailers at each terminal, and strengthening of our customers' road trailers to allow them to be lifted by the piggypackers.

In ANR terminology, intermodal business includes forwarding agents' consignments, containers, wagons on annual hire, piggyback traffic, and direct customer vanloads. The system has changed completely since the early days of the coordinated service when every consignment was handled manually. This traffic, known

Loaded trailers are lifted on and off rail flatcars by the giant 'piggypacker' shown here. Piggypackers at Alice Springs and Adelaide freight terminals have speeded-up freight movements. Previously specially designed prime movers were used to pull the trailers off the trains and deposit them on the adjacent hard-standing. *(Australian National Railways)*

TOWARDS THE TWENTY-FIRST CENTURY

in railway parlance as 'lcl' (less-than-carload) accounts for little more than 6 per cent of ANR's freight business.

Lingering still in the minds of many Territorians, especially those at government level, is the hope that some day soon there'll be a transcontinental rail line crossing the Territory from south to north. As this book was nearing completion the Northern Territory government had been presented with an economic study by Canadian Pacific Consulting Services which was said to prove the financial viability of constructing such a line. The government's response was so enthusiastic that it was casting around for venture capital to fund the project and run it as a private enterprise operation.

The government contended that the line would not rely entirely on Northern Territory traffic, as had been considered in the Hill report; a big selling point would be that of a 'land bridge' operation from Darwin to Sydney, Melbourne and Adelaide for container traffic and motor car imports, shortening the sailing time for overseas shipping between their home ports and Australia by days. The government has ploughed millions of dollars into the upgrading of the port of Darwin and this investment is expected to not only encourage 'land bridge' thinking but also to lead to greatly enhanced trade between Australia and its northern neighbours.

In the meantime there would appear to be little cause for discomfort among hauliers, as history has a habit of repeating itself.

An Australian National train coming through Heavitree Gap at Alice Springs with a mixed load of trailers and prime movers which will form road trains for the journey to Darwin and other destinations in the Top End. *(Australian National Railways)*

And Then There Was One

Cooperative business activities between government and private enterprise are rare, and even rarer are those between railways and road transport operators. But in the Northern Territory interaction between rail and road not only resulted in the adoption of the road train as the basis of the Territory's transport system; it also led to the formation of a company which is still to the fore in the road–rail transport scene, although its ownership structure has changed over the years.

Known originally as the Co-Ord and now named Co-Ord Transport Pty Ltd, it was formed in 1950 as the operating arm of the Territory Transport Association (see chapter, Organising the Unorganised) to carry out the contract for a co-ordinated road and rail service to bridge the railless gap between Alice Springs and Larrimah. It was formed with ten principal shareholders each holding one £10 share.

It was agreed at the time that in any disposal of shares they were to be offered in the first instance to existing shareholders. This was aimed at preventing infiltration and possible later domination by one or more of the large interstate transport operators. This rule was successful to a point; whilst it kept out the big forwarders it allowed in a 'local' operation which was, in fact, owned by a large transport and quarrying group in the eastern States and which eventually (in 1976) became the sole operator in Co-Ord. This was Fleet Owners Pty Ltd, owned by one of the best known but least publicised families in the transport and quarrying industries in the eastern states, the O'Neils, who at the time also owned Diesel Motors Pty Ltd, which was Australian factory representative and distributor for Foden vehicles, with agencies in all States and the Northern Territory. Another of the O'Neil's major business ventures was Australian Blue Metal Ltd, which used a large fleet of Foden vehicles in its quarrying and associated transport operations.

The founder of Fleet Owners, Mr Les O'Neil, could see the potential for road transport in the Northern Territory. His initial venture was in cattle transport in the early '50s in the Top End but his interest changed to general freight as the coordinated road-rail service got under way. It was widely thought at the time that whilst TTA operators may not have wanted a big firm in their organisation, railways commissioner Pat Hannaberry certainly did as he thought that the managerial and operational expertise of a successful and efficient company from what is vaguely termed in the Territory 'the south' would effectively strengthen both the TTA, and as a consequence Hannaberry's

brainchild, the coordinated road–rail service.

By 1963 Fleet Owners had acquired 50 per cent of the shareholding in Co-Ord. They'd bought out Lackman Agencies, Percy Colson, Len Tuit and Stan Cawood. Stan owned two shares, having earlier acquired Kittle Bros' quota in the Co-Ord operation. In 1966 D. R. Baldock & Co. became a Fleet Owners subsidiary and in 1973 Kittle Bros' tanker business (not in Co-Ord) was purchased and re-named Red North.

During the late 1960s and early 1970s Buntine Roadways gradually took over the remaining companies until the point was reached where Fleet Owners and Buntine each owned 50 per cent of Co-Ord. Then in 1976 Buntine sold to Fleet Owners, resulting in the whole Co-Ord operation coming under one owner.

Although some might have said it grudgingly, most of the original Co-Ord shareholders would have had to admit that the influence of the O'Neils brought a new level of thinking and operational expertise into the organisation. They showed what better equipment and sound management techniques could do and in turn the Co-Ord as a group was able to meet the standards of service demanded by Comrails and at the same time cope with an increasing volume of business and meet the pressure of keen competition from independent hauliers.

In 1963, as Co-Ord's business was climbing toward its peak, Fleet Owners had nine road trains, five of which were hauled by Fodens and four by Internationals. Four of the Fodens and two of the Internationals were powered by Cummins engines, and at the time the O'Neil interests in the Territory included sales and service facilities for Cummins and Internationals as well as Foden.

At a later stage the company introduced Macks in its fleet and finally went all-Kenworth. From the 150 bhp Gardners the company moved up to 175 and 220 bhp Cummins engines and today the power specification is 450 bhp and the motive power is Caterpillar.

From time to time the O'Neil family has been represented in the Territory by Denis, Colin and Gary (sons of Les) as resident directors of Fleet Owners. Among the managers who have guided the company's operations have been Don Merz, Michael Hughes and Peter Gunner. At one stage Peter Gunner was managing three O'Neil businesses—Fleet Owners, Baldocks and Red North—as well as being a member of the Alice Springs Town Management Board.

When Gary O'Neil returned to the O'Neils' Hy-Mix

Peter Baldwin.

Fleet Owners Pty Ltd was an early shareholder in the Co-Ord and after using Foden vehicles and then Internationals for many years the company adopted Mack as its principal road train power unit. *(Ken Moody)*

headquarters in Sydney in 1981 Peter Baldwin was appointed operations manager of Co-Ord Transport and Red North Trucking, with Ken Moody as Northern Territory sales manager.

Peter Baldwin has been associated with long-distance transport since 1981. He joined the interstate side of the business in what might be termed 'the fast lane'—driving for outfits engaged on overnight parcels express and newspaper distribution work up and down the Hume Highway, as well as a stint with the then-fledgling Kwikasair Express between Adelaide and Melbourne.

He gravitated to larger equipment moving at a more sedate pace when he joined East Coast Transport which was a Mayne Nickless subsidiary and later transferred to another MN company, Intermodal, where he became operations manager for the busy Intermodal branch at Morwell in Victoria.

When he moved from Morwell to the climatically opposite Alice Springs, Co-Ord Transport was running triples between Alice Springs and Katherine. Due to the restrictions on the operation of road trains north of Katherine, particularly in the hilly, twisting section of

the highway in the Pine Creek region, these units had to be reduced to doubles at Katherine, which in turn involved the operation of a shuttle between there and Darwin.

With the opening of the new Pine Creek section of the Stuart Highway at the end of 1982, triples were permitted to run right through to Darwin and that of course led to much improved efficiency and the company was able to trim back its trailer inventory.

Down through the 1970s the TTA-controlled Co-Ord had undergone considerable contraction of business due to a number of factors, and although the decline in road–rail traffic was felt by Fleet Owners its effect was minimised by the company's policy of concentrating on a core fleet and augmenting it with sub-contractors to meet fluctuations in demand. In 1973 the company had astutely diversified into liquid cartage operations by acquiring Kittle Bros' road tanker business; previously it had picked up D. R. Baldock & Co., which had a valuable copper ore cartage and general freight business between Alice Springs and Tennant Creek.

Another element which reduced the impact of a changing freight market was the transformation that

While body trucks pulling two and three trailers were the standard road train equipment, Fleet Owners continued to use Macks on line haul work between Alice Springs and Darwin. *(S. Reed)*

Red North is Co-Ord Transport's tanker operation. It was originally Kittle Bros whose tanker business was acquired in 1973. Caterpillar-powered Kenworths are used on this and Co-Ord Transport's line-haul freight operations. *(Peter Baldwin)*

came over vehicle technology and regulations in the '70s which led to a much improved capacity factor. The 60-tonne combinations of the Foden era were replaced by units grossing 115 tonnes and tankers carrying upwards of 100,000 litres. This was also the phase-out period of the body-truck prime mover and the replacement of the traditional body-and-three road train composition by the more economically viable and cost-efficient triple trailer set-up and conventional prime mover.

When Peter Baldwin came on the road train scene, freight movement had been going through yet another evolutionary stage. Back in the 1950s containers had completely changed the Territory freight scene. Thirty years later containers were being superseded (but not entirely replaced) by trailers piggy-backed on railway flatcars. And even the railway line to Alice Springs had been replaced, or, to be more accurate, had been rerouted and upgraded to first-class standard-gauge track, replacing the rapidly deteriorating narrow-gauge line which had served the Territory for just on 50 years.

The new line was opened in December 1980 and to match the accelerated trend toward the use of piggy-backed pantechnicons and other trailer equipment by transport companies, forwarders and wholesalers, the interchange facilities for road and rail at Alice Springs terminal were expanded and modernised.

Late in 1985 Australian National added to its handling facilities at Alice Springs and Adelaide high-capacity lifters which remove loaded trailers and pantechnicons from rail flat cars and deposit them alongside on the hard standing to await assembly into road train combinations. This equipment has greatly accelerated the movement of piggyback vehicles which previously were removed by 'yard goat' prime movers pulling them off flatcars and reversing them into parked positions, or (when loading them onto trains) reversing them along the full length of the string of rail flat cars.

In 1987 six piggyback trains a week were arriving at and departing from Alice Springs, in addition to numerous trains carrying crude oil from the Mereenie field and cattle from all parts of the Territory. Some of these trains consisted of up to 70 bogie vehicles and were 1,500 metres long.

Co-Ord Transport is still very much in the thick of the action and is still a household name in the Territory. Coordinated road–rail freight would probably represent less than one-tenth of the volume it did thirty years ago; today the company's predominant business is moving loads for freight forwarders and pulling trailers for various consignors.

The fleet inventory is six Kenworth prime movers with 450 bhp Caterpillar V8 engines, and 32 trailers, all 12 metres long, 27 of which are five-axled units and five with four axles (close bogies). Five sub-contractors' prime movers are also used to pull Co-Ord Transport trailers as well as their own units.

Red North's register includes three Kenworths, 13 tri-axle tankers and for both fleets there are 29 of those all-important converter dollies which Northern Territory road train operators use to convert semi-trailers to full trailers.

While all those individuals who played a role in the Co-Ord operation down through the years have left the industry, the O'Neil dynasty has endured, which is a tribute to the business acumen and flexibility of this family company's management.

And. . . something else that has endured is the red-and-white colour scheme of the company's vehicles, which was adopted originally by the Territory Transport Association in the 1950s to 'coordinate' with that of the Commonwealth Railways' diesel locomotives and rolling stock at the time.

Today and Tomorrow

Apart from Co-Ord Transport there's scarcely a trace in today's busy transport scene of the people or companies of the 1950s who established the road train as the Territory's principal freight and cattle transport medium.

The pioneer truck operators of prewar days who became the postwar road train tyros have moved off the stage and in doing so they've left behind a legacy which in its physical form is regarded with fascination and a degree of envy by transport operators elsewhere in the world and with awe and grudging respect by other road users in this country.

Through their efforts and the energies of those who have followed them road transport has shared in the economic growth of the Northern Territory.

Evidence of this is to be seen everywhere, every day; strings of cattle road trains move livestock to railyards, abattoirs and sea ports as well as to destinations across the borders of Queensland and Western Australia.

Fleets of road tankers owned by oil companies and independent operators keep up fuel supplies to the mines, various industries, airports, fuel depots and roadside service stations as well as moving crude oil from the Territory's Mereenie field.

In the big railyard at Alice Springs lines of piggyback rail wagons bring in pantechnicons and containers bearing the logos of national companies such as TNT, Railex, Ansett Freight Express, Ansett Wridgway, Southern Cross Van Lines, Woolies, Coles, Arrow Freight Lines, Brambles and many others, as well as those belonging to Northern Territory Freight Service and the Fadelli Bros of Tennant Creek, plus tarpaulined flat-tops for a myriad consignors and consignees.

Prime movers owned by Territory companies and owner-drivers and sub-contractors move in and assemble the units into road trains to be hauled to destinations throughout the Territory.

Up at the Top End, fuel coming into Darwin from overseas is distributed throughout the Territory by road tankers. Shell's fleet of seven triples—the largest oil company tanker operation in the Territory—provides a picture of 1980s transport technology and working conditions.

Each of Shell's road trains has a capacity of 100,000 litres although actual loads vary according to product: up to 105,000 litres of aviation gasoline can be accommodated as it is relatively light, but diesel fuel, being heavier, reduces volume to around 95,000 litres.

The company's tanker fleet is used principally to haul between Darwin and Alice Springs with some trips extended to Yulara, and from Darwin to Jabiru for the Ranger mining operation. Occasionally a Shell road train is dispatched to Kununurra in Western Australia. On the Darwin–Alice run the tankers also discharge fuel at various Shell roadside stations such as Dunmarra, Three Ways and Tennant Creek.

Shell has a preference for Mack prime movers in the Territory. They're the Superliner model (R721RS) with

Shots of Alice Springs railyard showing pantechnicons belonging to well-known national companies lined up ready to be assembled into road trains for the journey north. Many of these are hauled by prime movers by owner-drivers.

16.4 litre Mack V8 engine producing 343kW (460 bhp). A nine-speed Mack gearbox is preferred to a splitter-type transmission because of more favourable fuel economy and better drive axle tyre wear, as well as being less complicated from the drivers' viewpoint. Otherwise Shell's Macks are of standard specification.

However, the braking system for each triple has undergone modification by Shell transport engineers, with the result that these 50 metre, 115 tonne, 62-wheel rigs can be stopped in their own length without skid or axle-hop when moving at 70 km/h.

Each prime mover carries 1,400 litres in four fuel tanks; this quantity doesn't get the vehicle to Alice Springs and back so the tanks are usually topped up at one of the company's retail outlets on the return journey.

Two drivers are assigned to each road train; one takes it to Alice Springs and back, and on his return four days later the other does the next run down The Track. A sleeper cab is provided on each vehicle for drivers' use whilst away from base.

The driver's cabin of each prime mover is equipped with air conditioning, AM/FM radio, tape player and a small fridge. Each vehicle has a CB radio so that drivers can talk to their colleagues or other road train

drivers along the highway. The cab instrumentation is the usual Mack equipment, plus a fuel pressure gauge and a turbo boost gauge. In addition there's a handbrake interlock device linked with the power take-off as a safety measure. The company does not fit tachograph recorders to any of its road trains.

In busy times a Shell road train can be turned round in Darwin in under four hours; in other words it can be filled with product, undergo a basic maintenance check and be on its way south with a fresh driver in less than half a working day. After four return trips to Alice Springs the units enter the terminal workshop for a 12,000-kilometre service. The emphasis is on preventive maintenance to ensure top mechanical fitness because apart from any other consideration it can be an expensive exercise attending a breakdown hundreds of kilometres down the road.

Driving an oil company road train is regarded as the 'cream' of the transport driving jobs in the Territory. Handling a $500,000 triple bottom with at least $50,000 worth of product earns a Shell driver between $1,000 and $1,500 a week.

Since gaining self-government the Territory's population has grown at four times the national rate, the workforce has expanded by 40 per cent and many new commercial ventures have been established. The Territory's big pastoral industry is being complemented by a developing agricultural industry which has begun supplying vegetables and fruit to the local market as well as to Western Australia, South Australia, Hong Kong, Singapore and Brunei.

In addition to having a major share of world uranium, manganese and bauxite reserves, the Northern Territory also has large undeveloped deposits of lead, zinc, oil, gas, gold, copper and other minerals.

Owner-driver Laurie Pearson is one of a large number of self-employed operators upon whom the transport industry depends to move much of its freight. His Western Star rig is shown on a south-bound trip hauling empty pantechnicons from Darwin to Alice Springs.

TOWARDS THE TWENTY-FIRST CENTURY

The geographical position of the Territory, once regarded as hampering its development, could well be a key to its future prosperity because of its proximity to the fast growing economic bloc of the South-East Asian/Western Pacific Region. Enthusiastic Territorians foreshadow opportunities for the Northern Territory to become a land bridge connecting the southern states to Asian markets via Darwin.

Road transport and Territory development are interwoven. Companies new and old-established, large and small, specialised and general, form the pieces of a complex and comprehensive logistics pattern.

Darwin, with a population of 68,000 in 1987, and Alice Springs (30,000) are the Northern Territory's vital transport centres. A report by the Department of Transport and Works titled Estimates of Freight Demand by Surface Transport states that

the growing importance of Darwin as a staging centre for distribution of freight in Northern Australia was strengthened during 1984/85. Darwin was the destination port of some 700,000 tonnes of overseas freight including petroleum and bulk solid products.

Approximately 62% of all freight movements to the Territory were initially destined for Darwin, whilst 76% of all outbound freight originated from Darwin.

Looking at the general transport scene in the Top End, the report commented on freight traffic to and from Jabiru and said that despite the Federal government's restrictive policies on the export of uranium yellowcake

the potential importance of the mining industry to the Territory's economy and the freight industry in particular remains. The freight industry is ideally placed to benefit from significant increases in movements of sulphur, acid, quicklime, ammonia and construction materials.

The report added that 'Katherine is poised for an economic boom of a magnitude which it has never before experienced with the current development of Tindal Air Force Base and associated community infrastructure' and that 'considerable direct benefit for supply of goods and services will flow onto Darwin during the construction stage'.

This same report said that the freight industry is of singular importance to Alice Springs which is now 'the predominant staging centre in the movement of freight into the N.T.' It pointed out that an estimated 53 per cent of total freight movements into the Territory via the central transport corridor was handled through Alice Springs, and of this 49 per cent came into the Alice Springs railhead.

Contemplating the future effect the sealing of the Stuart Highway from the south in 1987 would have, the report offered the view that 'there was by no means wide acceptance' that an alternative to the present road and rail combination would provide a more reliable service; 'in fact, many forwarders and shippers [have] expressed some doubt that "southern operators" would impact to the detriment of already resident transport companies which had good performance reputations and sound client bases.' This could be interpreted as saying that Alice Springs' continuation as an important transport centre for the Territory seemed assured, given ANR's much improved service and freight handling facilities since 1980 and road transport's ability to successfully link with these developments.

In the event of the South Australian authorities' approving the use of triples from Port Augusta to the Northern Territory border, the cost of hauling individual trailers one at a time from Adelaide to Port Augusta would be a consideration as well as such factors as equipment utilisation and manpower. These elements

Drivers employed on Shell road tankers—and drivers of other companies' vehicles—have the responsibility for safely handling very expensive vehicles and very valuable payloads. They're professionals and hold the highest grade of driving licence in Australia.

TODAY AND TOMORROW

Road trains from the adjoining states of Western Australia and Queensland join their Northern Territory colleagues in the task of moving consignments of all descriptions. In the Territory there are no restrictions on the movement of three-unit road trains (triples) but in Western Australia, South Australia and Queensland there are defined boundaries, inside which triples must be broken down to doubles and then to semi-trailer configuration.

A road train driver's 'office' contains almost as many instruments and controls as a commuter aircraft cockpit. By monitoring them at regular intervals the driver is kept informed of mechanical performance and incipient troubles.

would have to be assessed in relation to the rates and equipment turnround times offered by ANR's piggyback service direct from Adelaide.

Back in 1934 when Britain's Overseas Mechanical Transport Directing Committee produced that marvel of the age, the eight-wheel-drive road train with self-tracking trailers as the answer to the transport problems of the Northern Territory which in those days was rightly regarded as one of the Empire's undeveloped regions, it bestowed on the nation a transport medium which not only led to the opening up of the Northern Territory but also put down the roots of a type of operation which is unique in the world.

World War II added its fortuitous contribution with the construction of two bitumen highways and the introduction of modern, powerful vehicles which advanced the technology of the road train and put it within the financial reach of those pioneering operators who could see the potential for serving the Territory with multi-unit vehicles in the absence of a rail service.

These and subsequent developments led to a type of vehicle which despite its size is not only acceptable to the public and other road users but is environmentally compatible and, more importantly, is essential to the economic wellbeing of outback Australia. Unlike its neighbours, the Northern Territory does not impose any area restrictions on the operation of road trains, and this freedom adds to their efficiency in serving the region.

The modern Territory road train has also generated drivers who have a professional approach to their job

and to the responsibilities entailed in handling the largest vehicles on the nation's roads. They're the holders of the highest grade of driver's licence in Australia which is, in a sense, a status symbol in the industry.

Road trains fit in with the Territory's road traffic pattern without fuss. Residents know and respect their size and weight, tourists are alerted to these aspects by leaflets issued by the Department of Transport and Works.

At night two piercing 'bull lights' high above the headlights usually indicate the approach of a road train. By day there's no such intimation; just two plates, front and rear, with large black letters on a yellow background announce to all concerned the presence of a . . .

ROAD TRAIN.

Most brides settle for a limousine or perhaps a horse-drawn carriage in some cases, but this Alice Springs lass got to the church on time in a road train prime mover! *(Peter Baldwin)*

GLOSSARY

articulated vehicle: a vehicle with a pivotal connection between the front and rear sections, e.g., a semi-trailer combination.

aux. box: auxiliary gearbox, sometimes referred to as a 'splitter' or 'joey box'. It reduces the gaps between the gear ratios in the main gearbox.

bhp: brake horsepower; power output of an engine.

body truck: a prime mover which carries its own load as well as pulling trailers.

bogie: two or three axles in tandem. (Note: not spelt bogey or bogy.)

bow trailer: ex-army trailer with rounded sheet metal front end.

B-train: a semi-trailer and trailer combination using a common bogie between the first and second units; also known as multi-trailer combination.

bull lights: very powerful aircraft-type supplementary headlights.

Coolgardie safe: a timber- or metal-framed box with wetted hessian sides for keeping food cool.

corduroy: saplings laid side-by-side to form a firm surface in mud or sand bogs.

crate: loose term for a cattle-carrying vehicle. Also applied to a lift-on, lift-off container for carrying small numbers of sheep and cattle.

dog trailer: a trailer with two or more axles, usually self-tracking.

dolly: a single- or bogie-axle module with turntable and drawbar for converting a semi-trailer to a trailer.

double bottom: a semi-trailer plus a trailer; usually referred to as a 'double'. Maximum length permitted in the Northern Territory is 33 metres.

epicyclic gearing: a system of planetary gears rotating around a central shaft, meshing with a 'sun' wheel on that shaft.

GCM: gross combination mass (weight), i.e., the manufacturer's maximum weight at which a vehicle can be operated with a semi-trailer.

GTM: gross train mass (weight), i.e., the manufacturer's recommended maximum weight at which a vehicle can be operated, pulling one or more trailers.

GVM: gross vehicle mass (weight), i.e., the manufacturer's recommended maximum weight at which a vehicle can be operated as a solo unit.

Holland Hitch: brand name for a quick-release semi-trailer and dolly fifth wheel (turntable).

hook-up: assembling a road train. (see note.)

hp: horsepower; a figure calculated by formula but not widely used nowadays.

Jake brake: Jacobs engine brake.

joey box: an auxiliary gearbox.

K or kay: capacity of a Queensland Railway K-wagon, between 18 and 22 beasts.

mud map: map drawn on the ground with a stick—or on a bar counter with a finger!

MTC: see B-train.

ox box: see 'aux. box'.

pig trailer: trailer fitted with two non-steerable axles, usually non-steerable.

pintle hook: a basic type of towing bracket.

prime mover: the hauling unit of an articulated combination. See also 'body truck'.

Ringfeder: brand name of a widely-used trailer towing coupling.

road train: a rigid vehicle hauling up to three trailers, or an articulated vehicle (semi-trailer) plus two trailers. Maximum length permitted in the Northern Territory is 50 metres.

splitter: an auxiliary gearbox.

spread tandem: a bogie with axles 2 m apart.

tractor: U.S. term for prime mover.

triple bottom: a combination of semi-trailer and two trailers. Usually referred to as a 'triple'. Maximum length permitted in the Northern Territory is 50 metres.

two-stroke: an engine which provides power on alternate strokes of the piston, as distinct from power provided on every fourth stroke of a four-stroke engine.

van: capacity of a former Central Australia Railway cattle van, between 11 and 18 beasts, depending on condition.

worm drive: rear (drive) axle with helical worm gears, as distinct from axles using planetary gears.

Note re *Hook-up:* it takes about an hour to assemble a road train, check air brake operation, hoses, couplings, electrical equipment, etc. on the prime mover and each trailer.

If not already in place, dollies have to be pushed under trailers and locked in position. The prime mover or other vehicle with towing eye and drawbar is used for this operation.

One method of assembly is to back the prime mover under the semi (No. 1 unit) and reverse this to connect with the dolly of No. 2, and then finally back these two on to No. 3.

Another technique is to reverse No. 2 on to No. 3, unhook, put the prime mover under the semi (No. 1) and reverse it on to No. 2. However, it is not always a matter of preference or style; two trailers may already be hooked up to the prime mover and a third becomes available later in the day, which means undertaking the skilful manoeuvre of reversing two units on to the third.

BIBLIOGRAPHY

Reports

The Beef Cattle Industry in the Leichhardt–Gilbert Region, J. H. Kelly, Bureau of Agricultural Economics, Canberra 1959.

Commonwealth Railways and Australian National Railways Commission, annual reports 1948–86.

Estimates of Freight Demand by Surface Transport 1980–87, Northern Territory Department of Works.

Guide to Vehicle Limitations and Safety Requirements, Department of Transport and Works.

Independent Economic Inquiry into Transport Service to the Northern Territory, 1984 (Hill Report).

Inquiry into Freight and Related Costs, Northern Territory Government, 1984.

Northern Territory Department of Mines and Energy, annual reports.

Northern Territory Department of Primary Production, technical bulletins and annual reports 1980–86.

Northern Territory Road Traffic Code, Department of Transport and Works.

Report on Port Augusta–Alice Springs Railway, Commonwealth Railways, 1967.

Report of a Study Group on Ways and Means of Exploiting Economies of Scale in Road Transport Vehicles for Certain Tasks in Western Australia, 1970 (Salter Report).

A Review of the Alice Springs to Darwin Rail Link, Department of Transport and Construction, 1980.

Road Train Specifications and Control Conditions, Highways Department of South Australia, 1986.

The Role of Commonwealth Railways Within the Northern Territory, October 1964.

Specifications for Road Train Prime Movers and Trailers, Main Roads Department, Queensland.

Standard Specifications for Operation of Road Trains in Western Australia.

Books

Abbott, C.L.A., *Australia's Frontier Province*, Angus & Robertson, Sydney 1950.

Bromby, Robin, *Rails to the Top End*, Cromarty Press, Sydney 1982.

Hill, Ernestine, *The Territory*, Angus & Robertson, Sydney 1951.

Further Reading

Lockwood, Douglas, *Up the Track*, Seal Books, Adelaide 1964.

Petrick, Jose, *Alice Springs Street Names*, Centralian Advocate, Alice Springs 1980.

Pike, Glenville, *Frontier Territory*, self-published 1972.

Powell, Alan, *Far Country: A Short History of the Northern Territory*, Melbourne University Press 1982.

Taylor, Peter, *An End to Silence*, Methuen, Sydney 1980.

INDEX